meditations on maximum velocity

Cole Coonce

2002
kerosenebomb.com

FIRST EDITION JULY 2002

Published in the United States by KeroseneBomb Publishing, a division of poverty and determination, fueled by consumption, Pabst Blue Ribbon and cheap racetrack tacos. Originally conceived at the bottom of a bottle of Bushmills, Famoso, California, 1997

Library Of Congress Cataloging-in-Publication Data

Coonce, Cole, 1961–
Infinity Over Zero: Meditations On Maximum Velocity / Cole Coonce

ISBN 0-9719977-0-5

1. Land Speed Record (world) — Meditations on. I. Title.

Photographs by Cole Coonce & unknown

KeroseneBomb Publishing
P.O. Box 8392 La Crescenta, CA 91224

kerosenebomb.com

Manufactured in the United States of America

CH_3NO_2

∞, 1962

CARBON UNIT RECOGNIZANCE

This manuscript could not exist without the energy of the following carbon units: Steve Collison, Kate "Basic" Peters, Ikky Shivers, Andy Takakjian, Anne "99" Thomas, the Vigle Institute, Danny Jo the Blind Hippie, Fred Vosk, Dave Wallace, AmC, Wayne "the Peregrine" King, "Jet Car Bob" Smith, Bill Kaska, Franklin Ratliff, Brent and Vicky Fanning, Pete and Leah Farnsworth, "Nitro Neil" Bisciglia, Jim "Postman" Post, Jack Logan, Dr. Robert Post, Dave Petrali, Vic Elisher, Robin Richardson, 'Blood, Pamita and Jeff Utterback, Jim "Monkeyman" Sorenson, Mark "Sparky" Hovsepian, Dawn "Sales" Mazi-Hovsepian, Nancy Cole, Steph, Brad, Jocko Johnson, Vic Elisher, David Tremayne, Ivan Samson, BZ, Cuz'n Roy, the Garo Foundation, Chris Martin, Bret Kepner, wrenchski, Carla Kaplan, Sara Lippincott, "Techno Tim" Gibson, Troy Cagle, Loyd Osterberg, Tom Hanna, "Kansas Al" Williams, the Goat, "Pistol Pete" Jensen, "Piston Pete" Millar, Craig Breedlove, Art Arfons, Fred Vosk, Mike Civelli, Ray Mueller, Jeri Sorm, Pit Crew Pete, Todd "Toothpick Elbow" Westover, Caz, Paula "Miss STP" Murphy, Don Jensen, RJ Smith, Terry Spohn, the Elena Ray Institute of Imagery, the nitromaniacs on the Header Flames bulletin board, Standard 1320, Drag Racers Inc., StOrMy Byrd, Bruno, and Bev from the Miner's Club.

Creditos Facile:
Infinity Jetcar photograph: *Bill Kaska, 1962*
Mach art direction: *Andy Takakjian*
Back cover photo: *Caz "ChaCha" Zugaib*
All other Photos: *Cole Coonce*

SSC, 1997

"The Smarandache Hypothesis asserts that there is no speed barrier in the universe and one can construct arbitrary speeds up to (the) infinite." — **AUTHOR UNKNOWN**

PART ONE:
HESITATION KILLS

HESITATION KILLS (WEST LA, 1996)

"Hesitation kills," Cuz'n Roy said, and laughed.

It's a Friday afternoon in Los Angeles; we are weaving through stop-and-go traffic on the San Bernardino Freeway and at that moment I negotiate a '71 Grand Prix through carnage comprised of upscale Westsiders in Lexus's, various sport utility vehicles and mini-vans, all of which had been snagged in a collision with a freaked and crying gaggle of immigrants in a chipped, varicose blue 1982 Toyota Corolla.

I see the pileup continue to metastasize so I punch the throttle, aiming the massive 2-ton projectile of Detroit steel bang on into the center of the chaos, which now resembles the entrance to a dark star. The eyelids on all four barrels of the carburetor open like the mouth on a porn queen and begin guzzling gasoline faster than a desert dog. Sundry automobiles continue careening and fishtailing, orbiting away from the spinning Toyota and its initial point of commotion as if by centrifugal force, creating a hole the size of a small crater that is plenty big enough for us to pass through unscathed.

In our wake I see disturbed yuppies already on cell phones to their insurers, lawyers and Immigration, speed dialing before their vehicles had fully reached a dead stop. Airbags distend like bulbous pimples and car alarms cycle in a discordant and paranoid arpeggio. Stalled automobiles point in five directions, the petals of a broken flower. Pieces of steel, plastic and colored glass litter the interstate and I keep the hammer down, with twin puffs of burnt blackie carbon punctuating our exit from the scene of this massive pileup.

"Man, this is like a bad day at a stock car race. Shouldn't we stop?" Cuz'n Roy half-chortles.

We both know the question is rhetorical. "What?" I reply. "And get caught up in that bureaucratic nightmare? Is that what Junior Johnson would've done at Daytona?"

We are en route to speed trials in the Black Rock desert, northeast of Reno. With that freakshow behind us, we can concentrate on the prodigious amount of ground we are to cover on this eve. Along the way, we will partially retrace the steps of one Craig Breedlove, a land speed racer who had built the first *Spirit of America* jet car in his dad's backyard in Venice in 1961. In the 1960s, Breedlove became the first guy to officially go 400, then 500, and finally 600 mph. These speeds were verified by stiff suits from a French organization, whose job description is to sign off on such esoterica. Now Breedlove was out at Black Rock, trying to reclaim the Land Speed Record from some Brits, who had held the title for over a decade. It feels right and patriotic to travel the roads Craig had taken to Bonneville in 1963, when he first achieved international notoriety and fame, stunning the motorazzi and the world at large with the first official 400 mph clockings. His goal is now 700 mph and beyond, ultimately puncturing the sound barrier itself. Mach 1. The Speed of Sound. There is no time for dicking around with cops, lawyers and insurers.

"Punch through the turbulence," Cuz'n Roy acknowledges. "It is the right course of action at the first sign of trouble. Otherwise you'll spill your beer."

Punching through the turbulence. It is a time honored approach to overcoming the pitch, roll and yaw of any journey with a potential for doom and immolation. Become at one with outrageous, incomprehensible velocity and use it as your guide. Once upon a time around 50 years ago, in pursuit of Mach 1, ace fighter pilot after ace fighter pilot lost control and stuffed sophisticated military airplanes into oblivion in the Mojave desert; conversely, Chuck Yeager commandeered a Bell *X-1* rocket airplane and kicked in the joystick towards the first successful supersonic flight (which is to say, he lived) by this approach: when things get weird and jittery, yank on the go-faster for more thrust. Damn the demons of chaos and instability. If you don't you are a footnote to history and mere allegory; if you do, you bask in glory...

"Hesitation kills," I repeat to myself. In an age of the neurotic, the paranoid and the self-absorbed, now more than ever definitive action and decisiveness are the only methods towards glory. Cuz'n Roy and I are on our way to see a guy attempt to turn Mach 1. In a car.

NO MORE PUSSYFOOTING

"When I drove *Thrust 2* to the record in 1983," recalls Richard Noble of his 633 mph jet car ride that reclaimed the Land Speed Record for Great Britain, "frankly, as a team we were damned lucky to get away with it. The car was within 7 mph of takeoff and with the huge dynamic pressures involved it would have gone upwards at 40G."

Noble and his *Thrust 2* machine were encroaching on the physical barrier of supersonic travel — and its incumbent aerodynamic disturbances. That would be the last campaign for a record in the subsonic speed range. From here on out, it would be a thrust-unlimited duel to Mach 1 between Richard Noble's *Thrust SuperSonicCar* (driven by Royal Air Force prodigy Andy Green) and Craig Breedlove's sleek new *Spirit of America* streamliner. The target speed is now the Speed of Sound — a velocity whose consequences could be fatal as supersonic shock waves would almost certainly send the vehicle careening out of control at between 740 and 765 mph. No more pussyfooting.

Suffice it to say, when the price of glory is quite possibly death you gotta' *really* want to go Mach One. It has to be in your blood. It has to be innate. For, in the same way that the laws of quantum mechanics tell us that the cosmos exploded and are in fact expanding, and the essence of this expansion is the behavior of subatomic particles, well, this same molecular information is at the root of a land speed throttle monkey's genetic code and drives its host harder and faster, ultimately creating speed demons infected with a primeval "sickness" of "Go! Fever," a fever that is a twisted, atavistic permutation of manifest destiny and good ol' honky imperialism. I.e., it is what makes people try to "discover" continents, climb Mount Everest in a blizzard, run four-minute miles, design spaceships, or travel at the Speed of Sound on land. I mean, if the universe is infinite, Mach 1 is not a physical barrier after all, it is just an illusory line, right?

It was no cosmic coincidence that the Mach 1 attempts would transpire in Black Rock, Nevada, an 80 mile chunk of parched alkali as expansive as the human imagination when it knows no boundaries. Breedlove and Green would attempt to travel at Mach 1 because that is what they were born to do — it is what we were all born to do, really.

JOCKO (1953)

The intersection of Lankershim and Riverside in North Hollywood. "Kustom Kar" builders the Barris Brothers — eventual manufacturers of the Batmobile, the Monkees' GTO, the Green Hornet's company vehicle, the Munster's grocery-getter and other funky, offbeat vehicles that raced into America's living room via the television's cathode tubes — hire a young apprentice, Robert Johnson.

Johnson is an astute learner and forward thinker. The guys in the shop wonder about his hygiene though... Seeing him rub his crotch absentmindedly, he is christened "Jocko." And despite his nickname's, uhh, *sensitive origins*, the moniker sticks like talcum powder.

THE TERRIFYING CRACK AND ECHO

Black Rock, Nevada, 1860. In the bleached and cracked playas and buttes of what was once Lake Lahontan, the Pauite Indians are under attack from Kit Carson and a buckskin battalion of pale faces. Carson and his troops are armed with 50 caliber round, lead balls that fire with a velocity at the muzzle of 1200 feet per second. The Pauite's armament is mostly sticks and stones; they are terrified of the white man's weaponry and the sounds whizzing by their heads. They fear the sound as much as they fear the imminent tearing of flesh.

Vienna, 1887. Logician and physicist Ernst Mach is attempting to isolate the psychoacoustical source and rationale for the psychological terror associated with gunfire. He tries to understand why soldiers engaged in battle with firearms are so emotionally volatile.

Mach endeavors to explain the how of what the Pauites already know: The sound of the air ripped asunder is an immediate reminder of one's own mortality. At any given millisecond, something as precious as life can be snuffed. "Shell shock." Faster than sound. Instantly. A crack and an echo.

YOU'RE NOT VICTOR BREEDLOVE (1961)

"The receptionist at the Shell office looked a little surprised when I struggled through the door with the model case and flip charts. I told her my name was Breedlove and handed her my card. 'I want to see Mr. Lawler, please,' I said. With no appointment or anything, there I stood in all my splendor.

"She opened the door to his office and said, 'Mr. Lawler, there's a Mr. Breedlove to see you,' and I heard this big, deep voice say, 'Send him right in.'

"I trotted through the door with my 'dog and pony show.' He looked up in amazement and said, 'you're not Victor Breedlove.' I later learned that Mr. Lawler had a Shell dealer named Victor Breedlove, whom he had been expecting.

"I took a deep breath and blurted out in one sentence, I think, 'No, sir, Mr. Lawler, I'm Craig Breedlove and I'm here to talk to you about a project that, I think, will not only benefit myself but Shell Oil Company as well, and I'm sure it will interest you because I am going to bring the world's land speed record back to the United States after an absence of 34 years, and after many people have tried and failed, and I have the car that can do it.'

"He looked up in bewilderment, took off his glasses, and said, 'You've got ten minutes.'" — **Craig Breedlove, the Spirit of America**

JORDAN (1996)

"If there is a divine purpose in Jafr, it is that God has placed it on earth as a warning of what hell is like." — **Howard Kent, publicist for *Lawrence of Arabia.***

It hasn't rained in five years.

If it weren't so dry, this burnt orange topography would weep from the sheer weight of its own isolation. The desert is motion in suspension and a set of quarantined co-ordinates whose desolation is inversely proportional to the outrageous expanse of nothingness.

Periodically — and apropos of not much — the winds gust and the sands pan across the hereafter; this is the Universe's small way of letting this uninhabitable Outback know it hasn't been forgotten about entirely.

But a lack of cosmic movement is the cruelest gesture of all. The silence confirms this sentiment.

Wild camels stare down spontaneous dust storms. After the winds die down, the next interruption to the parched and tedious desolation is the motorized fluttering of Bedouins crossing the desert in battered white Japanese pickup trucks. The murmur and obliquely reverberant rhythm of the camels is barely audible under the gear grinding and fishtailing of Muslims in mini-pickups. The marauding rumbling fades as the camels slowly scatter and the desert dwellers disappear into the their own dust.

When the commotion settles, the only sound remaining is the lonely brooding of bleached phosphate rock and the sulking of stone in what is the universe's driest and least efficient echo chamber.

∞

A Russian Antonov cargo plane unloads its burden at a military air strip not so many miles away. The Antonov is the size of an interstellar mothership. Its 75 tons of freight is an absolute Noah's Ark of arcane hardware and machinery: diesel 6-wheeled Supacats, a fire-fighting Jaguar XJR, a portable Airshelta hangar, microlight aeroplanes and *Thrust SSC*, a twin-engined jet car that weighs ten tons.

It is an ant farm of forklifts and traffic control. It is a military operation where nobody dies. In this part of the world, nobody dying is a refreshing change.

∞

Terra firma dissolves into a horizon of dust. It buttresses a heavy, two-toned sky nine times taller than the playa itself. The dusky blues and grays of the sky hint at how cruel and unforgiving this place really is... in the center of the sky, a billowing sun is burning orange. The grays and oranges of the sky and landscape co-exist as a sort of dialectic with the two-tones hammered into a third element. A synthesis.

Despite an integration of color, there is no syllogism here, nothing to be inferred or projected, no cubed or exponential meaning extrapolated from the two elements of harsh light.

It is. It just is. The synthesis is zero. The sum, product, and exponent of the synthesis is zero. It is an anti-syllogism. Which sounds like silence, of course.

∞

A renegade truck out of Iraq breaks the quiet. It scurries across the desert like a cockroach on a bleached snooker table. The trucker's freight is contraband of one sort or another... it could be guns, black tar heroin or black market Petrol. More than likely tobacco is the payload. Whatever the substance, it makes no never mind to the Sun as it continues its cynical sentry. Black globs of diesel exhaust puff and then dissipate, swallowed by a swollen sky.

It gets quiet again.

Off in the perimeter white smoke and dust complements a subsonic thrum breaking the silence while slowly changing pitch. The noise source is the jet car.

Eventually, flames pulse and belch out of a pair of Spey 202 jet engines. The engines are mounted on either side of the fuselage giving the race car the appearance of a spaceship on wheels. The vapors that buoy the flame are eye-watering. It doesn't sting, so much as it sours. The fearsome and leviathan silver engine burns a cheap fuel with a smell like cooked cough syrup. The jet spools up and up and up, reaching a whine that would shatter the wall of Jericho. The higher the pitch, the higher the decibels and the sicker the smell.

A group of mechanics and engineers crowd around the spaceship with wheels and perform a series of synchronized leak tests on the jet engines. The vehicle is 54 feet long, tips the scales at 10 tons, and has a surface composed of steel, carbon fibre and titanium. The men and women are sharply attired – matching khaki trousers, a variety of team polo shirts (red, yellow, gray, black), blue coveralls, tan colored boots, identical post-industrial sunglasses and green and red bomber jackets – and are a calm contrast to the chaotic pressurized air that billows out of the beastly, demonic jet engines' exhaust opening. In all the futzing, occasionally one of the engineers checks the time on a wristwatch with a SSC Machmeter as the face. The needles on the timepiece point to Mach 1, which represents high noon, natch.

They purge the afterburners on either of the jet engines. *PPPHHHWWWWUUUUHHHHHH*... (beat) ... *PPPHHHWWWWUUUUHHHHHH* goes one... 22,500 fucking lbs. of thrust at each belch of either afterburner ... *PPPHHHWWWWUUUUHHHHHH* ... (beat) ... *PPPHHHWWWWUUUUHHHHHH* goes the other... 110,000 fucking horsepower total... "This is one horny machine," one crew member mutters... On the horizon, a fleet of a Land Rovers retro-fitted with machine guns zoom towards the makeshift but immaculate compound in a flying wedge formation. The automobiles attract minimal dust, as the swirling pool of disturbed air puts the Rovers in a high pressure cocoon. It is like the winds know that inside one of these vehicles are some very important Muslims and the dust parts accordingly. Flags mounted to the skin of the automobiles buffet in the turbulence. The closer the cars come, the more frenzied the disturbance. The vortex summons Biblical stories, lost cities and civilizations, and Lawrence of Arabia. T.E. Lawrence was the last romantic vestige of British Imperialism here, but the caustic purging of Spey 202s conjure up the Empire's latest and perhaps final attempt at National pride. *Thrust SSC.* The Supersonic Car.

It is utterly atavistic.

The jet exhaust and the choreographed human commotion, the dust of the caravan and its flagellation of flags swirl into a single entity.

Before the military Muslims depart, the senior officer offers to cordon off the British Operation with the Land Rovers... and to shoot anybody who might get in the way.

THE END OF THE CENTURY (1898)

In 1898, the first official Land Speed Record was established by Gaston Chasseloup-Laubat, some French guy going a little over 30 miles per hour in an electric car named, loosely translated, "Never Satisfied"; to be blunt anything under 200 mph is of only marginal interest to me and will be acknowledged here in a pell mell, cursory fashion. With that being said, here's what I know about what happened at the end of the 19th Century, when this Land Speed record gag began:

In '02, France's Leon Serpollet leapfrogged over Count Gaston in a steam-engined *La Balleine* ("The Whale") at 75 mph. Later, the US made its presence felt via Henry Ford. In a successful attempt to crank up the profile of the fledgling Ford Motor Company, Ford slid his black Arrow across a frozen lake outside of Detroit at 91 mph in 1904. It was an absolute white knuckler of a ride and Ford admitted that even the memory of this adventure filled his heart and soul with terror. He was later succeeded by Louis Emile Rigolly, a Frenchmen who clocked a one-kilometer speed of 103.55 mph and therefore broke the 100-mph barrier.

Electric cars. Steam power. On some level, this turn of the century stuff is all just esoterica for the land speed fetishist. Besides Henry Ford, most folks can't remember (or pronounce) any of these guys names, nor can anybody but the land speed fetishist recite the speeds those guys recorded.

What is worth filing in one's gray matter is the following: It was around this moment when the discrepancy in what "officially" constituted a speed record began to take shape. In order to establish some semblance of credibility as per the timing systems and as to whether these attempts were aided with a tailwind, the *Federation International de l'Automobile* (FIA) intervened and attempted to establish order and protocol (within an hour, two runs in opposite directions, with the speed tabulated as an average of the two runs). To daredevil-hellcat Yanks such as Barney Oldfield and Ralph de Palma, guys who won early editions of the Indianapolis 500 as well as establishing ultimate speed records, this French bureaucracy and this two-run jazz was about as popular as UN helicopters in Montana; Oldfield and de Palma maintained that one banzai, balls out record run had as much validity as back-to-back runs sanctioned by some foo-foo timekeepers from across the pond.

History dictates otherwise.

LIVE WITH REGIS AND KATHIE LEE

April, 1996. Lincoln Square, Manhattan. Four city blocks have been cordoned off surrounding the ABC TV studios, in anticipation of a fiery display of raw thrust by the *American Eagle 1* jet car, a deconstructed fighter plane of an automobile whose design goal is to reclaim the Land Speed Record of 633 mph, currently the domain of Richard Noble, a land speed record racer who is also an Order of the British Empire. Television personalities Regis Philbin, Kathie Lee Gifford and their producers have signed off on the presentation of the *AE-1.* The racers figure a ring-of-fire dog-and-pony show on live television just might titillate some potential corporate benefactors enough to loosen its promotional purse strings. Conversely, if this stunt misfires, it could melt the plastic off of both Regis Philbin's mug and Kathie Lee Gifford's cleavage.

The *AE-1's* cash crunch is very real... Before the team can set its sights on the Land Speed Record, it needs to find a Corporate Sugar Daddy willing to pony up 250 large — yes, one quarter of a million bones — for design changes and sundry expenses. Thus far, the car is six years and $300,000 in coming.

This is Take Two, as they say in the biz, as the day before Regis and Kathie Lee broadcast their show from the New York Auto Show and did a bit on the *AE-1.* In an improvised moment of inspiration and *schtoink*, as cameras rolled Regis Philbin climbed into the back of the cockpit of the jet car while *AE-1* team members applied current to the engine. It failed to fire. On live national television. There was no jet fuel in the tanks...

The next day, however, outside of the studio, things will be different everybody says. The *AE-1* is fueled up and will light sure as sunrise.

Communications, microphones and cameras are hard wired to a control room five flights up and ensconced behind glass. Coming out of commercial, down on Columbus Avenue a stage manager with an intermittently-functioning headset folds three fingers in succession and then points to the talent, who introduces the jet car's Director of Operations. A red light glows on a handheld camera as the talent and the guest banter and make nice-nice for a few minutes with the Director of Operations explaining the team's plight re a lack of finances hindering their ability to reclaim the Land Speed Record from the British operation that set it in 1983.

Then things get weird. In a reprise of yesterday's coast-to-coast misfire, the jet engine won't light. Again.

It is a cacophony of confusion and futility, with the stage manager pointing his fingers and attempting to cue the *AE-1*'s pit crew to light 'er off and start making some noise with the J79 jet engine. The promotional pitch immediately degenerates into utter slapstick worthy of Buster Keaton. As power is applied repeatedly, the turbine blades spin harmlessly... a massive asses-and-elbows thrash ensues with the *AE-1* crew as Regis Philbin filibusters into the camera and a spokesman for the *American Eagle* tap dances around the reality that Middle (and Corporate) America is watching *and-here-we-are-screwing-the-pooch.*

The stage manager rolls his fingers, the camera's red light goes dark, and unbeknownst to the *AE-1* squad, bumper music rolls as credits burn across the screen horizontally. Finally, after their moment in the limelight has all but passed, the engine lights and rumbles and the small team of mechanics go through the various procedures designed to elicit oohs and ahhs and wows. The coast to coast audience doesn't hear or see the spectacle. Obliviously, the turbines plead and wail at an amplitude that would kill cockroaches in a lab experiment and if the intimation of the 48,000 horsepower isn't enough, the driver then purges the engine's afterburners and a 70-foot orange flame bursts aft of the deconstructed post-industrial monstrosity. Windows shatter and eardrums are permanently cauliflowered.

It is for naught. This ersatz, shambolic Gotham *Götterdämmerung* is a fallen tree silent in an empty electronic forest. New York City cops survey the broken glass, key their radios and shrug their shoulders while chomping on donuts or knishes and sipping coffee.

Via videotape playback, the next morning Regis and Kathy Lee relive the moment on their show, the third consecutive day the *AE-1* gets national exposure. Still the money never comes.

MIGRANT APES IN THE GASOLINE CRACK OF HISTORY

Rocket cars. Rocket dragsters. It was only a matter of time before the technology designed to put a man on the moon and vaporize entire cities was appropriated by the speed demons on wheels...

It's simple: the common method for propulsion of the rocket dragsters utilized the following method: pressurized nitrogen forces the hydrogen peroxide onto a silver plate and the ensuing, instantaneous chemical reaction creates a tremendous cloud of hot stream that is force fed out of a nozzle, creating thrust.

Rockets summon, tickle and reanimate many primal notions dormant within the collective human consciousness... they tap into the memories of fire and they evoke the spirit of the transcendental, the exaltation and elevation of the human body and of the human spirit... *"They wanted to escape from their misery and the stars were too far for them"* — thus spoke Zarathustra and Friedrich Nietzsche about the very banality of existence... rockets are the stuff of Jules Verne books *(From the Earth to the Moon)* and Fritz Lang movies *(Frau Im Mond)*, of Arthur C. Clark and Stanley Kubrick and 2001 whose symphonic score (Richard Strauss' "Thus Spoke Zarathustra") observed a human destiny far beyond the confines of Planet Earth; of the Ancient Chinese and tossed bamboo tubes filled with saltpeter, sulfur and charcoal as part of ceremonial fires and noisy explosions scaring away evil spirits. A full millennia subsequent, this is the stuff of the Sung Dynasty attaching tubes of powder to spears and using the projectiles to repel the invading Mongol hordes... *"thunder that shakes the heavens"* was the Chinese description of the dual elements of physical devastation and psychological terror... the Mongols appropriated the technology for use in their conquests of Baghdad and from there rocketry spread into Europe... as the Dark Ages gave way to the Renaissance, Sir Isaac Newton solved the theorem of equal and opposite reactions, which became his Third Law of Motion and a pithy explanation of how a rocket generates altitude and velocity... this is the stuff of unmanned rockets built from the blood of indentured Hebrews, subjugated into aiding the Third Reich as it bombed the shit out of London in its quest to establish a Master Race; of the Space Race and the rocket to the moon with spacemen in aluminum suits establishing beachheads on extra terra firma... this is the stuff of our id and a Jungian subconscience — of "migrant apes in the gasoline crack of history," William Burroughs said — of apocryphal legend and honky imperialism and of dusty teenagers ratchet-strapping forgotten solid-fuel rockets onto the hoods of their rusted Chevy Impalas and smashing man and machine into the eternal oblivion of desert stone...

THE ROAD TO BURNING MAN (1996)

"For my next act, I will set myself a-fire," — **Craig Breedlove, moments after nearly drowning in a brine pond in Bonneville while becoming the first man to travel 500 mph.**

Picture this: a transmigration towards the center of being, the Pauite Spirit Land where, according to Injun' tradition, white and red brothers had been separated at creation, Black Rock, Nevada.

Picture this: a Blind Hippie and three compatriots on the road to the Burning Man festival there, a sort of free-form techno-pagan celebration with colors and music and a giant, sky-scraping wooden effigy of a stick man set on fire as a sort of act of atonement for the sins of post-industrial America.

If the culture is to seek penance, the Black Rock desert is as good a place as any. Injun' Conflict and conflagration, war games, amateur rocket launches and sundry manifestations of tweaked machismo have been perpetrated on this very chunk of longitude and latitude. Atonement is a nice gesture, but its really to ease the soul of those still breathing, as those who have vanished and vanquished have been incorporated into a landscape whose scale and magnitude renders such gestures superfluous and futile.

Still they come: in vans, cars and caravans.

Roving bands of naked percussionists — Marching Drug and Bong Corps, if you will — jammin' on high and so blissfully oblivious to their own arrhythmia that it eventually becomes a rhythm, snake through various camps of pierced performance artists and tattooed torture artists, Fuller-ites with portable Geodesic domes (!), etc., etc.

The Burning Man. It resembles a star-shaped power line stand that supports the high tension lines cutting across the Mojave between LA and Vegas. The resurrection of a skeletal Trojan Human with nothing hidden, its structure as blank as the desert that houses it, its message empty excepting whatever meaning any one of the gatherers wants to foist upon it. And with that done, the whole thing will be set on fire, of course. These projections, like the edifice itself, which will be consumed by fire at the culmination of the festival. Woodstock meets the World's Fair, whose finale is Jimi Hendrix electronically vomiting out the Star Spangled Banner while the Hinderburg immolates. Or something.

The festival is held on the Black Rock dry lake bed, a location with serious overtones of ancient civilizations of Pauite Indians and genocide, and WW II war games.

This dry lake bed is a flat ball of string with the triumphs and transgressions of Western Man and the Noble Savage he supplanted all intertwined. The spiritual, the cosmic and Western Man's "fucked male energy" are all there... it is the only logical place to set the Man on fire and attempt to purge the sins of Modern Life and some how get right with nature.

Beyond its status as a pagan festival, Burning Man is a gesture. It is a metaphor. A reactionary statement about life at the ass end of the 20th century, whereupon technology has taken a strange turn.

The whole gag was form over function. A bio-mechanoidal convergence. The least functioning the sculpture the better. Technology is inextricably intertwined with our lives, nay, our very central nervous system(s). Thematically, Burning Man is a commentary on technology gone awry, a re-enactment of *2001*, when the mainframe computer on the space station in *2001* went haywire and makes a cognitive decision to lock the pod bay doors in attempt to deprive the astronauts of their oxygen. The astronauts were in a battle of wits with the computer and the computer was kickin' some serious Homo Sapien ass. So anyway, Burning Man is/was a contrived attempt to dis-empower technology, to relegate it to its proper status as a tool and not the command center.

Technology is an extension of humanity, and takes the Venn Diagram one step further, it is an extension of nature. Burning Man was a contrived and somewhat precious attempt to detune technology to the basics: punch cards, strobe lights and pulse jet go-karts...

All of which is sheer spectacle and an exercise in entropy and pointlessness.

The festival ends with thousands of post-modern hippies, punk rockers and other bohemian-types wiped out on the dry lake bed. They were drugged out, drunked out, fucked out. The Man is cinders, caught in the ethereal, *basso profundo* winds that blow across a desert bed that one sci-fi writer referred to as "the afterlife."

There was nothing left to burn.

The only thing left was to "pack it out." Dutifully, the Blind Hippie begins to help clean up the trash. The next year he returns. And stays.

VESUVIUS (POMONA, 1996)

En route to Black Rock, and with the motorized class struggle in our rear view mirrors, we continue to fight our way through the crosstown traffic on the San Bernardino Freeway, arguably the most constipated thoroughfare in Los Angeles. As we pass through East LA, traffic is really beginning to tighten up and the radio man says that just beyond Pomona the freeway was an absolute parking lot. Cuz'n Roy and I take a slight detour. We go drag racing.

Top Fuel cars are running out at the drag strip in Pomona that same day, which is pretty tough for us to blow off: aye, getting dosed by nitro-powered projectiles reaching a terminal velocity of 300 mph in 4 seconds, the ground shaking like Vesuvius, buckets of raw, liquid explosives seeding the ionosphere like the Devil's cornfield. It sure beat sitting in traffic, watching the temperature gauge needle weld itself to the red line. Once the sun set in Pomona traffic would thin to a tolerable density and we could ball the jack into San Berdoo and Barstow and continue to retrace Breedlove's steps at night, as least as far as Tonopah, Nevada, out by the missile silos and the proving grounds of Area 51. All things considered, an afternoon at the drag races seemed like the perfect overture for a trip to the desert...

The detour makes sense on many levels, not the least of which being that Breedlove hisself had raced on this very chunk of asphalt back in early 1962, shoeing a railjob propelled by two small block Chevies with pump gas for its fuel. It was a deconstructed machine known as the *Freight Train*, and as part of the race team's schtick, they often wore railroad engineer's caps in the Winner Circle. Breedlove drove the car only for a couple of weekends as a prelude to his initial Land Speed Record attempts, and well before the choo-choo hats became part of the wardrobe...

Indeed, throughout the 60s and early 70s, Breedlove used the drag strip as a test bench for various aerodynamic theories and propulsion systems, but whenever the fastest man in the world returned to the quarter mile asphalt, one got the feeling he was really slumming and passing time until all systems were "go" for another crack at the Land Speed Record out on the Salt Flats.

Cuz'n Roy and I park the '71 Grand Prix at a taco stand that stood behind the drag strip's timing tower, hoof it a couple of blocks into the pit entrance gate, then grab some track steaks and a couple of beers and cop a squat on some aluminum seats near the finish line. Top Fuel cars come roaring by our perch in pairs at speeds of 300 mph or so ("*WHH-HHAAAAAAHHHHHHUUUUUUHHHHHNNTT!*") and as often as not — due to finicky track conditions and an envelope of smog that was starving these rapacious dragsters for oxygen — blow up overamped engines and propel shrapnel into altitudes of absurd elevations ("*PPPOOOFFF!*"). The dragsters pound the pavement with such ferocity that car alarms are triggered in the parking lot after nearly every pass. The explosions are a great spectacle, but the car alarms bum our high.

"When does that fucking noise stop?" I blurt. "Is that constant squeaking, squealing and honking the soundtrack to our entire existence nowadays?" It is the noise of fear, dread and neurosis, and it had invaded the otherwise peaceful confines of an afternoon at the drag races. It was one thing to hear the sounds after an accident on the freeway, but quite another to have it interfere with our enjoyment of gratuitous explosions at the drag strip. I take a hit off of my paper cup and tried to block the shrill sounds from the parking lot out of my consciousness.

Another fuel dragster blazes by on fire, the crew chief having miscalculated the fuel mixture and atmospheric boost levels, the infernal roar drowning out any superfluous noise from the parking lot. As flak rains from the heavens I tell Roy I feel like Robert Duvall in *Apocalypse Now*, dodging fragments of molten metal while trying to maintain a cogent discourse. In this instance, rather than debating Duvall's take on whether or not the Red Chinese used surfboards in Vietnam, the conversation is about the strange turn the land speed record took once Breedlove shunned the traditional internal combustion engine used by both passenger cars and Top Fuel dragsters in favor of jet propulsion that was, in essence, liberated from the trash bins of the military industrial complex.

THE FLYING CADUCEUS

As track workers mop up the space age detritus from the last failed attempt down the drag strip, Roy goes to take a piss and I hang on the fence thinking about guys other than Breedlove who did second-hand shopping from military boneyards: Dr. Nathan Ostich, who showed up at the Bonneville Salt Flats in 1960 in a contraption he tagged the *Flying Caduceus*, a needle-nosed machine shaped like a tight-wad's pencil and sporting a J47 jet engine as a propulsion system; Walt Arfons followed suit with his *Green Monster*, a jet car that looked like an armadillo run over by tractor tires and used a Westinghouse J46 engine out of a Navy fighter for power. Then there were more: Romeo Palamides' *Infinity*; Gary Gabelich in Bill Fredrick's *Valkyrie*; Art Arfons and HIS *Green Monster*. For a brief instant in the early 1960s, there was a small battalion of gallant, courageous men out at Bonneville who had strapped such devices onto rolling frames of steel, albeit with mixed (and sometimes tragic) results...

VERY EXPENSIVE SHIT

After the oil and broken hardware is finally mopped and broomed off the drag strip, another pair of fuel cars march down the asphalt at terminal velocity and begin shooting out pieces of burning titanium through the exhaust, a spectacle reminiscent of roman candles at a fireworks display on Independence Day. The heat generated from the explosions is quite palpable and makes one feel warm and even patriotic, in a fuzzy, non-jingoistic sense. Is this the Spirit of America? As referenced by the moniker Breedlove assigned to his speed machines that debuted on the Salt Flats in the summer of 1962? Whatever it is, it is more than apparent by the repeated extravagant and Teutonic displays of noise and fire that it is our God-given right as Americans to burn up precious metals in a public display of sensory overload and fiduciary carelessness.

"It's amazing the stress these Top Fuel guys are subjecting these aluminum engines to," I say to Roy, damning the dangling modifier, "... the same engines that Chrysler built for their street machines back in '63 or '64."

Another Top Fuel car went by on fire, burning off its parachutes.

"Too bad they melt after four or five seconds of use," Roy laughs.

"We live in a time and place of entropy, where you can blow very expensive shit up and laugh about it — as long as you keep it between the guardrails..."

GAS AND DUST, THE DEVIL AND DARK MATTER (1887-1912)

"*The inertia of any system is the result of the interaction of that system with the rest of the universe. In other words, every particle in the universe ultimately has an effect on every other particle.*" — **Ernst Mach, Mach's Principle of Inertia** (1893)

You are in either Bonneville, Black Rock, or perhaps Al Jafr. Pick one. While meditating on the desolation, you assume that space is merely emptiness. An absolute void. The desert merely nods in the affirmative.

Your inference is wrong. The desert lies. You are not the first to be hornswoggled by such supposedly empirical observation...

Ernst Mach — the man who uncovered the mystery of the speed of sound — was an empiricist and a logician. A logical positivist. He presupposed that space is merely emptiness. The Void. The Quantum Vacuum. He was wrong.

Space is loaded with stuff that won't glow in the dark in any way that astronomers can spot.

This stuff is loaded with a so much mass that its gravitational field tugs and affects the velocity of everything else in the universe (including Land Speed racers).

Even though the mathematics of the day insisted upon the presence of a form of mass that instruments could not and (cannot) detect, Mach insisted that space was empty. If you couldn't see the matter within the space, nothing was there. (He also insisted that the atom existed only as an abstraction, but that is another riff altogether and tangential to this one ...)

Space has to have mass for inertia to tug on heavenly bodies. It takes the form of dark matter. The Mach Principle states that inertia depends on the reciprocal interaction of bodies, however distant; in other words, a body in motion tends to stay in motion unless acted upon by another force.

Dark matter is stuff the cosmologists of Mach's day could not see; suffice it to say there is enough gas and dust that the vacuum as a condition of complete and absolute void does not exist.

Despite what the physics and the math of the day indicated had to be there,

Ernst Mach made no never mind for the stuff in between the heavenly bodies – a pretty big snafu, cosmologically speaking.

Not even Einstein was able to suss out the Laws that truly guide (and guide us through) the Cosmos...

Dark matter: The entropy and chaos of the cosmos... Its presence was undetected, yet its gravitational pull tugs on all things. It is entropy that guides us, and it is entropy that acts as a force that slows us down... entropy equals inertia, and entropy is a force that acts counter to the infinite... and yields the finite...

The devil lurks in the entropy that tugs on our every thought and action like so much dark matter; he lurks in the banality that is Life on Planet Earth.

Yes, ***"every particle in the universe ultimately has an effect on every other particle."***

Specks of dust and pockets of gas gravitate towards a darkness so black we cannot see it and whose magnitude is so massive we cannot come to terms with how to measure it. The stuff we cannot see and don't know how to measure made Einstein blink and made Ernst Mach draw a line in the sands of epistemology.

Ernst Mach is synonymous with "inertia." But his own tug and resistance was not gravitational, it was intellectual.

The desert bleaches everything white as stone. It is a blank slate, according to a friend of mine who used to work in a junkyard. What the empiricists call "tabla rasa." On a meta-level, perhaps my friend is right. The desert rarely puts up an argument. But it ain't empty. And it puts up more resistance to human endeavor than the pull of a dark star on a cosmic body or spaceship set on warp speed.

By extension, a blank slate is perfect tableaux upon which one can foist his dreams. It is the perfect setting for the Land Speed Record. It is also the perfect setting for failure.

THE FLOOD (JORDAN, 1996)

"*Come Friday and anybody with any sense was in full* Lawrence of Arabia *mode with goggles, scarves and Arab headgear much in evidence, and it was needed, since a sandstorm was now in full flight and showed no sign up giving up, even for the benefit of a handful of Brits far from home who just wanted to run a jet car. Briefly, the sun came out at the Southern end of the track and hopes rose momentarily only to fall again. The Jordanian Air Force guys from the base had done a sterling job with watering trucks and graders to fill and flatten the Bedouin track even more, but this is an open desert and apart from a short time either side of a run, nothing can be done to stop (bandits) if they want to cross...*

"... time was slipping away as the weather got worse and worse. The pressure was still on since the car had to be ready for any break in conditions, but it was destined not to be. Just when the mods were complete and SSC *sat there ready to do its stuff once more, the heavens really opened. Thunderstorms of truly biblical proportions swept the area causing major floods and widespread damage. Thanks to the policy of keeping people on the desert at all times, the advancing tide was spotted early and the site evacuated in the nick of time. Even so, a couple of vehicles only just made it, having to be towed out as the desert turned to porridge before disappearing under water.*

"With no chance of conditions improving until early 1997, there was no option but to pack up, return to the UK and plan for 1997. So, part one of the attack on the Sound Barrier was over. Plan as you may, there are some things you can't control and the weather is one of them. These were the worst conditions since 1991 and you'd have thought that the Middle East was the one place on Earth safest from such conditions. But then again, this is record breaking and record breaking always attracts bad weather." — **Robin Richardson, *Thrust SSC* Team Member.**

THE TWENTIES (1920)

"Everything was going well and the record appeared to be in the bag, when, suddenly, at a speed of more than 200 m.p.h., the weakened rear tire blew out... the Black Hawk *swerved to the left, skidded for several hundred feet, then jumped into the air in three great leaps. (Frank) Lockhart was not strapped in, and he was catapulted out of the car. The unconscious driver was dead when he reached Halifax County Hospital. The record set by Ray Keech still stood."* — **Paul Clifton, THE FASTEST MEN ON EARTH.**

By the end of the 20s the *back-to-back-turnaround, two-way-average-within-an-hour* system was established as the criteria for holding the record. The LSR wars crank up throughout the remainder of the 20th Century with Brits Henry Segrave, Sir Malcolm Campbell, George Eyston, Richard Noble and Andy Green as well as Yanks like Craig Breedlove, Art Arfons (Walt's half-brother) and Gary Gabelich; on flat tableaus such as the beaches of Wales, Denmark, and Daytona and fossilized badlands such as Verneuk Pan, South Africa; Bonneville, Utah; Lake Gairdner, Australia and Black Rock, Nevada.

Art Arfons, a guy who crashed at 600 mph and lived, told me over the phone that "the real trailblazers were the ones at Daytona; Eyston and Cobb and them guys." Art Arfons also had this to say about the rich, gallant British aristocrats who broached the 200 mph benchmark, "Those men really had to be something else."

Arfons litanized the British Land Speed Heroes, the men who had dominated the Salt as America attempted to dig itself out of its economic Depression and as it slugged it out in World War II. American involvement in the Land Speed Record had ended before the Stock Market Crash of 1929... After that, the daredevils and speed maniacs seemed more content with drag racing than the massive and expensive undertaking of an ultimate Land Speed Record...

March 1927. It is a battle of the Bluebloods. Great Brit Henry Segrave punctures the 200 mph benchmark for automobiles, clocking 203 mph on the "treacherous sands" of Daytona Beach in his *Sunbeam.* His source of motivation was a pair of 12-cylinder Sunbeam Matabele aircraft engines. A year later Segrave's mark is raised by Malcolm Campbell — a rigid, regal man with an angular mug and a buzzard's beak of a nose who claimed to be a pirate in a past life but looks more like the Human Fly with his bug-eyed goggles — who clocks 206 on a pass that nearly had Ol' Malcolm singing "Nearer My God to Thee"; while blazing across the beach at 200 mph, Campbell's *Bluebird* encounters a sand ridge which serves as a catapult and launches the hapless, passive car and driver 100 feet into the air. Cowabunga! Campbell lives and splits the beach scene in search of some Salt Flats — preferably in the colonies of the British Empire — that could safely accommodate his target speed of 250 mph.

FELLOW TRAVELERS

•

May 31, 1959, Riverside Raceway: The Russians dominate the heavens with Sputnik, a satellite designed to determine the density of the upper atmosphere and return data about the ionosphere via a pair of radio transmitters.

It's Memorial Day weekend — when the US of A honors its war dead — and Eisenhower/martini-shaker America is having enough problems coming to terms with the Russkie's satellites that continue to buzz the stratosphere whereupon an Ozzie & Harriet-type couple is motoring down the surface streets near Disneyland and they encounter what looks like a spaceship strapped-down on the back of a flat, open trailer, being towed by a 1956 Chevrolet station wagon.

In the front seats of the Chevy are a couple of beat looking young men, "Jazzy Jim" Nelson and "Jocko" Johnson. In the back is a lone black man, pit man Eddie Flournoy.

As the couple pass the spaceship-time machine looking thingie, they do a double take. The Harriet-type drops her jaw. The Ozzie-type scratches his crewcut. As disturbed as they are about the Communist threat of interstellar superiority, they are unsure if these are the guys they want on "our side."

∞

After Jocko and Jazzy unload their streamlined dragster off of the trailer, the world stops in its rotation: On this day, the *Jocko's Porting Service* entry, a rear engine dragster blanketed in aluminum lovingly hand-formed by Jocko, sets a quarter-mile elapsed time record, as driver "Jazzy Jim" stops the clocks in 8.35 seconds. To Jocko, it is an empirical display of the equation wot says: horsepower less drag equals an ungawdly acceleration. His stealthy car slithers through the slipstream and into the history books.

In a direct contrast, at an Air Force base in Kansas, Glen Leasher in the *Sullivan Martin and Leasher* AA/Fuel "rail" claims a quarter mile speed record of 185 mph the day before...

Dragster were called "rails" or "railjobs" for a reason: They were either sedans stripped of all body work or were purpose built chassis that were nothing but tubing. *Jocko's Porting Service* was different: The damn thing looked like it was from another planet, but was influenced by various land speed record setters such as the *Bluebirds* of Malcolm Campbell, George Eyston's *Thunderbolt* and the *Railton Special* of John Cobb, which, at the time of Jocko and Jazzy blasting into the record books, held the Land Speed Record at 394 mph for over a decade.

(To avoid confusion, it helps the reader to remember that the Land Speed Record is the average speed between two timers set exactly one mile apart. This is after a running start of as much as six miles. It is the average speed of two timed runs, back-to-back within an hour, run in opposite directions. Conversely, drag racing records are measured by timing lights triggered 66 feet before the finish line and 66 aft, for a total distance of 132 feet, which is 1/10th of the distance of the race course (a 1/4 mile equaling 1320 feet.)

Because the drag strip runs are more of a sprint and less of a marathon, the use of nitromethane — a highly destructive fuel — was used by drag racers such as Jocko Johnson, whose specialty was "porting" the cylinder heads' combustion chambers for burning nitro, a rather delicate science as the porter had to re-engineer the heads on an engine designed for a passenger car that would normally burn gasoline. Johnson had "porting" down to a science, but he was the first drag racer to also factor in the science of aerodynamics, which had previously been the domain of the Land Speed Record guys and aerospace.

Although the LSR crowd had tapped into decreasing both wind resistance and drag, they did not utilize exotic fuels in the rather prodigious amounts that the dragster guys did, who had no fear of "tipping the can" with the "yellow stuff" or "liquid horsepower."

The LSR competitors made horsepower another way: with gobs of cubic inch displacement, via engines that had come out of fighter planes. To see these giant, beastly machines blubber down the Salt Flats of Bonneville with massive puffs of black smoke billowing out of the exhaust was a truly unique spectacle.

(In the 30s, the Germans had burned nitro with an automotive, streamlined vehicle, albeit with tragic results: Berndt Rosemeyer, a national hero of the Third Reich, was killed while racing on the autobahn at a speed of 280-something mph in the *Auto Union GP*, whose design pre-saged that of the Top Fuel dragster (supercharged engine, with nitromethane as a fuel) by a quarter of a century . The *Auto Union GP* was ultimately co-opted by the Third Reich, much to the consternation of Ferdinand Porsche, the car's designer, who ultimately shuttered the project, as a political gesture as much as anything else...)

But the salient point among all of the digressions is the reality that Jocko Johnson had created a package that had the best of both worlds: a streamlined dragster that had plenty of downforce without much drag (the opposite of thrust) and aided by a powerful badass hemi, huffing on nitro.

Streamlining rarely paid off on the drag strip. The weight penalty of the added body work negated the benefits of slipping through the air stream.

The *Jocko's Porting Service* 'liner is history's exception.

SHOT GLASS (1887)

Two central Europeans are firing a gun into a bottle, breaking glass and making sparks as the bullet rips through a charged glass coil. A flash of light illuminates the projectile as it hurtles through space.

Ernst Mach is examining a photograph of a bullet in flight. His brow is furrowed. In the frame is a bunch of scrunched up air, gathering around the leading edge of a bullet.

He is exploring the notion of the vicious severity of war wounds as a function of compressed air pummeling the flesh, as opposed to the projectile itself. He is holding a visualization, empirical proof, of what would later determine to be a sound wave.

Using a kind of redundancy and "absolute proof" as his methodology, Ernst Mach figures out that the terrifying crack and echo from a gunshot is because the bullet is traveling faster than the speed of sound.

"Mach Numbers" enter the field of physics as a form of measure. The concept of "supersonic" enters the idiom of psychology. The sound of air is terrifying...

This shock wave became anthropomorphosized by fighter pilots in the 1940s, as they danced and died with the shock wave that forms at the Speed of Sound. The fighter pilots considered this waveform to be a Demon. (Read *The Right Stuff* for a 400-plus page explanation of this...)

Mach's Demon is a very lithe contortionist. He is made of air molecules that can warp, tear, compress and fan out when pummeled by a body in motion passing through the transonic region.

A VISUALIZING SYMBOL (1912)

Ernst Mach insists that acceleration can be defined as only relative to the distant stars... Albert Einstein hammers out equations for this, and thus explains gravity in his General Theory of Relativity.

Mach has heard that he is being hailed as a predecessor to Relativity. He is not pleased.

Vienna 1912. Einstein and Mach meet to address the atom as a "visualizing symbol." Mach not only refuses to accept the existence of atoms, he thinks a lot of Relativity is bullshit and he tells Einstein so.

The human mind has its own inertia, I reckon. Even the human mind that developed Universal Laws *about* Inertia.

∞

According to Grolier's, Mach "was suspicious of any thought (including scientific hypotheses) that was incapable of being reduced to direct observation..." This leads us to the Cosmological Battle between Inertia (Mach's Principle) and Gravitation (Einstein's General Relativity); as far as Special Relativity goes, Einstein never did the math to Mach's satisfaction... The Mach Theorem of Inertia not only disagrees with Newton's notion of absolute time and space, but it also challenged Einstein to explain what was affecting the orbit and velocity of both celestial bodies and photons... Einstein proves to be more or less right with General Relativity... Mach feels that space is empty (his fallacy), while Einstein alludes to gravitational forces (later shown to be "dark matter")... Unfortunately, empirically speaking, by that time Mach croaks... Forthwith Einstein coaches the scientific community from the sidelines on the best way to bomb the shit out of the Axis Powers. Again, from Grolier's, "Mach died in the very year that Einstein published his major paper on general relativity; neither of these two giant intellects was ever fully in accord with the other."

THE CURATOR OF TECHNOLOGY

Washington, DC, October, 1997. The appetizer of nachos arrive, moments after the dispatching of the first round of margs. The salsa is white-people tepid. I am having dinner with the Curator of Technology from the Smithsonian, and we are discussing the intersection of Ernst Mach's research in Vienna.

"Mach espoused 'sensationalism,'" the Curator says, "the concept that sensory data — color, space, time, tone — comprise the limits of one's world. Now, the question is: Why, when he was mainly interested in such considerations as this, was he also interested in the flow of air over moving objects at high speeds?"

"The faster you go," I say, crisping a chip, "the fewer limits to your very existence. If color, space, time and tone are the limits of our experience, speed is a means to break through those limits."

I lick a swath of salt off my glass. I tell him it is my understanding that Mach was studying the "bow wave" and the mysterious "bang" that happens when a bullet whistles past someone's ear. His interest was the physiological effects of shell shock. Ergo, he ascertained that bullets were traveling at the speed of sound...

"The sound of the bullet is as damaging as the ripped flesh from the bullet," I tell the Curator. "That is the damage of fear. I don't know why Ernst Mach was interested in the flow of gasses over moving objects, but I do know he used a bullet." I take a drink. "To me, the great irony is that the human-guided devices that either broke the sound barrier or gave-it-the-ol'-college-try, were bullet-shaped. The Bell *X-1.* The *Spirit of America* is shaped like an arrow. Art Arfons' stuff is shaped like a shotgun shell.

"Whatever the example, the drivers became at one with the bullet. They became the bullet."

We order another round of margs.

THE OTHER X-1

July 23, 1966, Union Grove, Wisconsin. On this day, an afternoon as hot and as sticky as taffy, the Space Age comes to the local drag strip in the guise of a revolutionary new dragster concept. After three years of testing and two years of construction, the *X-1* rocket car, built under the aegis of the Reaction Dynamics Corporation (basically a three-way partnership between a couple of shade tree propulsion experts as well as an expert fabricator and welder, all working out of a garage in Milwaukee), finally makes it maiden voyage down the pavement...

The *X-1's* rocket engine has no moving parts and burns 9.5 gallons of hydrogen peroxide. By design, it shoooshes down the 1/4 mile pavement like a shot, and runs out of fuel 1000 feet into the run. Even after coasting for the length of a football field before entering the timing lights, the *X-1* is still the quickest and fastest machine on a drag strip, effortlessly eclipsing the speeds and elapsed times of the state of the art nitro-burning dragsters that roar through the speed traps in full song, week after week across America.

Reaction Dynamics' goal is to design a supersonic vehicle with a target speed of 1000 mph. The first step is to use the drag strip as a means to shake down their ideas.

The throughline for this project goes back to Germany in the 20s. As a pup, Richard A. Keller ("Dick") saw a photograph of Fritz von Opel's rocket car, the black brautwurst-shaped roadster that exploded and killed Max Valier. Dick was smitten with the stark white lettering on the car, which spelled out "RAK," short for "raketen" (*Kraut fur* "rocket"). It was an eponymous coincidence as RAK was young Keller's initials also. Of such coinky-dinks, does the trajectory of history twist... Likewise, at a drag strip, the fortuitous meeting of Keller and Ray Dausman with Top Gas dragster racer Pete Farnsworth also tweaks the course of history.

August, 1967, U.S. 30 Drag Strip in Crown Point, Illinois. Chuck Suba, an All-American boy with a healthy sense of curiosity and a clean cut appearance not unlike that of Eisenhower's favorite son, has been hired to pilot the *X-1* rocket car.

This day is a day of destiny.

A gurgling sound bubbles out of the rocket's decomposition chambers, like Frankenstein on day old pizza. *DRAG RACING Magazine* reports that Suba "holds the steering yoke vertically, 90 degrees off axis, and aims the front of the car between his third and fourth knuckle, like a sight on a revolver.

"The rocket engine's exhaust is 4 times the speed of sound... a noise like an afterburner kicks in and suddenly he is off, riding on the head of a bullet." The *X-1* zips to a 5.41 second elapsed time — the quickest ever on a quarter mile drag strip. By a bunch.

∞

Documentation of the *X-1*, and its follow-up, the *Blue Flame* (both being preeminent rocket cars in the history of maximum velocity) is rather sparse, as is accurate information about Reaction Dynamics, the small business that operated and designed these machines. I know they were based out of Milwaukee, but that is about all I know. So I fly out to Wisconsin on a whim. Once there, I cold call Reaction Dynamics co-founder Pete Farnsworth and arrange to meet him and his wife Leah for Chinese food.

It is thirty years after the *Blue Flame* set the Land Speed Record. Its driver, Gary Gabelich, might call this meeting of conversation and won ton ala Wisconsin "blenderized karma." As the Farnsworths and I sit down in a restaurant whose decor can only be described as "cavalier and relaxed rusticana," I take notice of Pete's prosaic build and underspoken demeanor. There is absolutely nothing about this guy that says "*I-was-part-of-the-intellect-behind-what-once-was-the-quickest-car-on-the-planet-and-I-still-have-a-rocket-dragster-in-my-barn-as-some-weird-totem-and-memento-to-the-days-when-I-set-the-world-on-fire.*" Nothing. His accomplishments are absolutely hyper-intense, but the guy is more laid back than a back lot security guard. His wife Leah is small in stature, but there is nothing diminutive about her worldview and opinion. Both strike me as no nonsense. During the course of dinner I begin to understand something that I never knew: that holding the Land Speed Record could be as sweet and sour as any Chinese pork.

Between forkfuls as brackish as Bonneville, I masticate and ask Pete about his transition from Top Gas dragsters to the rockets:

But how did you go from reciprocating engine drag racing into the more, you know, thrust driven stuff?

PETE FARNSWORTH: It was a matter of necessity, really. I was working full time and racing full time and it just became a twenty four hour a day thing to try to maintain a fuel dragster and work 8 or 9 hour a day too, so I was looking for a way to build an exhibition car of some sort.

Um hmm, what, what year was this?

PETE: Probably about '63, '64, when the jet cars were just starting to tour the circuit. As I have mentioned, we know (amputee jet car driver) Doug Rose quite well and he was running for Walt Arfons at the time and broke away from Walt and started his own car, the *Green Mamba* (jet dragster) and uh, we figured "these guys have cars that will run all day long, they don't have to do a massive amount of maintenance on them." I thought the next step up from a jet car would be a rocket car — and I started looking around at propulsion systems that were available in the early 60s and there basically wasn't any.

I was out at Oswego Dragway with a gas dragster and an acquaintance from out past in Chicago — we both grew up in Evanston (just north of Chicago) and Chuck Suba had run a shop there, building race cars and doing specialized tune ups and things like that, and he had one of his customers that, uh, I was an acquaintance with - his name was Dick Keller and um, Dick was out there and happened by our pit and recognized me, and we got to talking. He asked me what we were doing and I said, "You know, running a gas dragster now, but trying to put together a rocket car for exhibition." He said, "Well, that's funny, cause a friend of mine, Ray Dausman, and I had just finished building a twenty five pound thrust rocket engine."

Um hmm.

LEAH: And they were both going to go to Chicago where, um...

PETE: ... the Illinois Institute of Technology and uh, Dick worked part time as a research assistant into gas technology, which was the research arm of the American Gas

Association. So that was our first tie-in with the gas association was the fact that Dick knew people in the industry.

So that connection was made even before you guys ran the X-1?

PETE: Yeah, he was working there at the time when we got together. We started out as DFK Enterprises, for Dausman, Farnsworth and Keller and um, I believe that was 1965. We formed that and this was after a discussion meeting about whether the 25 lb. thrust motor they had built was scalable for something usable for drag racing — and all indications it was so, I decided from what I had heard from all this that this was the way to go because it was throttle-able, it was a reasonably safe fuel to handle and uh, hydrogen peroxide didn't have any possibilities of explosion, (it is) reusable safe to handle as long as you didn't pour it into a pile of rags or something and it wasn't going to spontaneously ignite...

Um hmm.

PETE: We were having truckers trying to drop off great big drums of nitromethane while — you were thinking about your kids taking a nap — that was what they did one day when I was at work and they came with a 55 gallon drum of 98 percent nitro next to benzol straight from California. The guy didn't have a loading shoot, so we decided we were going to take the back off a semi trailer...

LEAH: Well, it was labeled as cleaning fluid...

PETE: Um hmm, "cleaning solvent."

LEAH: Cleaning solvent, you know, "no problem, it's just a solvent."

PETE: Well, my wife panicked, went down to one of my garages and grabbed a bunch of old tires and they rolled in down and dropped it off onto the old tires. If it had gone off it would have leveled the neighborhood -

LEAH: See that's why I'm so gray.

(laughter)

PETE: She'd had to cover for me a lot.

Was the design goal ultimately to go to Bonneville and take the LSR?

PETE: No no....

Exhibition money?

LEAH: Um hmm.

(discussion turns to Pete Farnsworth and Chuck Suba towing the X-1 *to California in an effort to get the car approved by the National Hot Rod Association for exhibition runs at their tracks.)*

PETE: My idea to start with was just to build and exhibition car and Dick and Ray had ideas of going to Bonneville for the Land Speed Record. They started to use it as a stepping stone and I wasn't involved with the land speed record at all. At that time I had interest in it, but I was following it since I was a kid. You can't help it if you're in Hot Rodding to not read about Bonneville, but I had never been there.

HOT ROD did a nice article on it and then we went over to NHRA (in California) and uh, we had contacted them before that we were coming out, (because) we couldn't even get anyone to come out into the parking lot and look at the car... Finally, I think it was Bernie Partridge came there and he took one look at it and he said, "No." I explained the car to him, Chuck and I did, and he said well, "We'll let you know." So we went back in and in a while they came back out again, you know, didn't invite us in at all. *(laughter)*

PETE: In a while they came back out again and said, no we can't do this - and explained that they were supported by the automotive industry and that the automotive industry would not want this sort of competition at the track, and from that standpoint I could see it, so they basically said, "No, we're not going to let you run."

And one thing was that they said that the car was so fast that it would have too much kinetic energy if it got into the crowd. Well the top fuelers were much heavier and they were going proportionally pretty fast, they had more kinetic energy than we did, but they flat refused to consider it.

LEAH: That was a real heavy disappointment to send the car all the way out there and...

Sure, and you had to know in hindsight that they had their mind made up even before they saw it... then again, you guys were so far ahead of the curve that, whether it was collusion with the automotive industry or not they just couldn't deal with it.

PETE: I think they saw that after we ran the car and we were the first to go below 6 seconds — we clocked a 5.90 in Oklahoma City and, uh, Labor Day weekend of 1968 - that was the last time the car ran and we went 6.03 and 5.90. Nobody ever recognized it except the Guinness Book of Records, which did recognize it and so we were in there as world quarter mile elapsed time record holders. We were two miles an hour short of what Art Arfons did with his J79 *Green Monster* Car. He had gone 267 mph and we went 265 but we weren't even running all the way through to quarter mile with it (because of) the fuel tank's capacity. We never had enough fuel to go all the way through and considering we were coasting going through the trap and we were running 265. We probably figured the terminal speed was probably 280, 285 something like that when we shut off and coasted. But uh, that was basically the end of the *X-1*, we ran it down at the meet at Oklahoma City. We had already started on our promotion with the Gas Industry people and they were there observing what we were doing the day we set the world record (for the drag strip).

Within a month we had signed a letter of intent with them to build the *Blue Flame*.

AMERICAN EAGLE ONE POSTSCRIPT (2001)

The *AE-1* project is aborted shortly after the "Live with Regis and Kathy Lee" comedy of errors. Some of the team members started another project with a pre-owned F-104 Starfighter (an airplane nicknamed "the Missile with a Man in it" by its designers in 1957).

AE-1 alumni Ed Shadle and Keith Zanghi shod the fighter plane of its wings, install aluminum wheels and the J79 turbojet off of the *AE-1* and re-invent their entry into the LSR as the *North American Eagle,* now optimistically billed as an "800 mph world land speed record challenger."

Before being christened as the *NAE*, and after some research missions out of Edwards AFB in Mojave, CA, this particular plane had spent nearly 30 years in surplus in South Central LA, rusting, decomposing and exposed to elements while graffiti artists had their way with it. Ed Shadle tells it this way:

"It was in very sad shape with holes punched into it, a lot of missing panels, the wrong tail cone and was basically gutted. He asked $25,000.00 for it. I sat down with the team and we had to make a decision. He was the only show in town we could afford so we passed the hat and we came up with a plan. We offered $15,000 up front in September 1998, with a $5000 payment in January of 99 and the final payment in July of 99. Keith Zanghi paid the freight bill of $3000 to have it transported to Spanaway, Washington.

"Upon arrival, we were pretty disappointed in the condition of the aircraft but we were certainly proud owners of this beast. We knew there would be much hard work ahead of us but when you are as tenacious as we are, it didn't seem all that bad.

"We weren't sure which aircraft we had because there was so much paint and graffiti all over the aircraft you couldn't tell what its number was."

When asked about the metamorphosis of monikers, Shadle explained thusly:

"*Yes, we originally had it named* American Eagle One *but when (driver) Gary Swenson dropped out in 1996 and we had picked up some sponsorship from Canada we decided to rename it* North American Eagle *in order to give some recognition to the Canadians. After Rick Kikes decided to quit the project completely in 1998 and give back our investments, we moved on into my current project which of course is the F-104. My extraction from the old project gave me the right to the name, the website and the aluminum wheels. The sponsors also went with me. Keith Zanghi and I teamed up together to form the new project in 1999. Last I heard, the old car was sitting out behind a drag racer's shop near Portland Oregon, rusting away with grass growing up through it. Swenson bought out the remaining ownership from Kikes so Swenson is the owner but last I heard of him he was in Peru growing potatoes.......*"

POMONA SEX MACHINE (POMONA, 1996)

Nearby a couple of old time railbirds are smoking nails and have overheard Cuz'n Roy and I ruminating about the dueling topics of a) the absurdity of these race cars stressing a pushrod engine to 8000 rpm in four seconds; and b) the Spirit of America. One of the bleacher bums — the more portly of the two – is sporting a t-shirt with the caption, "This Ain't A Beer Gut...This is a Fuel Tank for a Sex Machine." He asks if we need tickets for the races for the rest of the weekend as he had extra. We tell him thanks but no thanks as we were just passing through, en route to see Breedlove attempt his supersonic record runs out at Black Rock, Nevada. We tell him that we would be on the road right now if the San Bernardino Freeway wasn't so bollixed.

The skinnier guy chuckles, takes a pull off of his beer and relates how he and his partner knew Craig from the old days of car club gatherings on the Westside of LA, as well as when Craig hisself was running dragsters out here all those years ago, back in the days before there were very many freeways, when the hot rodders congregated at hamburger stands like the 19 in Culver City ("... on the corner of Jefferson and Sepulveda," the skinny guy said, "named after its 19 cent hamburgers"), the Clock Drive-in ("Sepulveda and Venice, across the street from the Shell Station") or the Foster Freeze on Hawthorne Blvd. On a Saturday or Sunday afternoon they took surface streets to the sundry drag strips such as Saugus, Santa Ana, Riverside, Fontana Drag City or Pomona — that is, if they bothered to take it to the drag strips at all...

"One night at the Clock, Craig Breedlove was draggin' it out in some guy's 3-window deuce," the skinnier old timer says. "Craig crashed out by the railroad tracks and just about broke his friggin' neck..."

"He went through the roof..."

"...We thought he was dead until the guy who owned the deuce called the police and an ambulance."

"... I can't believe none of us went to jail."

"After that, Craig took it to the strip," the sex machine says. "Eventually, he ended up driving for John Peters and Nye Frank for awhile, in 1962. Two blown and injected small block chevies. They called the car the *Freight Train.* The whole crew wore engineer's hats."

Both bleacher bums chuckles at the memory of the train engineer's get-up.

"Craig didn't drive the *Freight Train* very long," the fat man says as he exhales on a butt and pitches his cup. "It probably wasn't fast enough for him."

STOVEPIPE VISION

The brevity of Craig's tenure in Pomona back in those days had little to do with engineer's caps. It had to do with vision. Ingenuity and a dream. It was to reclaim the Land Speed Record for America, something that hadn't happened in over thirty years previous, since April 22, 1928 the date on which Ray Keech turned a two-way average speed of 207 mph at Daytona Beach in a jalopy with three Liberty v-12 airplane engines (and the year before he won the Indy 500).

From the 1930s on, the LSR had been the domain of British aristocrats and playboys who — as often as not — were knighted for their efforts by the King and the British Empire for achieving speeds of 300 mph and beyond.

The irony is that when Breedlove conceived of the *Spirit of America*, he had to turn his back on Detroit in order to bring his vision of American ingenuity home. To his way of thinking, nothing that had its origin on the drafting tables of the automotive sector would get the job done. He needed some serious propulsion in order to reach 400 mph way back then, and his design required the kind of power that only a military jet could provide... Sure, he once took a chopped and channeled '34 flathead Ford and modified it for extreme speed, setting records out at the dry lake beds when he was, in his own words, a "punk kid." But really, even as he dabbled on the drag strip and recorded speeds approaching 180 mph in Peters & Frank's gasoline-powered *Freight Train* in '62, he was already otherwise occupied with leftover thermodynamic devices discarded by the military industrial complex, beginning in 1959 when he procured a "spare" J47 engine out of a fighter plane that had been destroyed in the Korean War. (Craig bought the engine (sans afterburner) from a technical school for $500, where it was being used in a study aid for technical design.)

But still, 400 mph or not, the swapping of a proper hot rod for a turbojet-powered "stovepipe" dubbed the *Spirit of America* was heresy. Anathema. Betrayal. He was a drag racing Iscariot. The more closed minded members of the hot rod community were aghast.

"I used to race Breedlove on the streets on the Westside of Los Angeles," the teetering sex machine rattles as the center of gravity of his fuel tank warbles like jello, "but that was before he climbed into that wienie roaster and went out to the Salt."

The California sun sets over the hills just beyond the adjacent Brackett Air Field as the last pair of fuelers whisked into the impending darkness, blowing by as if they sailing on the tradewinds of Hell. There was an awkward silence as track workers clean up the last vestiges of metallic fragments littering the top end of the drag strip.

As Roy and I swill the remaining dregs of our plastic cups, the conversation briefly 180s back to illegal drag racing on the streets of Los Angeles; kids are still grindin' the gears on city streets, I say, albeit in Japanese cars instead of souped-up '34 Fords. The conversation shifts. Cuz'n Roy and I continue to riff with the railbirds about our misadventure earlier on the freeway that afternoon. I say that one doesn't have to worry about go-cat wild hot rod hoodlums barrelin' down to the Foster Freeze on Hawthorne Blvd. anymore. Greater civic threats are entertainment lawyers and soccer moms on the freeways with **DARE** stickers pasted over the one that once read **BABY ON BOARD**.

Apropos of nothing and for whatever reason, car alarms were going off in the parking lot again as the skinnier bleacher bum tossed another butt and shook his head. "Los Angeles is a different place now," he mutters.

SWINDLER'S SALT (1928)

Emblematic of how pushed the competition had become, Malcolm Campbell engages on a journey into a chunk of real estate that was completely uninhabitable, but was the perfect backdrop to implement his vision. Using kaiser blades and machetes, B'wana Malcolm pushes through the thick brush of South Africa with his shark-shaped *Bluebird II* streamliner en tow, in search of a fabled chunk of salt known as the Verneuk Pan (loosely translated, "Swindler's Salt"), all the while ignoring the fact that this is the habitat for puff adders and cannibals. The nearest source of water was five miles away — and it hasn't rained in five years.

Drought, serpents and the headhunters are least of Campbell's tribulations, however. Once the trail is blazed onto the Pan, the intrepid explorer discovers that the virginal "course" is fraught with shale that would shred *Bluebird II*'s Tulip tires to ticker tape. Rather than hightail it back to Daytona, Campbell orders his crew to remove 12 miles of shale and lay down some white line. They do... only to the witness the fruits of their labor completely torn asunder by a ferocious turdfloater of a storm.

Meanwhile, back in the Western World, Henry Segrave is lighting up the timers at Daytona, streaking to a 2-way average of 231 mph in his *Golden Arrow* (powered by a Napier Lion seaplane engine) as Campbell and his minions hike back out of the jungle with the bitter memories of a disheartening ordeal in their wake. Ultimately, the Napier aircraft-engined *Bluebird* hits 200 mph at the Pan, but for all practical purposes Campbell's campaign has been mau-maued by the uninhabitability of the "Swindler's Salt." It's time to get back to the beach.

MAXIMUM THRUST (KAPUT) (1929)

Since Fritz Lang's *Frau Im Mond*, it was more than obvious that rockets were the only form of propulsion that would put a *mensch* or *frau* on the moon...

Rocket engines were useful in that they did not need to induct oxygen into its combustion system. Its propellant system carried its own oxidizer, which is necessary when one is propelled and elevated to heights beyond the earth's atmosphere and whereupon there is no oxygen. (No oxygen, no fire. No fire, no thermodynamics in the thin, rarefied air of the cosmos...)

Jets, however, sucked in copious amounts of oxygen. Due to this system of propulsion, they become less efficient at higher altitudes as the air is thinner and less oxygen is available for combustion.

In aerospace, that is how it shakes out. On land, there are different reasons for using different forms of propulsion.

∞

The first documented LSR rocket car explosion involved the *Opel RAK 3*, built in Germany in the 20s and campaigned by Fritz Von Opel and Max Valier. The initial runs in Berlin were followed by a few attempts made on rails, during which *RAK 3* pushed the world speed *rekord* up to 158 mph with clusters of solid fuel, black powder rockets arranged in a cylindrical cone. After a successful flight with the *RAK 1 Friedrich* rocket propelled aircraft, the experiments conducted by Opel as a pioneer in rocket propulsion end in 1929. Patron Shell Oil (who were floating the nearly bankrupt Valier) insisted that the propulsion system be modified from a water 'spiritus' and oxygen combination to a paraffin-based system; a subsequent test ended in a holocaustic explosion that killed Valier, moments after his aorta was punctured by metallic fallout. It was high stakes techno-mechanical vaudeville, with Valier a mortal victim of his own schtoink ...

The morale? The folks cutting the checks may not have the best approach to maximum velocity. The trick is to take their money and not their ideas...

THE BLUE FLAME AND THE DATING GAME

You're saying that the Gas Company people were in Oklahoma City in '68 when you guys set the drag strip record?

PETE FARNSWORTH: Right, and we signed a letter of intent with the natural gas company contingent upon the fact that we could get tires from Goodyear that were capable of very high speeds.

The *Blue Flame* was designed to go 1000 miles an hour structurally and aerodynamically, we thought. You know, that's speculation...

You start getting into and beyond transonic and supersonic regions and all kinds of...

PETE: Well, we wind tunnel tested the model, at Ohio State University's wind tunnel. (We did) subsonic, transonic, supersonic (tests). And uh, so anyway we signed this letter of intent. Suba was going to be the driver. He was a super personable guy, very knowledgeable, smart as a whip, this guy was General Manager of the repair department of the biggest Buick dealership in Evanston, Illinois when he was 19 years old. Really sharp.

But anyway, two weeks after he set the quarter mile ET record, he jumped into a friend of his top fuel car at Rockford Dragway, to try to figure out why they had a handling problem. They couldn't straighten it out and he got out the edge of the drag strip and they had a 55 gallon barrel marking the end of quarter mile — marking the edge of the track and he clipped that with the front wheel and then totaled it.

That's asinine.

PETE: Asinine of him to run the car that way. He didn't know, it was only a couple of days or weeks or so after that that we got the okay about the land speed record driving and he never knew about, I mean he knew about it, he was part of the idea but the fact that we had actually gotten it.

That is so brutal. So now, so now the search is on for somebody to shoe the car and you're thinking target speed, 850 to 1000 miles an hour.

LEAH: And the Gas Industry at that time, when Chuck died they wanted to pick out a driver, someone who would do TV interviews and be Mr. Gas America, it had to be someone dynamic that was going to be in favor of, they really did cooperate in the search for someone else.

Okay, so Reaction Dynamics was kind of an umbrella corporation that would exempt you guys from liability if something weird happened with a car and also maybe tax reasons too...

PETE: Tax reasons too. But um...

So the search is on for a driver, how did that go?

PETE: Well, we Dick Keller and I, both knew (Top Fuel racer) Don Garlits real well. You couldn't ask for someone who was more knowledgeable or observant of things that was going on with a car, so he was the first choice — he was the only choice at that time, we never even thought about anybody else and Don agreed to drive it, so months went by and we got further along with the design and we were going to have a press conference with the Gas Industry in Los Angeles for the announcement — the driver and the project — and just before that happened Don called us up and said he had to back out of the deal. He said he had sponsor pressures or something, that they didn't want him to risk his life driving this car and he was making pretty good money at that time with his various sponsorship deals and as I remember it that was mostly why he had backed out if it.

So all of a sudden here we had the press conference scheduled and nobody to drive so we quick made up a list of people who we thought might be acceptable and Danny Ongais who raced for Mickey Thompson at that time was the first one that we thought of, he was pretty versatile and a nice guy. Art Malone was on the list and Craig Breedlove and we made up a list of ten, Gabelich who we had met because he flew out from Los Angeles, he wanted to run the *X-1* rocket car, after we weren't going to run it anymore.

After we interviewed him we realized he had done an awful lot as well and he explained he worked at North American Aviation as a test astronaut and had done high altitude sky diving with the power capsule, done all sorts of stunt stuff, you know diving off Hoover Dam. He was a genuine...

... Was diving off Hoover dam was that part of his duties with North American?

PETE: No, no that was strictly a...

He had a weekend off?

(laughter)

PETE: He was an adventurer. In fact he drove the *Beach City Chevrolet* funny car, (note: which burned to the ground.)

He drove the Valkyrie *(jet dragster).*

PETE: The *Valkyrie.* He had run the *Moon Eyes* Invader, I believe at that time, the Allison-powered car that belonged to that guy who could port headwork, Jocko's Porting Service...

Jocko Johnson — yeah.

PETE: Yeah, he drove that car out on the Salt Flats. So he had this tremendous background of experience behind him and that tying in with the Space thing, he was (Mercury Seven astronaut) Wally Schirra's exact size and he did a lot of space checkout for Wally Schirra.

It was explained to me by somebody basically that if Gabelich survived it then it was okay for the astronauts to try it.

(laughter)

PETE: Well, that may have been.

I mean, you can't have one of the Mercury Seven getting killed before lift off...

PETE: Gabelich was a very personable fellow. Good with people, likable and uh, not a bad looking guy either. He was on the *Dating Game* TV show, the kind that gets the girl and he did get the girl.

LEAH: He was his own product.

PETE: Later on he became the subject on the *Dating Game* and the girls vied for him. So he's already in with the TV stuff and all that stuff. We personally went to Breedlove and figured he had the experience out there. He didn't want anything to do with it because he didn't build it and I'm the same way...

That's just the confirmation I'm looking for because Craig told me that you guys went to him and somebody else said that he was not even in the loop.

PETE: Oh no, (after Garlits) he's the first one we went to.

Excellent. So was his Goodyear sponsorship a conflict of interest?

PETE: Well, the way he explained it that he didn't design and build the car, he didn't want to drive it. And we had no idea what he would want in the way of money cause he had already been running you know, he had held the record at that time, why should he break his own record, you know there was all sorts of reasons.

But that was part of Shell Oil and Goodyear's thing, too, you know "you're the first to go 400, 500, 600 mph; you haven't reaped the benefits of the 400, 500, 600 yet." He explained to me it would be prudent for him, because he wanted to go Mach One, his car was called Sonic One *at the time and — it would beneficial for him to have an adversary who took the record away — and then...*

LEAH: He could get the sponsorship to come back with his own glory instead of ours...

PETE: So anyway he basically turned it down. Next we went to Mickey Thompson to talk to (funny car driver) Danny Ongais and uh, Mickey wouldn't even let us talk to Danny.

"My guy."

PETE: That's right, he never contacted me, you know, that's it — so we never did talk to Danny and so here we are, we're out there in Los Angeles, no driver, so we called Gabelich. Gabelich was just tickled pink. He loved to do it. Didn't take him long to accept and so we presented that to the Gas Industry and they met him. They decided yeah, this guy can handle the job as far as the p.r. end of it, from there we had our press conference and we all went back to work and Gary was our driver.

I remember the Purple Gang Top Fueler that he drove with the big purple plumes and kind of the feathers coming out of the crash helmet.

(laughter)

PETE: Say if you don't mind I'm going take a couple of more pieces...

(TAPE ROLLS OUT)

INFINITY AND THE NOTES WITHIN THE NOTES (1997)

Four hippies are traveling east out of Grass Valley, CA in a beaten '89 Ford Taurus station wagon, brownish yellow as sun-beaten adobe and trimmed with a personalized California license plate that reads "EIEIOM." Like a perpetual motion machine powered by cough syrup, the Taurus chugs up and over the Donner Summit, gathers downhill momentum and coasts across a state line that gradually smears into the funky, gaudy Babylon of Reno. After exiting the interstate at Fernley, the Ford heads north on a ghostly two lane highway snaking towards a dry lake bed some ninety miles up the road, burning the proverbial midnight oil in a grimy crankcase.

With an eggshell of a summer moon as their beacon and a hissy, unbiased cassette tape of Schoenberg compositions as their soundtrack on a factory stereo with no noise reduction, this ragtag new age entourage journeys past the ramshackle shanties that serve as suburbs of the nearby Indian Reservations. It is a menagerie of adobe shacks, satellite dishes aimed at the heavens, rusted Chevy Vegas and sandblasted pickup trucks with weathered bumper stickers that read "**SURE YOU CAN TRUST THE GOVERNMENT JUST ASK AN INDIAN,**" and sundry forsaken hardware (washing machines, refrigerators, teevee sets) whose sole practical application is that of lawn sculptures. This scene is supplemented by a lunar-lit landscape of buttes, mesas, the placid veneer of Pyramid Lake, and lava rock that had been spit up 150 million years ago out of the parched and ancient Lake Lahontan. As it climbs into the thin air of the high desert, the dingy Ford is conspicuous as the only object in one hundred square miles to exhibit any motion, a reality punctuated by its dull, low octane ping.

To these travelers, this pinging was another intermittent, syncopated rhythmic element that accompanied the cassette tape of Schoenberg.

Among the four hippies is Danny Jo, a blind visionary riding shotgun and meta-grokking to the sounds of Schoenberg, as his exceptional sense of hearing was piqued by the minor detonations inside the combustion chambers of the engine. (The sound of vehicles in motion always spoke to him, as did twelve tone compositions by German cars with umlauted names.)

Schoenberg used every note in the Western scale — all twelve tones (the black keys and the white keys) that was his modus operandi and his signature as a composer. His critics considered this technique busy and gratuitous. To the blind hippie, however, these compositions were not busy enough (!) and when the low octane pinging subsided, to compensate the blind hippie would begin riffing on the notes within the notes.

The notes within the notes. It is interesting how the mind travels. The notes within the notes reminded Danny Jo of the Ancient Greeks and their conundrum about infinity — and the infinities within the infinity. Between 0 and 1 were an infinite amount of fractions *(1/2, 1/10, 1/100, 1/100,000,000, ad infinitum).*

The higher the denominator, the lower the value. The higher the denominator, the closer you are to zero. But you can never get to zero. That's the paradox of Infinity.

The knowledge warms him with glee. He begins to meditate with *"In-fin*-uhh*-tee"* as his mantra.

As the Taurus passes by the shells and hulls that dot the Reservation town of Little Nixon, the blind clairvoyant's meditation is interrupted by a flaming telepathy, as Danny Jo begins to involuntarily decode spiritual overtones of massacred Injuns. Furthermore, he is enveloped by sound patterns of what he considered an extraterrestrial presence. He feels both death and... the presence of spaceships in the desert.

Despite the exotic and transcendental nature of these telepathic interruptions, the blind man considers both signals not only superfluous to his purposes but even ultimately distracting to his mission, and he begins to filter out these pulsations by dialing in the sound of a freight train as it chugga-chugga'd down some lonesome railroad tracks. And from listening to a videotape of *Bad Day at Black Rock*, that old Spencer Tracy flick, he knew that Gerlach was nothing more than the intersection of railroad tracks, the highway, a gypsum mine and a prehistoric lake bed. This must be the source of the sound of the train.

A train is the perfect construct to drown out the other psychic noise. The blind hippie remembers to back when times were bad, when he lived near the railroad tracks in Olathe, Kansas before he had found himself a good woman with a gold station wagon, and how he had to create a way to tune out the extraneous din that clouded his head and his being. Once, in the midst of a particularly vicious and dark argument with his woman, he had heard a railroad engine off in the distance. As it moved closer, the freight train began to drown all of the infernal hollerin'. And when both the train and the domestic situation had passed, the blind hippie unchained his relationship with that harridan shrew — not unlike a boxcar at the station — and moved out west to find him a peaceful woman with good karma. So from that day forward, in order to create a device that would reject the negative vibrations and that would streamline the metaphysical signal-to-noise ratio to an acceptable level, he had fabricated a sort of post hypnotic suggestion for himself in the guise of an oncoming train steaming its way down the tracks, whose sound suggested to the blind hippie that good tidings were coming. His heart was filled with glee. An oncoming train. A Juggernaut of Positive Vibrations. And by extrapolation, A Glorious Portent for the Millennium.

FELLOW TRAVELERS POSTSCRIPT (1959)

Two weeks after the *Jocko's Porting Service* streamliner knocks the drag racing world off its axis, it implodes. Reasons given were "downforce versus insufficient substructure." Besides being the only streamliner that ever really accomplished something *profound* on the drag strip, really, the Jocko-liner had *ALL* the elements: Completely avant garde, yet thoroughly functional. A hep cat driver named "Jazzy Jim." Low ET of the Universe. Cover of *DRAG NEWS*. Then it *self-destructs* two weeks later.

I mean *there's* your folklore. So ripe it can make one itch.

NOTHING IS STATIC (THE GREAT AMERICAN SOUTHWEST, 1996)

The journey continues. Night has fallen and a cassette tape of Link Wray rumbles on the car stereo. Cuz'n Roy and I burn down a rather deserted stretch of desert in time with the music, the swanky and ferocious beat acting as a syncopated counterpoint to the soothing thrum of the Pontiac's smoothly percolating 400 cubic inches of internal combustion. These are the only sounds to permeate the mute omniscience of the California moon and interrupt the stillness of the surrounding darkness.

I pull on a styrofoam big gulp of jake, thick as motor oil and twice as sour. The brackishness of the caffeine is exacerbated by the faux liquid creamer, which has a consistency and overbite reminiscent of a night in Akron, Ohio. Despite the brutality of the acidic bile in my styrofoam cup and the realization that if I didn't drink this stuff we would never reach Black Rock, Nevada in time for Breedlove's record runs, nothing could harsh the mellow of a night that seemed to be in harmony with the cosmic consciousness.

"The sound of a well-tuned V8 is the sound of the universe at peace with itself."

Roy agrees. "It is the perfect rhythm section for a twangin' guitar," he nods, reaching to crank up the volume pot on the tape player.

Like Link Wray, Roy is a North Carolina boy and he grew up around the souped-up V8s of stock car country. He is a strapping, towheaded country mouse with a build informed by a generous helping of corn beef hash. Neither of us are particularly mechanically inclined, but we both have a profound appreciation for an internal combustion engine and all of its trappings, not the least of which was the different ways one can sound depending upon fuel type, air/fuel induction system and cam grind.

Roy can find harmonic overtones from a variety of fountainheads, but he has a real penchant for picking out the symphonies buried in thermodynamic sources... He knows that machines are part of the great cosmic *om.* Many times at the drag strip as I fought for elbow room amongst the bleacher bums and professional photographers Roy would just stay in the parking lot and recline in the front seat of the car, content to kick back with a sixer and listen to the different types of drag racing machines gear up and wind down across the pavement. It is music to his ears, like the sound of bird calls to somebody in the Audubon Society.

"It sounds like you are down on compression in the number seven cylinder," he says during a lull in the cassette.

I am colored impressed. Roy's appreciation of the sonic qualities of an eight-cylinder internal combustion engine makes sense when one factors in that his birthplace, Ranlo, is not more than a three beer drive from a triumvirate of company towns whose main industry nowadays is stock car racing and its spinoffs. In recent years, surrounding cities such as Charlotte, Hickory, Rockingham, Winston-Salem, Spartanburg, South Carolina et. al., have all blossomed and roared with commerce as garages, shops, wind tunnels, checker flag themed coffee shops and other havens for horsepower research and development for stock cars replaced or supplanted the region's rather moribund textile industry. Each of those cities is a point on a circle that envelops the modest digs of Roy's childhood in the podunk burg of Ranlo.

The conversation turns to North Carolina and its recent history. We talk about textile mills and relatives with missing fingers; we talk about how Link Wray and how North Carolina has changed since the days of rockabilly and moonshine. We talk about the jail terms of the first wave of stock car racers.

Ahhh, the checkered history of stock cars in the Crimson State. The phenomena that became stock car racing as an industry transpired the moment when federal revenuers and local Good Ol' Boy law enforcement were empowered by the sudden ubiquity of inexpensive radio technology in the 1950s and 60s. This finally allowed them to stop (or at least stem) both the rampant bootlegging of corn liquor and its coefficient, tax evasion. Sure, a hot headed soda cracker moonshine runner could out drive the local sheriff's deputies, but good luck in outrunning radio transmissions carried on modulated electromagnetic waveforms that travel at the speed of light. So the daredevils who were at one time runnin' shine and who were the object of hot pursuit from law enforcement became stock car drivers. Many had gone to jail at one time or another (and another), but these days they are respectable businessmen and/or tooth-capped spokesmen for boxes of Corn Flakes and laundry detergent, pitch men racing for maximum exposure on the boob tube and catering to the needs of the racing crowd and its Fortune 500 sponsors, their tawdry occupation of outrunning the law now firmly excised in life's trail of exhaust.

"A bonafide hillbilly guitar player can't get a job in county music no more," Roy muses. It seems the landscape had been gentrified with corporate stock car bucks and Starbucks, he says and in reference to the motorsport that was once the domain of moonshine runners, he adds that, "and all of those famous stock car boys can't talk about their vacations in the big house neither."

Stock cars in the Deep South. Corn liquor squeezin's. Hillbilly guitar players. None too shabby a cultural backdrop for life east of the Mississippi, but for Cuz'n Roy these trappings were not enough. As a kid, he had been exposed to the surf and drag culture of California via exploitation films and sound recordings. Throughout Roy's youth it was, by day, surf guitars mixed in with hillbilly honky tonk on a dime store phonograph or transistor radio and, by late night under the blue cathode glow of a rabbit-eared teevee set, beach movies with gratuitous dragster crashes shoehorned into the plot and then the world fell into a sine wave and a test pattern. This imported culture shaped and informed Roy's appreciation of California and fired up his sense of wanderlust.

(Early in our friendship while watching the vintage surf and drag trashploitation flick *Bikini Beach* on videotape, he told me in solemn tones that, "Every time I went to a drive-in movie theater in the deep South and I saw these beach movies with dragsters racing alongside those majestic mountains, or whenever I heard a song by the Beach Boys on my AM radio, I knew there was something going on in California I needed to experience.")

Back in those days, for kids in the hinterlands, pop culture — late night television, AM radio, surfing and drag racing magazines, etc. — taught its impressionable viewers that California was not just a place on the map, it was the end of the line for the Manifest Destiny. It represented an ideal, opportunity, the last stop on the trail that began at the Gateway to the West, a logical extension of the last chunk of real estate within the borders of the Continental US. In fact, it is where the pavement ends and where vision begins for passengers riding the American Dream, a notion encapsulated in the idiom of Breedlove's choosing, "the Spirit of America."

As a transplant, Roy is the natural guy to tap into what that meant, i.e., to figure out what resonance and deeper meanings, if any, could be summoned from the whole Spirit of America gag — as a phrase, as a concept, as an approach to life. It is 1996. California had changed; America had changed... all of which is natural, as life is nothing, if not change.

The drive continues. California became Nevada. Posted speed limits are ignored. The conversation dies and the mix tape of surf music spools out. I eject the cassette and scroll through the dial of the AM radio. We find a rock and roll station out of Reno, which through a quirk of electromagnetism, is able to transmit all the way to I-15 east of Stateline, Nevada with minimal fritzing. Late night radio in the American Desert is truly freeform and tonight the screed from the deejay in Reno is particularly temporal and metaphysical...

"... *Nothing*-uh *is static*-uh," the voice from the radio says through some static, while a disjointed organ solo section of a vintage Pink Floyd space instrumental meanders in the background. *"Things move both forward and backwards, as a function of space and time, but things move, my friends. Stars move, galaxies move, everything moves away from everything else. And the further away they get*-uh, *the faster they move, which indicates the universe is expanding and constantly changing. Only when something ceases to move, does it cease to exist. Can I get an amen*-uhh*?"*

We lose the station not long after that and drive more or less in silence for the duration of the trip. And so it goes into the black vacuum of the Nevada desert. Vegas. Beatty. Tonopah. Hawthorne. Reno. By 3 AM, all are road signs in our rear view mirrors. Nixon. Little Nixon. Black Rock. We spend the night in Gerlach, Nevada, with me on a pool table and Roy on the floor of a joint called Bev's Miner's Club, whose back door is a crack in the lip of the dry lake bed. This next morning we drive out onto a ridge overlooking the dry lake bed, share a batch of campfire coffee with some backpacking survivalists, brush our teeth with salt and bottled water, and then spit the wash on gypsum dust white as the fossils of time.

THE THIRTIES (1930s)

Henry Segrave dies in 1930, attempting to set a new water speed record. Campbell continues to "endeavor to prove the supremacy of British workmanship and material" and fires off a volley for God and Country. His latest *Bluebird* is also a test bed for the Old Sod's Air Ministry, who bequeaths Campbell with a new, secret aircraft engine. It clocks 250 mph in Daytona, a watershed performance. Campbell is knighted by King George V.

And although Campbell has stormed through the 250 mph zone virtually unchallenged, this feat merely serves to raise the bar to 300 mph for this land speed pole vault. And Campbell's new threat was fearless and formidable: Captain George Eyston, decorated World War I officer and shoe of the massive, 6-ton, eight-wheeled, dual Rolls Royce-powered *Thunderbolt.*

But Campbell once again prevails, this time at Bonneville, where on September 3, 1935, he tallies a record speed of 301.13 mph in his now Rolls-Royce-powered vehicle. This just antagonizes and cranks up Eyston's sense of both pride and honor, however, as *Thunderbolt* returns to terrorize Utah's potash desert floor with a series of gonzo runs; after a succession of 300+ mph saline sleigh rides where the clutch disintegrates, on November 19, 1937, Eyston's goggles are blown off as he blasts through the measured mile en route to a record of 312 mph. Outrageous.

The following summer Eyston engages John Cobb in a duel. With an enclosed cockpit and *Thunderbolt's* aluminum body painted black, Eyston goes 345 on August 27, 1938. Cobb goes 350 a week later. Eyston's titanic *Thunderbolt* gets lean and mean: Eyston shitcans the radiator and stabilizing fin and recaptures the LSR at 357.50 mph in September. Eyston continued his assaults on the salt that year until, finally, *Thunderbolt's* rear suspension wishbone snapped at nearly 400 mph. Eyston retires — only to help brainstorm on the Invasion of Normandy in WWII.

During the war, the Land Speed scene goes dark, as fuels and metals are rationed...

JOHN COBB'S NITRO (STUFF WAS STILL GOOD)

"1965 at Bonneville, I made friends with the Mobil Oil guy, and mentioned we needed some nitro. He said, 'I have some.' There was a corrugated tin shed in back of the Texaco station that he had a key to, he gave me the key and said 'help yourself to what you want.' I had Bob Knapp's Chevy pickup and when I opened the door, there was about 60 drums of fuel in the shed left over from John Cobb's land speed run. I thought about all of the racers that parked next to the shed over the years and never knew what was in it. Seeing as how he said to help ourselves and I was by myself, I found a stack of pallets, I put one down and rolled a barrel onto it, then up onto two and so on up to the bed of the truck. I got two drums of nitro and one alcohol, before I could no longer move... Stuff was still good from 1948." — **Chassis builder, drag racer and land speed racer, Kent Fuller.**

D-Day becomes V-Day, and more attempts at cracking 400 mph transpire. John Cobb resurrects his unique 4-wheel Railton 'liner (now coined the *Railton Mobil Special*), a sleek manta ray of a streamliner with independent suspension and a Napier-Lion 12-cylinder aero-engine mounted in each curve of the S-shaped chassis. At Bonneville on September 16, 1947, John Cobb lays down a scoriating two-run average of 394 mph. Asked to describe the runs, one of which tripped the timers at 403 mph, Cobb exercises the British gift for understatement when he says, "Everything happens quite quickly." Yes, things do happen very quickly at those speeds. Empirical proof? Cobb is killed attempting the water speed record at Loch Ness in 1952. He never cracks the 400 mph barrier; his record remained unplucked like a grape on a vine until...

1959

Breedlove begins construction of the *Spirit of America* streamliner in his parent's backyard... At Bonneville, Athol Graham turns 344 mph in his homemade, Allison-powered *Spirit of Salt Lake* streamliner... garbed in black leather and an oxygen mask, California hot rodder Mickey Thompson makes some ramp-up laps in his *Challenger I*, a four-wheel drive streamliner, whose chassis consists of steel purchased from a junkyard and whose power comes from four Pontiac engines. Thompson reaches a peak of 363 mph.

The rains come.

1960

"*I don't believe in boundaries.*" — Ken Norris, co-designer of Donald Campbell's Bluebird CN7 car.

The Great Confrontation at Bonneville: Thompson is back with *Challenger I*. Malcolm's kid, Donald Campbell, unveils his own *Bluebird*, a turbine-powered machine five years and many millions of quid in the making... Out of a chicken feed mill in Akron, Ohio, Art Arfons is on the scene with the *Anteater*, an aardvark-shaped car with an Allison engine... Nathan Ostich debuts his *Flying Caduceus*, a turbo-jet on wheels... after five weeks of record runs Thompson turns a one-way speed of 406 mph in 1960, but fails to back it up nor break Cobb's record, succumbing to a blown engine on his return run... Arfons breaks and splits... Ostich crashes and lives... Donald Campbell crashes and lives... Graham crashes and dies...

"I felt I knew enough about driving at very high speeds to tell that Graham, driving his car through only two wheels, could not hope to deliver enough horsepower to the Salt to go more than 355 MPH... I got up at the crack of dawn on August 1 and went out to have a look at the course. I had a spooky feeling that morning, which I explained to myself on the grounds that Graham was driving awfully fast for a man who had only made a couple of runs on the Salt... I headed down to the north end, where Graham's pit was located, found him and spoke with him for the first time. I offered him any and all the help I could give... But he looked at me as though from a remote distance and said, 'Look. I've gone 344. I don't have anything to learn below that speed.'

"I tried to point out that he had changed the car radically since that time and that the surface of the Salt changes almost from hour to hour. But his mind was completely preoccupied... It was at this point that a heavy premonition settled upon me. I gave up talking and drove to where I knew it would happen and set up my movie camera... Graham took off at 11:02 that morning and 47 seconds later he was doing well over 300 MPH when he got sideways in front of my station. The tail section peeled away from

his car; the car leaped high into the air, crashed upside down and then bounced and slid for a good half mile.

"I was one of the first to the wreck, hoping to reach Graham in time to do him so good. But it was too late. His roll bar had withstood the impacts but the upper tip of the firewall which was between his back and the engine somehow bent forward and had chopped his spine just under his crash helmet. I walked back in his tire tracks for a mile, analyzing what had happened. It was crystal clear. He had been accelerating very hard and his car had begun to drift off the black line. If he lifted his foot at all, he didn't lift it very much. The tire tracks showed he just got farther and farther off course until he got sufficiently sideways to trip over his own wall of air." — Mickey Thompson, CHALLENGER.

AFTERBURNERS AU GO GO (1962)

The assault on the 400 mph barrier cranks into high gear via the intrusion of some wily Americans who sully what theretofore had been the sanctified sandbox of European aristocracy. After the shootout between Eyston and Cobb concludes, the Yanks begin kicking up dust storms on the Salt Flats in contraptions so stripped down, coarse, and primitive that the Brits kinda' viewed them as uncouth tinderbox folk art.

Perhaps most emblematic of this mindset is Akron, Ohio scrap yard scavenger Art Arfons, a drag racer who terrorized the strips with Allison aircraft engines until the National Hot Rod Association pulls the rug on both his ingenuity and his aircraft engines, and tried to relegate Arfons to a circus act. In retaliation, Arfons doesn't get mad, he just turns up the boost on a mighty mastadon of mutant machinery that he has christened *Cyclops*, and aims his crosshairs on the Salt Flats, leaving the drag strips in the rear view mirror of his memory. "I had an Allison (aircraft engine) for ten years and I couldn't get to 200 in the quarter mile," Arfons recalls about the '60s. "I wanted more horsepower." It is difficult to ascertain what was the bigger monster at this point: the race car or Arfons himself.

∞

"I had three children by my twenty-first birthday," remembers Breedlove, reflecting on the transformation of the LSR tableau from the domain of Euro high society to working class 'Merican motorheads like himself. "I was financially strapped. Even if you could afford the Merlins (aircraft engines) or what have you, the costs of developing the transmissions and the gear trains and so on and so forth was really prohibitive. When I saw the jet engine, I went, 'Oh boy — there's no way we can go wrong with that.' In '61 we located a J47 engine at Airmotive Surplus down on Alameda Street in L.A," he continues. "They had a whole batch of 'em coming in that were Korean War vintage. The engines were being scrapped out for $500. I had a sponsor, Ed Perkins, who had an aircraft fastener company. I talked Ed out of 500 bucks and that became the first engine for the *Spirit of America*."

But the prodigious-yet-cost effective horsepower that aerospace technology provides to the salt flat racers did not come without a price: And in 1962 drag racer-cum-jet setter Glen Leasher pays it — in full. While driving the J47 powered *Infinity* at maximum velocity, the jet car veers off course. Glen corrects at full burner and the stress and torque loads the suspension, precipitating a possible wheel or axle failure; the motor explodes and scatters its remains — as well as Leasher's — across the measured mile of Bonneville potash.

Regardless of Leasher's fate, however, the fuse of the paradigm shift has been lit. Taking bald exception to the stateside jet set, however, is the progeny of Sir Malcolm hisself, Donald Campbell. Piloting an immaculate, brand new turbine-engined, axle-driven re-invention of his old man's *Bluebird* streamliner, Campbell is caught in an awkward transition, as he sets a water speed record with a jet engine, yet rigorously maintains that any proper heir to the LSR throne would not be thrust driven like the abominations Breedlove and Arfons were disgracing the Salt Flats with; By 1960, Campbell sinks over three million dollars of other people's British Pride to ensure that the stateside vulgarities never triumph. And this was just startup lucre; by 1963, after a spectacular 500 foot hurtle across Bonneville, the venture capital doubles. As *Bluebird* is humpty-dumptied back together, Campbell seeks a new venue for his mission. He takes aim in Lake Eyre, Australia.

Meanwhile, Breedlove petitions the FIA to sanction his impending incursion on the LSR but the FIA sniffs its nose and harrumphs at Breedlove's request, noting that the *Spirit of America* a) is not wheel-driven; and b) only has three wheels, therefore it is a motorcycle, not an automobile. Craig shrugs his shoulders and shrewdly summons the FIA's kid brother, the FIM (*Federation Internationale de l'Motorcycle*), seeking its approval and timing resources. The FIM is down with the *SOA*'s request, under this criteria: Breedlove's cigar-shaped streamliner fits the description of their "Unlimited Sidecar" category (!), and they will happily sanction the record runs if Craig adds thirty kiloliters of ballast to one side of the vehicle, as to mimic a sidecar sans passenger (!!). Done. *Spirit of America* cranks out a two-way average of 407.45 in the summer of '63 to reclaim the LSR. Breedlove is officially the first man to travel at over 400 mph on land — all accomplished in a "motorbike" with a virtual sidecar. Brilliant.

Amidst the controversy and hullabaloo over the *SOA*, Campbell continues to sojourn in his *Bluebird*, albeit with mixed results. His Australian expedition is hammered by monsoons, weather conditions that enable Breedlove to score the LSR uncontested back in the States. Indeed, the weather in Australia was so disheartening that Campbell's benefactors begin to view this whole land speed record thing as a multi-million dollar boondoggle and yank their sponsorship. Finally, on Friday, July 17, 1964, Campbell goes 403.1 — twice — with a backup pass so brutal that it rips the wheel from out of his hands. Both Campbell and the FIA claim the de facto record runs went down in Australia, that this was the "real" LSR. Latter day pop psychologists would refer to this way of thinking as "denial," for history remembers Breedlove's run not as a bogosity on a tricycle, but as triumphant; it remembers Campbell's run as valiant as Paul Bunyan, but unfortunately a day late and a few quid short. There indeed had been a changing of the guard in the 1960s at the Salt Flats, as it became not only the domain of new technologies with godawful gobs of horsepower, it also becomes distinctly American.

Equally important, Breedlove has trumped the FIA, who were now sucking hind teat as far as sanctioning prestige goes. With its ego bruised, the FIA swallows its pride and allows jet technology into its competition, opening the floodgates for folks like Arfons, "the junkyard genius of the jet set," the man who set out to conquer the LSR in a post-modern mongrel contraption that featured a '37 Ford truck axle, depression-era Packard steering and a top secret fighter plane engine. Breedlove, Arfons and their ilk were now legitimate.

How legit? Even as the FIA and the hot rod set thumb their noses at the exploits of a tricycle that strapped a military surplus jet just on axis of where the sidecar should go, the Beach Boys write and record an eponymously monikered B-side about such an endeavor. So... What is more relevant? The approval from pop stars that sold more records worldwide at that time than Beatles or the signing off from a French bureaucracy?

SPIRIT OF AMERICA

(Doo doo do duh) Spir-it of America,
(Ahh hah huuhhhh) Spir-it of America
(hah hunh huh hhu-unn-hnnn) Spir-it of America...

The Bonneville Salt Flat had seen some strange things
But the strangest thing yet was a jet without wings
Once there's a jet it played in the stars
But now on the ground, is the king of all cars

(Ahh hah huuhhh) Spir-it of America, Spir-it of America
(ha hah huuhhhh) (Ahh hah huuhhhh) Spir-it of America,
(hah huh ha-ha-ha-unn-uhh) Spir-it of America

Half airplane, half auto, now famous worldwide
The 'Spirit of America' the name on the side
The man who would drive 'er, Craig Breedlove by name
A daring young man played a dangerous game

(Ahh hah huuhhhh) Spir-it of America, Spir-it of America
(hah hah hhuuhh) (Ahh hah huuhhhh) Spir-it of America,
(hah huh ha-ha-ha-unn-uhh) Spir-it of America

With a J47, a jet for his power
Craig Breedlove had averaged 407 per hour
For man and machine had given fair warn
They set a new record on that warm August morn

(Ahh hah huuhhhh) Spir-it of America,
(hah hah hhuuhhhh) Spir-it of America
(Ah hah huuh) Spir-it of America,
(ha hunh huh huh-unn-hnn) Spir-it of America

- The Beach Boys, 1963

500 MPH

In October of '64, Walt Arfons makes his presence felt at the Salt Flats with his *Wingfoot Express.* With Tom Green pushing the pedals and pulling the parachutes, this bulbous, bulky flounder of a 'liner reels off a new record of 413.2 mph at Bonneville... three days later Art Arfons and the *Green Monster* turns 434 mph ... Breedlove clocks 468 ... and so it goes, a month long game of ping pong with a target speed of 500 mph.

Walt Arfons makes the mod to his wienie roaster (now dubbed *Wingfoot Express II*), modifying the thrust from his jet engine with JATO (jet assisted takeoff) rockets. The car is now denied sanction by United States Auto Club timing, the American sub-contractor and corollary to the FIA, because of the alteration. Just as the jets had initially caught the powers that be off guard, so had the rockets. The technology was ahead of the intellectual capabilities of the sanctioning bodies...

On the 15th, Breedlove strikes paydirt — and a telephone pole. After bursting through the 500 mph barrier on the first lap, Craig turns his *SOA* around and is chewing up black line in supreme fashion, easily generating enough thrust to backup his provisional record run. Through the speed trap, however, chaos envelopes the vehicle: At 539 mph the parachutes shred like CIA phone records and, like a domino, Breedlove's brakes melt into goo-goo muck. The barreling machine is vacuuming up salt like June Cleaver on benzedrine, and begins swerving off axis from the infinite black stripe burnt into the salt and continues barreling towards an imminent peril. After the rampaging bull of a streamliner snaps a telephone pole into kindling, it hits an embankment which launches the race car and dunks 'er into a brackish brine canal. Breedlove swims to the surface and climbs onto the stabilizing fin at the stern of his streamliner, the only portion of the vehicle not completely submerged. "For my next act, I will set myself a-fire," a wet but euphoric Breedlove tells stunned camera crews. His two-way average speed is 526.61 mph.

NOW I'M GOING TO DROWN

The following transcript is verbatim from a portable recorder operated by voice-over announcer Jim Economides and his recording engineer, Bill Robinson. While producing a vérité sound f/x record, they were stationed at an observation station manned by United States Auto Club timer Joe Petrali. After Craig went zooming past their stations with his parachutes shredded to ribbons, Economides and Robinson gave hot pursuit in their rented vehicle, whereupon they continued to roll tape at the final rest of the *SOA*. This is unexpurgated documentation of the return leg of the record run, when Breedlove became the first driver to eclipse the 500 mph mark.

Breedlove sounds adenoidal and like a chipmunk, giddy and vaguely bi-polar. He also sounds very glad to be alive.

∞

USAC Official: He's on his way... he's standing on it... they say he's really standing on it now... nice and straight... he's really rolling... into the mile...

VOICE: I see a smoke trail.

USAC: ... something fell off of the car... that must be the chute... wait a minute, something fell off of the back of the car... he lost his chute...

VOICE: I hope it was his chute...

USAC: ... he lost his chute...

VOICE: Before he hit the trap or after?

USAC: He didn't say it's out ... I see him coming... he's really coming along, he's really pouring it on... here he comes...

VOICE: ... heads up....

USAC: He's approaching the finishing line ... he's past the finishing line...

VOICE: ... he's got no chute...

(*ppppphhhhweeeeeeeeWHHHHHAAAAAAAHHHHHHH.....*)

VOICE: ... OOHH!!!

(trucks and support vehicles roll, horns honk, general commotion as reporters dictate to machines)

VOICE: ... what a thrill for the people...

VOICE: He's in the water...

USAC: He's in the water...

VOICE: He's in the water...

USAC: Better roll the ambulance down here... roll the ambulance... I'll roll down there... okay... I'll roll ...

(tape rolls out)

∞

BREEDLOVE: (*deep breaths and laughter*) Unnnhhhh, hunnhhh...

VOICE: Suppose you'll get a water speed record on that too?

BREEDLOVE: I think so.

VOICE: Who do you think you are? Cobb or somebody?

BREEDLOVE: What a ride! Uhh hnnnuhhh... "*FOR MY NEXT TRICK!*"

(*laughter*)

(*more laughter*)

VOICE: (*unintelligible overlapping dialogue*)

BREEDLOVE: "I'll set myself... a-fire... "

VOICE: ... son of a bitch...

BREEDLOVE: I went over the top of that 10 mile light. Did I break it? Did I break the record?

VOICE: Yeah...

BREEDLOVE: Okay.

VOICE: We didn't wait to see...

VOICE: You went right over the top of it...

BREEDLOVE: If Petrali missed the time on that, boy, he's out of business.

(*laughter*)

BREEDLOVE: I'm not doing it again!

(*laughter*)

VOICE: Jeez-us

VOICE: Look out now...

(*shutters click*)

VOICE: Holy Mackerel...

VOICE: See you had to swim there... That was an underwater job!

VOICE: Yeah.

VOICE: Craig that was a tremendous run, though. It looks like you broke the record by a big margin.

BREEDLOVE: I obviously did!

(*laughter*)

VOICE: It can't stand another one though ...

BREEDLOVE: Hey, you did a pretty good job with that course, old buddy...

(*laughter*)

VOICE: He was really steerin'. I thought you were going to go right by here and you might not make it in this water...

VOICE: I tell you that was the last we expected...

BREEDLOVE: PHHWEEEHHH!!

VOICE: ... to see of ol' Craig Breedlove...

BREEDLOVE: (*off mic and distorted*) Roy, you wouldn't believe it!

VOICE: I'll tell you one thing, you're spectacular, man.

(*commotion*)

VOICE: I wonder what the people are going to...

BREEDLOVE: (*shouts*) WHAT'S MY TIMES? NOBODY WAITED TO GET IT!!

VOICE: Nobody waited to get it!

BREEDLOVE: How fast did I go?

VOICE: Let's all get in this four-wheel drive...

BREEDLOVE: (*shouts*) HOW FAST DID I GO??

VOICE: (*off mic*) Nobody heard, Craig.

BREEDLOVE: Hey... Hey Bill... For my next trick I'll set myself afire! (*laughs*)

VOICE: Well, you did a beautiful job on the car. (*laughs*)

BREEDLOVE: (*deep breaths*) Hunnnnhhhh! Hunnnnnhhh... Did you see what I did to that telephone pole, Nye?

VOICE: Jeez-us...

BREEDLOVE: I damn near drowned... look at the racer!

VOICE: Craig, here's your dad....

(*commotion*, *heavy breathing*, *more commotion*, *unintelligible*)

VOICE: Oh my god... Oh my god...

BREEDLOVE: I'm okay, Pop.

(*commotion*)

BREEDLOVE: At least we went 500... (*deep breaths and laughter*) unnnhhhh, hunnhhh...

(*commotion*)

BREEDLOVE: I damn near drowned in that thing! I couldn't get out!

(*commotion*, *overlapping dialogue*)

VOICE: You know, you should get a skin diving license.

(*commotion*, *overlapping dialogue*)

BREEDLOVE: (*unintelligible*) ... spectacular. If Petrali missed that time he's fired!

(laughter) (*film camera rolls*) *(commotion, overlapping dialogue)*

VOICE: He's the first guy to try and set a Land Speed Record and a Water Speed Record at the same time!

BREEDLOVE: (*off mic*) I lost my steering at the *(unintelligible)* mile.

VOICE: You did?

BREEDLOVE: The brakes just burned up.

VOICE: They did?

BREEDLOVE: I put my chutes out after I cleared the mile because I lost my steering.

(*commotion, overlapping dialogue*) (*film camera rolls*)

VOICE: You put out both of them didn't you?

BREEDLOVE: Well the first chute, I pulled it, it just went to shreds. I felt it go to a ribbon. Then I hit the... I waited for a while and I tried to hit the brakes and the brakes just wouldn't go... I was pumping the brakes and then nothing, no brakes at all. Then I hit my other chute and nothing happened. I didn't have any... I just took that...

VOICE: No steering...

BREEDLOVE: ... steering and I turned it clear around like this. It finally started...

VOICE: (*interrupts*) Did you see that...

BREEDLOVE: ... coming around.

VOICE: ... telephone pole that you sheared?

BREEDLOVE: Yeah, I know. I hit the pole.

VOICE: With your right fin or what?

BREEDLOVE: I just saw that pole coming and I went just like that...

VOICE: (*whistles*)!

BREEDLOVE: ... and then I hit the pole. I thought I had it when I hit the pole. I saw that telephone pole coming and I went "Ooohhh" and I gritted my teeth.

(*laughter*) (*film camera rolls*) (*commotion, overlapping dialogue*)

BREEDLOVE: (*loud, over laughter*) I gritted my teeth and that pole just sheared off like nothing. You know, "DOUMM" and no pole! *(breathes in)* UUNNHH... I looked up and I thought, "Oh Boy! Another chance!"

VOICE: (*giddy laughter*)

BREEDLOVE: I looked up...

VOICE: (*giddy laughter*)

BREEDLOVE: ... I hit the water and the water started slowing me down and I seen (sic) this big old bank coming up and I thought, "OHHH NAWWWW." (*laughs*)

VOICES: (*giddy laughter*)

BREEDLOVE: I hit the bank and it just went right over the top there. I was flying through there about thirty feet in the air and I thought, "NOW I'M GOING TO DROWN!"

VOICE: (*uproarious laughter*)

BREEDLOVE: I couldn't get the canopy off. I tried to get my belt done. I couldn't get my mask off and the water was filling up like that...

VOICE: ... Next run scuba gear...

BREEDLOVE: ... and I thought, "What a way to go! After all this and now I'm going to drown!"

VOICES: (*uproarious laughter*)

VOICE: Next run, scuba gear, baby!

(*shutters click*)

BREEDLOVE: (*giddy laughter*) I broke the racer! *(giddy laughter)*. Everything's okay... How fast did I go, dammit? *(giddy* *laughter) (shouts)* DID WE BREAK THE RECORD?!

VOICE: (*shouts*) WHAT WAS THE TIME?

BREEDLOVE: (*shouts*) WHAT WAS THE TIME? *(giddy laughter)*

VOICES: (*commotion, overlapping dialogue*)

BREEDLOVE: (*clears throat*) Will somebody tell me how fast I went?

(*giddy laughter*)

VOICE: Hey Craig! You set a boat record!

VOICES: (*giddy laughter*) (commotion, overlapping dialogue)

VOICE: C'mon, let's go and (*unintelligible*).

BREEDLOVE: I want to find out how fast I went, man!

VOICE: Where? In the water or in the...

BREEDLOVE: Hey Al! What was it?

VOICE: 526.

VOICE: 539 for the kilo.

VOICE: 535.

(*truck pulls up*)

VOICE: 526 average. 535 coming back.

VOICE: (*reading off time slip*) Mile is 539 point eight nine. The kilo was 535 point four-oh. And the average for both ways was 526 point two eight. And the kilo was 527 point three three.

(*tape rolls out*)

THE SIDE OF A BARN

Upon word of Breedlove's conquest, Art Arfons dutifully 180s his converted school bus out of his shop in Akron and hauls his jet car operation back into Utah. "It was really competition between Goodyear and Firestone," is how Arfons explains his return to Bonneville. "They were the motivating thing.

"My car wasn't real streamlined," Arfons continues. "When Breedlove went 500, he told Goodyear they could go ahead and put their ads out because the *Green Monster* was about as aerodynamic as the side of a barn and I would never go that fast." Barnyard aero or no, on October 27, 1964, Arfons unloads his wienie roaster and rips a new mark of 536.71. With winter eradicating further record runs, Arfons, the rubber city son-of-a-chicken-farmer, could claim bragging rights — at least until the snows thawed.

Meanwhile, Breedlove scores a J79 and begins to construct a new *Spirit of America*, sub-titled *Sonic 1.*

The Arfons/Breedlove transonic tennis match resumes at Bonneville the next year.

BURN BABY BURN

In the interim, after Breedlove set the world on fire and after he threatened to set himself on fire, civil unrest almost beat him to the punch.

While cloistered in the claustrophobic confines of his South Central LA shop on Compton Boulevard, the Watts Riots begin and spread like a virus. The flames lick at the door and Breedlove's shop help (Tom Hanna, Quinn Epperly, Nye Frank and others) arm themselves on the roof on his industrial building

The city is on fire and it is the *Spirit of America* against the world. Among the angry and the downtrodden, the Spirit of America is a fraudulent symbol. To an underclass struggling to find its place in society, 600 mph is a bourgeois construct, another manifestation of Honky Imperialism.

The guns and the molotov cocktails are drawn. The Great Society versus the tendrils of the military-industrial complex. Perhaps, in calmer moments, Breedlove and his endeavors can be viewed as a symbol of self-help and stick-to-it-ineness. Of the Aristotelian decree that "All men by nature desire to know." But to those in streets, this whole jet car was a variation on the Thoreau didacticism of "we do not ride on the railroads, it rides on us." To those it the streets, the *Spirit of America* was a jive turkey mutha'. Burn, baby, burn.

"This was '65. I was involved in the building of the car. When we were building the car, the Watts Riots went on. I was there when they started. The heart of the Watts Riots was about four blocks away from where we were. We were trapped. We couldn't leave the building. I can tell you that we were frightened enough... our concern was that someone was going to torch the building. Here was this car — we've committed to Goodyear and Shell and we've got to deliver. This is how stupid we were: We had guns. We were in there with whatever kind of guns anybody could come up with. We were defending the fort with molotov cocktails rolling in under our feet. We had National Guard trucks rolling back and forth down the street and so on..." — Tom Hanna, Aluminum Fabricator and Spirit of America crewmember.

The *Spirit of America* wins the standoff in the ghetto that summer.

That fall, in the new four-wheeled, pop bottle-shaped J79-motivated *Sonic I* streamliner, Breedlove whooshes to 555 mph on November 2. Five days later, Arfons loses a tire while upping the ante to 576 mph. Art is nearly asphyxiated from smoke enveloping the cockpit as fiberglass shattered and the vehicle careened haphazardly across the Salt Flats.

November 15, 1965: Breedlove records an average of 600 mph; He is the first human being to officially go 400, 500, and now 600 mph. Two days later, in an attempt to push the envelope even further into the stratosphere, Arfons's white knuckle symphony turns completely discordant. He goes into orbit at over 600 mph, after losing a front wheel. Art gets the 'chutes out as the other wheels let go. This is the dénouement. The transonic match of Russian Roulette is over. Breedlove held onto the record.

"I shared a room with Walt Sheehan, Breedlove's engineer from Lockheed. He would bring the paper reels out of the recorder — the car had a recorder that was connected to strain gauges, the same thing they would use as if it were an airplane test project. In those days what you would do is develop those reels just like it was a photographic negative. So we had to beat it back to the motel room, take our showers and convert the bathroom into a dark room and use the bathtub to develop the print out for that day's run. And from that, extrapolate what needed to done to take the next higher step." — **Tom Hanna.**

FROM THUNDERCAR TO DRIFTWOOD (1964)

After he set a Top Gas record in 1964 with *Thundercar*, an Allison-powered streamliner — a machine that defied convention (fully enclosed, contoured and tapered body, motivation by an aircraft engine) except for the fuel it burned, pump gas — Jocko Johnson retires from the digs, popping in occasionally to port heads for some hitter engine builders in both drag racing and sports car racing.

He shutters Jocko's Porting Service and assumes the life of an artist. His hair, couture and lifestyle become more bohemian. The hippie revolution is germinating. Jocko appears equally at home with the now-withering beat movement as well as the hippie gag, as he becomes a wood sculptor, creating art pieces out of driftwood.

THE EARTH'S CURVE

Newton figured that space and time are absolute. They ain't. Had he done his calculus at the Bonneville Salt Flats, he might have come to a different conclusion.

Time. He might have asked the Donner Party as they ran into trouble crossing the salt lake how many minutes were in an hour, how many hours were in a day and how many days were in a week. The Donner Party were misled and bamboozled by a slick-as-owlshit map seller who sugar-coated the distance across the tremendous and treacherous lake bed. They didn't have to resort to cannibalism until they reached the Sierra Nevada Mountains, but the interminable delays as they negotiated their way across the sweltering and sodden salt flat delayed their arrival until wintertime and an unforgiving blizzard.

Space. From where the Donner Party crossed the salts of Bonneville to where Art Arfons skimmed across the salt like a stone at 600 mph, the earth's surface bends like the whistle on a locomotive as it makes it way closer to the station.

The bending of space and time is a crucial aspect of Einstein's Theory of Relativity, as gravity warps, compresses and expands spacetime itself. Time slows down and time speeds up. Synchronized watches give conflicting readings from different points in the solar system. Watches orbiting the globe maintain a different reading than those static on planet earth.

All of this wisdom is burned inexorably into the Salt from millenniums of harsh lessons. Human experiments are redundant. Tautological.

On a human level, spacetime is not so much gravitational, as it is physiological: just ask Art Arfons how time stood still when he was bouncing across the Salt Flats in 1965 at over 600 mph, as he tried to re-take the Land Speed Record from Craig Breedlove. Art crashed when a wheel spindle broke, launching the car in the air for a distance of nearly two football fields, before it touched down and continued caroming across the desert. As the second ticked off while he was in the air for those 527 feet, time was stretched like a rubber band in suspended animation, then snapped back to nothing at all.

Aristotle, Galileo, Newton, Einstein, and others have all argued about the state of Space and whether or not Space itself is a body in motion. Ernst Mach was critical of Newton's definitions of time and space as absolute. He denounced the theory of absolute space as "a pure thought-thing which can not be pointed to in experience."

Mach's rebuttal of Newton was part of his research investigating Doppler's then controversial law which described the relationship between perceived frequency of sound and light and the motion of the observer relative to that source. Einstein owed much to this research.

Sound and light bend depending on the velocity and proximity of the source. Like the Earth turning its back on the Sun. Like a train heading toward a station. Or a motorcar approaching the speed of a bullet on the desert floor.

The cosmos and the desert have their own empiricism, and they really don't care if this knowledge is something humanity can or cannot grasp. Regardless, it will dispense harsh lessons in physics and relativity to those who dare challenge the cosmos' sense of superiority. "I don't remember nothing until they tried to get me out of the wreckage," Arfons says.

IT WASN'T FOR NOTHING THAT WE DID IT

You got Gabelich hired as a driver and I assume...

PETE: He was hired by the Gas Industry, we didn't hire him. He had his own deal with the Gas Industry which was fine with us because we didn't have anymore in our account.

When you say The Gas Industry you mean... ?

PETE: The Institute of Gas Technology, which was the research and development arm of the American Gas Association at that time, was overseeing the project for the American Gas Association. It was a promotion of the safety of and the usefulness of liquefied natural gas. They were trying to promote it as a hypersonic fuel for aircraft and, of course, I think they probably succeeded in that now, but you know in certain areas, they were pushing at it.

LEAH: And the gas industry as a whole was trying to push natural gas as a modern fuel, and they were looking for something that would spark an interest in the younger people in gas.

How did you incorporate LNG with the hydrogen peroxide?

PETE: It was the fuel. Hydrogen peroxide created the oxygen. We added the liquefied natural gas to the engine as a fuel to burn and then we ignited it.

So the hydrogen peroxide was the oxidizer and LNG was the fuel, but with the X-1 *car, what was...?*

PETE: There was no fuel, it was just peroxide, forced through a catalyst pack at a 600 to 1 liquid to gas ratio and creating about a 1300 degree temperatured mixture of oxygen and water vapor.

Steam.

PETE: Um hmm.

The catalyst pack was?

PETE: Silver. Silver screen, chemically treated and it had nickel for port screens.

So as you guys got to Bonneville, it's like 1970 I think, and...

PETE: Dick went out there in 1969 when Mickey Thompson was running the *Autolite Streamliner*. He hired a survey crew out there and we did a full length survey of the course: how flat it really was, you know, how much of a dip and what sort of undulation the surface had, (there is) so much suspension travel we had to figure on at speed. So he was out there when Mickey was running and got the survey confirmation which we then sent to the engineers at the Illinois Institute of Technology; they were nine graduate engineers working on masters degrees for thesis on various aspects of the design of the *Blue Flame*: structures, dynamics, aerodynamics, wheel design, all sorts of things.

I was the liaison between our company and my title was Manager of Vehicle Engineering, that's what it was.

So this was not a couple of hot rodders building something in their backyard.

LEAH: The *X-1* was. We built the *X-1* during the week in our family garage — we parked it on the street. *(!)*

So anyway, you're acting as a liaison between Reaction Dynamics and the Illinois Institute of Technology and so you got a bunch of...

PETE: Our company presented the basic layout of what we wanted to do and then they would work on refining those ideas: location of center of gravity and how it worked with the aerodynamics. We worked back and forth between the engineering students and the engineering staff at ITT...

(*stop tape*)

... I'm not sure I got this on tape, I want to be sure I'm

hearing this, you said there was some scale wind tunnel testing, subsonic wind tunnel testing...

PETE: Supersonic.

And which wind tunnel was this?

PETE: It was Ohio State University. We paid them to build the wind tunnel model to the aerodynamic specs and wind tunnel tested up to Mach 1.120. 1.15 I believe. It was around 850 miles an hour that they wind tunnel tested it to and structurally it was built to hit a half-inch steep bump at 1000 miles an hour. There was nothing out on the Salt Flats that high, although there was deviations and dips which we thought maybe would be a problem, but as it turned out the 350 pounds of nitrogen pressure in the tires, the tire moved itself out of the way, it just made ruts.

So the tires were 350 psi and they were filled with nitrogen?

PETE: Yeah, they were built by Goodyear, designed by Mike Hopkins.

Now I got the impression that at some point Firestone originally was interested in this car, and uh, they were never in the loop with this?

PETE: They were interested in our quarter mile car, the *X-1*.

Right, but then they pulled out.

PETE: Humpy Wheeler, who is a big deal in stock car racing now with tracks, worked for Firestone at that time and we had contacted them. They provided tires for the *X-1* to start with, then later on when we became associated with Goodyear. Goodyear gave us tires for the car, the *X-1*.

Okay, so basically, as I understood it, Firestone pulled out of the "tire wars" altogether and nobody saw it coming.

PETE: So we went to Goodyear and Goodyear supplied us with tires.

And with that, we got the letter of intent that Goodyear would be making us these tires and went to the Gas Industry and they then signed the contract to let us build the car, once they were assured that we could get tires. It wasn't until afterwards that we found out it would be three years before we would get the tires.

Yikes.

PETE: We already signed all the contracts and everything and we were too much of novices to nail down all the specifics in the contract, we were just young people at the time and didn't have any business experience as far as contracts. So we learned.

Do you think that partially because Firestone pulled out and so Goodyear has no real incentive?

PETE: They already have the record.

(With) Breedlove's Sonic 1 *car.*

PETE: But, uh, they were not interested in having their record broken by someone else so they decided — they didn't help us financially at all. They built the tires and provided us twelve tires tested and did the balancing on them and Cragar Industries built the wheels. Did just a beautiful design, we designed the wheel, they manufactured them and just did a super job on them, they made 12 wheels and Goodyear mounted them, spun test them on Walt Arfons' spin testing machine and while they were spin testing it, they had the machine break while it was going 850 miles an hour with a tire up there.

So the tire took it, but the machine didn't ?!

PETE: I think there was a four-inch shaft driving that thing and the shaft snapped. They said there will be tire marks in that test cell that will be there forever.

Okay and just to wrap this part of it up — Goodyear developed tires, specifically for this project...

PETE: They were going to and when they couldn't deliver them soon enough we ended up using the front tires off (Breedlove's) *Sonic 1* car, only they were re-engineered for our car — same molds, but the insides were quite different and they'd come up with new fibers and double the bead wire and change the internal construction using the same molds that the front tires on the *Sonic 1*. Those were 35 inch diameter and because of it the car grew a third in size and tripled and cost and we lost the vehicle to the Gas Industry because we immediately overspent.

Wow.

LEAH: Also our original contract with the Gas Industry called for them making payments here, here, here, and here. Those payments were contingent on the fact that we had this much work done before each payment by a date and we had to prove we could do it — well we were doing fine until there was a national steel strike, you cannot build if you don't have steel. Finally they settled, and it was just going to be touch and go for us to possibly make the next point and the truckers were waiting for the steel strike to get over. When the steel strike was over, the truckers shut down and said, "now it's our turn" and we had no steel, and we couldn't build, the fellas went back looking for other part time work, no paychecks, there was nothing.

PETE: Six months nothing happened on the car.

LEAH: The Gas Industry said we're taking our car, they took the car and they left and we were sitting there devastated. No work...

PETE: The car went to Chicago, got put in a shed and it was on the wheels by that time, but the propulsion system wasn't finished, it hadn't been tested.

LEAH: It was no longer our car, according to the contract we didn't own it.

PETE: We lost the ownership of the car, because initially it was going to be our car.

LEAH: It was a very hard time, that was during the time when Ray Dausman said his part of the work was done. He had developed this propulsion system, he had seen it through, he didn't walk out on the company, he saw through everything that was his part, but he couldn't deal with this devastating loss and saw no need for his talents to stay there. So he sold his share of the company and got on with his life basically and the rest of us twirled until we could re-negotiate.

That's brutal.

LEAH: It was brutal, you know we think of it very sadly. It was out of our hands, the Gas Industry knew that we weren't just scuffing around with the thing. "Well, send us more money, we'll build it," you know, they were aware of the steel strike and the trucker's strike, but there was nothing we could do, so then we re-negotiated and...

PETE: They ended up owning the car and they agreed to pay us to finish the car, and because they had twice the money into, more than twice the money of the original contract and just to finish it, get it to the testing point, and of course it cost a lot more to run it.

So the last part of the car as far as buttoning it up finally was you guys were kind of out of the loop at that point or you were just hired employees?

PETE: We were basically hired employees.

So Reaction Dynamics was still involved with the car?

PETE: Oh yeah, we were doing all the work, but we were doing for the Gas Industry.

Was there a positive out of that, were you like, getting a paycheck at least?

PETE: Once we started working on it again, then everybody went back to collecting paychecks and you know everything was basically the same except that we didn't get the car.

LEAH: It wouldn't be our car and we spent about a week as a family agonizing over what this was going to mean, but you don't meet too many people with the determination of Pete and he was going to have that car finished. If we didn't have it, we didn't have it, but he had said it would be done, he'd given his word, he signed the papers and...

PETE: We decided that it still needed to be done, I mean it wasn't for nothing that we did it. We wished we'd been able to go back.

(*TAPE ROLLS OUT*)

How much would you say was LNG and how much would you say was hydrogen peroxide? 50/50? 90/10?

PETE: I'd say when we finally ended up running it, well, we had, it jetted so that the flow 25% of what the full flow of the engine would be and we flowed in 25 % by volume of LNG, no wait a minute — yeah it was about 25%. 30 gallons of LNG and 160-something gallons of hydrogen peroxide.

What was remarkable about this car was that it was really the last hurrah for the rocket guys, I mean Bill Fredrick was trying something similar, but by that time it was so hard to get fuel in the US, hydrogen peroxide, you know?

PETE: I guess you can get it, but whether or not they would allow you to import that much into the country I don't know.

Well, (drag racer) Brent Fanning was telling me that there was one manufacturer left in Europe that would manufacturer at a percentage that a decent rocket, which I think is above 85%.

PETE: Yeah, it will run about 70% but it's very poorly, it runs poorly and very inefficiently, 90% and above is better, 98% is better yet.

Spoken like a true drag racer.

PETE: 98% is military. That's torpedo fuel.

MISHAP AT BLACK ROCK! (1996)

The morning is superficially calm. A palpable tension tightens amongst the spectators and the engineering types milling about the barren floor of the dry lake bed. Once or twice the *Spirit of America's* jet engines spool up and purge its afterburners and then shuts down. There is an aura of confusion around the streamliner as it sits in its staging area for hours, all the while with Craig Breedlove suited up and strapped into the womb-like cockpit of his homemade missile. Desert winds begin to kick up dust and storm clouds blew in and cast a pall on the entire landscape. The mood seems to darken with the weather, which acts as a tangent to the reality that the *Spirit of America's* permit from the government expires in a couple of days...

∞

MISHAP AT BLACK ROCK! Breedlove's Record Attempt is Off! (NR Wire Service)

Black Rock, NV. October 28, 1996 — While attempting to break Richard Noble's Land Speed Record of 633.468 mph, Craig Breedlove's Spirit of America *jet car crashed and was severely damaged. The attempt took place two days before his Bureau of Land Management permit to use the Black Rock desert expired.*

On the first leg of the required back-to-back runs, Craig was well on his way to breaking the record, which is based upon two timed one-mile averages, when at a speed of an estimated 675 mph a burst of wind lifted the back of the car and pushed it up onto one side. Major damage was inflicted on the rear axle and rear frame of the car. Craig was unhurt, but obviously disappointed to be so close to the LSR after many years of research and development with his GE J79 powered vehicle.

The car will be brought back to the team's compound in Rio Vista, CA to assess the damage and make repairs, but it appears unlikely that another attempt at the Land Speed Record could be made until early next Spring, permits allowing.

Breedlove is in the throes of a duel with Richard Noble

OBE, who is campaigning a LSR vehicle piloted by Royal Air Force "Top Gun" Andy Green, to be be the first to eclipse the Speed of Sound on land. Currently, Noble and Green and their Thrust SSC *twin Rolls Royce Spey jet-powered machine are testing in the Jordan desert in preparation for their impending Mach One effort at Black Rock.*

Breedlove's ill-fated record run was his first attempt at reclaiming the LSR from Richard Noble, the first goal en route to ultimately breaking the Sound Barrier. Breedlove uses a single J79 — capable of 45,000 horsepower — mounted on the fuselage, directly behind the driver, an engineering approach in stark contrast to Noble's system of using twin 202 Spey turbofans, each capable of 50,000 hp, mounted on either side of the cockpit in what, in essence, is a 10-ton, rear wheel-steer Batmobile.

Breedlove's mishap occurred after a promising day of testing the day before. He was able to hit 563 mph, but did have some trouble with the parachutes...

YOU DID MOST THINGS RIGHT

From the ridge, Cuz'n Roy and I watch what is the fastest U-turn in history. Breedlove catches a crosswind at 675 mph as his *Spirit of America* streamliner "Wrong Way" Corrigans itself, assuming the attitude of a rather elliptical traffic circle. Breedlove bicycles — and nearly destroys – his cherished, cherry jet car while traveling at a speed of over three football fields a second (!). While up on two of five wheels, the machine begins making a hard right towards some nearby hot springs and foothills, buzzing and nearly t-boning a motorhome parked not too far from the photoelectric timing traps, missing it by less than a "Hail Mary!" pass into the end zone.

"It looks like the Tazmanian Devil out there," Cuz'n Roy says as Breedlove attempts to correct the precarious trajectory of his race car.

A retired couple stand on the roof of the motorhome with binoculars out and watch the streamliner kicking up dust lickety-split, the smoke of cherry-colored coals from a portable barbecue wafting past their eyes and nostrils, the acrid haze adding to the disorientation they experienced when they notice that the *Spirit of America* — and by extension — themselves are in serious trouble.

"Christ, Martha, look at this," the snowbird mouths to his mate. "He's got 'er on two wheels and he's heading right toward..."

He never gets the rest of the sentence out as Breedlove boogies by the startled occupants of the motorhome like a transonic rodeo rider, as Craig hangs on by a proverbial leather strap... Miraculously, nobody is hurt as the race car somehow avoids contact with the motorhome. After a banzai blast across miles of gypsum dust, Craig gets the chutes out and calms 'er down, but the streamliner is bongoed like a skateboarder's knee, sustaining structural damage to a right wheel fairing and the chassis.

"Hesitation kills," Cuz'n Roy said, and laughed.

∞

That afternoon the mood at the post-record attempt press conference is dusty and grim. I stick a micro-cassette recorder in Craig Breedlove's gypsum-caked kisser and ask him to summarize his approach for recapturing the LSR and for going Mach 1 vis-à-vis an aerodynamic approach that seems to hasten instability at transonic speeds, Breedlove is uncharacteristically terse: "We don't want a lot of downforce because it creates drag," he says.

"But could your low weight, low drag, and low downforce approach, a combination rather vulnerable to powerful crosswinds, a phenomenon that is rampant in the desert outback of Nevada, is that the right way to go?"

"Anytime you walk away from a 675 mph crash, you have to say, 'Well, you did most of the things right,'" Breedlove maintains.

"So what happened exactly?"

"In my mind, I had no thought that there was any crosswind condition whatsoever," he says. "We had called down for wind condition earlier and it was at 1.5. The timing wasn't ready and we already had the engine fired but they said, 'Shut down,' so I was all ready to go. I actually sat in the car for forty minutes waiting for the timing to get back on. We re-fired the engine and had a compressor shake, so we had to shut down and check for that — then re-lit again. In the meantime, the weather conditions had changed: It had gone from a nice, bright sunny morning to big, dark clouds and I was having trouble even seeing the course."

I hear what Breedlove is saying, but my mind ramps up into extrapolation mode as he continues to describe that moment when a bad case of "Go! Fever" short-circuits logic... the story is as follows: with the permit to run dwindling and bad weather encroaching, Craig knew his window for making history was finite... When the *SOA* crew fired the J79, it developed a fluid leak and was shut down. As the crew tightened some fittings with their wrenches, a cloud cover blew in over the playa, obscuring Breedlove's vision. He continued to wait, and kept his game face on still strapped into the cockpit. Finally, the clouds lifted and Craig could see the 13-mile black stripe, his empirical guidance system down the course... Four hours after the original time of departure, all systems were go and Craig requested another wind profile...

"There were some decisions made because of the weather closing in that were just not prudent decisions; I kind of caught up in the 'I've-got-one-chance-to-do-it' mode," he rationalizes. "When I called Chuck just before leaving the starting line, I asked was the course clear because we had a problem with policing the course, when Charlie came on and said the wind was at one-five, I thought, 'One-five, okay... one-point-five.'"

In his zeal to go 700 mph Craig inserted a decimal point in the wind profile... He interpreted the transmission as "1.5" not "15" mph. The profile of Breedlove's latest speed machine could withstand a crosswind of one-point-five mph. But a gust of 15 miles an hour blew his precious rig around like a corrugated styrofoam cup tossed out of a passenger-side window. "The omission of the decimal point didn't click," Craig concludes. "I didn't know that I had the sidewind. I was confused. I wouldn't have run had I known what the wind was.

"The other problem, of course, was that the car was much faster than we had anticipated. (I was) trying to watch where my mile-marker was, trying to look at a digital speedometer the size of a postage stamp and back off the afterburners while trying to figure how long I need to stay out of the engine and when I could go back in."

When the car tipped up on its side and went into a skid, "I had dirt in the windshield, and I really couldn't see what was happening... I thought I'd probably had it, that this was going to be it."

I click off the recorder, shake my head and thank Craig for his time. One observer — a desert rat who watched the entire spectacle through a telescope and was eavesdropping on the interview — says to me after I shut down off the micro-cassette that, "Craig's lucky he wasn't smashed into quantum foam" and then drifted off into the eye of an oncoming sand storm.

Meanwhile: Richard Noble, Andy Green and *SSC* were frantically evacuating the flooded desert in Jordan, as a monsoon nearly wiped out their entire operation.

The next available permit for speed trials in the Black Rock Desert would be in September, 1997.

Cuz'n Roy and I drove back to Los Angeles.

PART TWO:

PICK YOUR PART

PICK YOUR PART (1999)

"One day I found myself sitting in a physics class trying to understand how to calculate the instantaneous acceleration of some particle inside the nucleus of the atom, which particle may or may not even exist, and I didn't even care if it existed or not because all this horsefeathers had nothing to do with engines or anything else that I cared about even in the slightest, teensy bit." — **EJ Potter, MICHIGAN MADMAN.**

"Just to know that you were going to a hard top track was a thought that acted like a supercharger on the jets of that mental carburetor called the brain. But this nuclear-physics jazz was — well — not exactly for the birds, but certainly for the new type of square that the scientific age was producing. The old-type atom buster was a kind of beatnik who neglected the barbershop and dribbled shreds of pipe tobacco into his beard. The new model was apt to have a clean crew cut over an Ivy League lab jacket..." — **Philip Harkins, *The Day of the Drag Race*, 1960.**

BZ catches me as I am out the door. It's a Friday on the second week in March and my quest for information on something known as *Infinity* is taking me to Bakersfield to interview an old timer known as "the Goat."

In a rare twist of meteorology, it is actually cooler there than it is in L.A. where Santa Ana winds blow hot and caustic like some sort of cosmic halitosis and the masses of people — including my pal BZ — are stupefied by the preternaturally scorching heat and are acting strange as vaporlock.

He is calling from a pay phone on the corner of Tuxford and Glenoaks

Boulevard, down the street from the gates of the Pick Your Part in Pacoima where he has just been fired. They cut him a check during lunch and sent him home. He tells me he is in no mood to talk about his former job.

"So tell me about Bakersfield and this search for *Infinity.*" He exhales into the tinny mouthpiece. I can hear the sweat on his forehead.

∞

Bradford Ramon Zukovic — BZ to his friends — is the son of Slavic emigres ("Where Nicky Tesla was born," he told me) and has an uncommon command of advanced mathematics as well as an atavistic appreciation of Americana, most specifically its coefficients of automotive culture and technological enthusiasm... His math theory is a little more together than his sartorial sense, in that his belt makes it through all the loops, but there is something off about the way his pants fit. Before he worked at a junkyard, he was a science teacher at a junior college in Glendale, whereupon he seamlessly insinuated his own ideas about bleeding edge theoretical physics on his English As A Second Language class, mixing it in with classic Newtonian theory.

(I thought this was slick. His employers disagreed apparently...)

He abhorred the dumbing down of the curriculum at Glendale Community College. Because of his thorough dissatisfaction with the feel-good and self-helpish tone of contemporary academia that ignored Classic Theory in any discipline (the 3 r's as well as science), BZ ended up working a forklift at the junkyard in Pacoima. This career switch came down after vehement opposition from faculty and administration. There would be no more of his foisting of nanotech and quantum mechanics to unsuspecting English-as-a-second-language types who just wanted to get through enough General Ed to score a job behind some cosmetic counter at the Galleria in Eagle Rock...

∞

"The search begins in Bakersfield at the US Fuel and Gas Championships. 'The Smokers Meet.' The drag strip is out in the orange groves just north of Bakersfield."

I then tell BZ that the Goat had promised to give me the skinny on Glen

Leasher, the driver for the *Infinity* jet car, an ill-fated (and mostly forgotten) LSR project that had crashed with tragic consequences at Bonneville in 1962. (Leasher had driven a AA/Fuel Dragster for the Goat months before his ill-fated Land Speed Record attempt; I had tried interviewing the Goat over the phone, calling him at his speed shop in San Francisco, but this proved futile as he was an octogenarian drag racer and, by extension, rather hard of hearing. Even with all the noise, I decided it would just be easier to just yell into the old man's hearing aid at the drag strip...)

Just as an automated operator interrupts to tell him his allocated time is up, BZ asks me to pick him up by the taco truck on Glenoaks. Over the tremolo effect of more nickels being plunked into the coin slot, I say I'm on my way.

Once he gets in the car he opens up and starts talking about his latest former day job, telling me that the junkyard had let him go for reasons of subterfuge, insubordination and malingering, as he was caught having parked his forks behind the shade of a towering pile of crushed Gremlins and Pacers in the American Motors section of the scrapyard. He tells me that when he should have been loading a 1950s luxury car onto the piledriver, the boss man found him reading a book on a drag racer who changes careers and becomes a wrench on an atom smasher (*"The Day of the Drag Race"*) instead.

"Check this out," he says, pointing to the dog-eared hardcover that got him fired. "I found it in a dumpster outside the library at Glendale Community College."

"My god, they were throwing that away?" I am appalled. "Is every vestige of hot rodding culture going to be trashed in some sort of do-gooder save-the-planet purge?"

"Probably. You should read this book sometime before they do. It proves that even in 1960 some folks knew that the real r&d was going down in atom smashers and not at the drag strip."

This re-ignited an ongoing argument between the two of us as to what was a cooler proving ground: Particle accelerators or the drag strip.

"Atom smashing. Sounds like great work.... if you can get a government grant. Which not even you can get nowadays, eh?"

He ignores my question about government grants for a minute or two. Perhaps he was absorbed in a moment of self-awareness, brutally cognizant of how remote the possibilities are of ever milking the teats of Uncle Sam when one is wearing an oil-stained blue jumpsuit, slurping on an horchata and carrying a sackful of greasy tacos while riding shotgun in a '71 Grand Prix that needed the upholstery replaced. He processes these thoughts and begins dealing with them tangentially...

"That's the great paradox, isn't it?" he deduces. "If books like *The Day of the Drag Race* were part of the curriculum on even a Junior College level and were to show kids that hot rodding can hone one's math and science skills — or better still that the *real* hot rodding is going on at the speed of light, then I'd be in a white coat right now trying to find out what happened to the particles of anti-gravity that were necessary to keep the galaxies from collapsing on themselves moments after the Creation of this Universe..."

"There is more than one kind of white coat."

"Look, if our government has one purpose, it is to cut checks to the people who are trying to separate the bay leaves from the broth in the great cosmic, primordial soup."

We eat ceviche and lengua tacos and wash them down with horchata while I drive. We have ample time to discuss both the cosmos and *Infinity* before we got to the drag strip in Bakersfield; as much as anything, however, we discuss the philosophical and utilitarian ramifications of working at a scrapyard. I tell him that I wondered how he had been able to live with himself while under the employ of Pick Your Part, and that crushing abandoned and surplus automobiles was beneath his dignity, particularly when it means the destruction of irreplaceable gas guzzlers of yore. I say this was, karmically speaking, somewhere between a book burning and replenishing the poison at a gas chamber at Dachau. If he hadn't been fired and had continued "... 'just following orders,' if you will," someday the vehicle he carted to its demise might be the very '71 Grand Prix that he was cruising in right now, confiscated by agents of the Air Quality Management Department and crushed to neutrinos, as a symbol of profligacy and as an incorrigible gross polluter.

"You know there is a government program to destroy these things so an oil company can get particle emission credits," I tell him. "They pay folks 500 bucks to get non-operational beaters off of their front lawn, figure how much carbon dioxide the vehicle would have contributed to the smog theoretically, and then allow the oil company that much more leeway with pollution from their refineries. 'Remove the filters and stoke the furnace.' Pardon the pun, but it's an utter shell game."

BZ agrees. "It's a bureaucratic rimjob."

The casualty in this bureaucratic flimflam was the American muscle car. He tells me of the litany of endangered classic luxury and muscle cars that he had recently carted that much closer to their ultimate extinction: A '59 Chrysler Imperial. A 1960 Dodge Polara. Desoto Adventurers. A '62 F-

85 Cutlass. Buick LeSabres. Pontiac Bonnevilles. A '58 Nash Ambassador. A 1950 Olds Futuramic 98 with a whirlaway hydra-matic drive.

The scrapyard was a museum, he says, and some of these forgotten automobiles were pieces of sculpture. To relegate these arch, epic pieces of American iron to an industrial-strength compacter was an abomination against preservation and decency...

"No matter how decrepit the vehicle, the thought of their imminent destruction always made me well up."

I just listen. I think he mistook my silence as some kind of rush to judgment...

"Look, besides the fact that I needed the cash, I took the job to get next to the contours of those elegant machines, okay?" He pauses for a second, searching for the right phrase. "There is a certain existential beauty in their corrugation and decay as they rust and rot in the excruciating heat of a summer in the forgotten wastelands of the San Fernando Valley. Everything is temporary. Even triumphs of engineering and art. Even triumphs of the intellect." He looks out the open window at the freeway offramp where the LAPD once beat the living chicken livers out of Rodney King, tosses out his straw and plastic lid and then takes a last drink from the dregs of his horchata, which leaves a crescent rice milk moustache on his upper lip.

We ride in silence for awhile...

"So what happened today?" I finally ask, and then turned my head, my gaze distracted by roller coasters as we motor past an amusement park in Valencia. "What finally made you snap?"

"They told me to load up a trashed '57 Pontiac Star Chief on to my forks and take it out to get crushed. I couldn't. The tailfins alone were entirely too majestic — I just refused to be an accessory to its destruction. So I hid it out by the Pacers and Gremlins in the AMC section. Nobody goes there except the — and when I say this, I mean it with respect — the kookiest of car collectors. You know the type: the ones who think the push buttons for the transmission were a neat idea. Lupe Garou. Phhewwww," he whistles and then pointed his forefinger at his noggin and rotated it counterclockwise.

"So while I was kicking back, one of the other fork operators saw the tailfins through the glass bubble of a Pacer and reported it to the dispatcher." He exhaled and sighed. "Christ, they were pissed off, yelling at me in both Spanish and English. I told them to fuck off and that this was Pacoima, not Nuremberg."

"At least you got fired."

THE VELOCITY OF A STEAM JET

We continue to climb. As we blaze up the Grapevine the temperature gauge on "the Batmobile" (BZ's pet name for the '71 Pontiac) slowly creeps onto the warning track. The higher the elevation the thinner the air density, the hotter the Batmobile runs.

We stop for petrol, carbohydrates and radiator water on the Gorman exit. As we gas up, I let some pent-up steam out of the radiator, gingerly easing off the cap with a couple of delicate quarter turns, a task performed with a deft touch worthy of a safe cracker. Or so I thought. The cap was really fucking hot, however, and the pressurized steam ultimately overwhelmed my sense of finesse and just as BZ set off the Junior Food Mart's binging and bonging photocells on his way out of the store — *BHHAAWHHOOSSHHH* — a geyser of boiled and excited ethylene glycol baptizes the parking lot.

In the adjacent bay, a mini-van full of dapper, rather well-to-do Middle Eastern immigrants are genuinely spooked by the ferocity of the discharge, recoiling reflexively as they watch me dive for cover away from the molten volcano of anti-freeze. Theirs was a look of contempt and concern, not one of appreciation for how Nixon-era gas guzzlers such as my '71 Grand Prix fueled the development of a leisure class in whatever oil baron country they emigrated from in the first place.

After things cool down and the radiator is flushed, we motor onto I-5. BZ is showing some concern about the thick heat and the thin air. "You need to get the radiator re-cored on this beast. That might let it run cooler."

"These things came out of the factory running hot... I've tried everything: re-coring the radiator, cleaning the water passages, a bigger fan, a smaller fan. Nothing works. This chunk of Detroit steel is always going to run hotter than a blowtorch."

He looks dubious. Even with a dried, pasty rice milk moustache.

The windows are down and we both eye the temperature gauge with minimal conversation. I could see BZ getting rather edgy, leaning over the console and drawing a bead on how precarious the radiator situation really was. I began trying to calm him down by inserting some levity into what was a dicey situation. I knew there was no guarantee we would make our destination and could end up stranded 4000 feet up on the Grapevine.

"Let's pretend this is a rocket car and we are monitoring the thrust."

"What for?"

"We can just pretend that we have a hot water rocket engine under the hood, not unlike the *Neptune* rocket car that Walt Arfons ran back in '66."

I knew that Arfons' steam rocket had been based on the principle of water superheated and pressurized in a closed container and then flashing into vapor and escaping at the vent, which acted as a venturi and produced a supersonic flow of steam... Pressurized steam and "action and equal and opposite reaction" and all that...

"Yeah? What happened with that car?"

"The ran it once on an air strip in Akron, Ohio."

"And?"

"Uhhh, it crashed on its only test run."

"You might want to find a more positive example, sir."

I thought of Max Valier. I say nothing.

BZ IS SILENT

BZ is silent.

"Hey man, you gotta' believe Walt Arfons was onto something," I bellow over the purr and gurgle of the Pontiac. I knew — or at least, felt I knew — the failure of the *Neptune* had nothing to do with the fact that its steam-powered engine was just a hot-rodded, modified surplus fuel pump from a Titan Missile.

"It crashed because of aerodynamic issues and a nasty crosswind, nothing related to thrust."

BZ is still silent.

"It was one of those great ideas that only made one run down the drag strip," I say.

"If it only made one run, don't you think that by definition it would be a bad idea?"

"Perhaps."

Again, I thought of Max Valier. Again I say nothing.

FAUSTIAN BARGAINS IN THE ROCKET AGE: SUMMONING PAN AS A MEANS TO TEUTONIC ENDS AND JET ASSISTED TAKE OFF (1939-1965)

"I figured that if the car went half as fast as his mouth, I was in trouble." — **Craig Breedlove, in reference to Bobby Tatroe and the *Wingfoot Express II* rocket car.**

Neptune was actually the second rocket car built by Walt Arfons. The first was the *Wingfoot Express II*, a moniker originally hung on completely different set of hardware, a J46 powered jet car that set a LSR of 413 mph in 1964, (numbers surpassing Breedlove's mark of 407 mph). The second *Wingfoot Express* was the first land speed car to use rockets and the only car to ever use JATO (jet assisted take off) bottles. Each 'bottle' was actually a solid fuel rocket and could only be used once at a cost of $1,000 each. Arfons started out with 15 mounted in the back, but that wasn't enough thrust and Arfons installed an additional ten bottles. Officially, the car reached a speed of 476.6 mph one way in October of 1965.

The car was built sturdy enough to break the sound barrier — its ultimate goal — but the weight penalty of the structural reinforcement necessary to withstand supersonic pressure waves became its Achilles' heel, as it tipped the scales at 6,500 lbs. On the run of 476 mph, driver Bobby Tatroe reported seeing 605 mph on the speedometer once, but this was in the middle of the run and by the time the *Wingfoot Express* entered the measured mile its rocket fuel was spent and it coasted impotently through the timing traps.

Fascinating was the taxonomy of the solid fuel rocket bottles themselves. These devices were originally the property of Aerojet-General Corp and were developed in the 40s by the notorious 'Suicide Squad' of Pasadena, a motley quartet of rocket scientists, whose members were linked to Guggenheim and Cal Tech. The chief engineer and designer of the solid fuel JATO system was the man who was the most infamous of the group, Jack (nee John) Parsons, a disciple of black magick, pagan practices and deviant sexuality, all of which were used as devices wired into his summoning of 'Universal Knowledge.' This supernatural wisdom was then harnessed and focused into test sessions at the The Devil's Gate, a small rustic canyon adjacent to what is now the Jet Propulsion Laboratory.

In its original application, the JATO system was instrumental in generating enough lift to propel Allied bombers and hefty cargo planes into hostile skies, and was in fact crucial in hoisting the Army Air Corp — and by extension, the Allied Forces — to triumph in both the European and Pacific Theaters.

On the Salt Flats of Bonneville, Walt Arfons had no such luck with the Aerojet devices, however, and was never able to generate enough thrust to overcome the heft of his endeavors; he failed to claim the LSR with the JATO system; conversely, in an ironic twist of fate after his exile from the rocket science community, Parson was blown to molecular molasses in his home when he dropped a vial of hypergolic chemicals in 1952.

CLASSIFIED JET ENGINE (YOU CAN'T HAVE IT)(1964)

"He even tests that jet engine in the backyard. You can't conceive of it unless you've seen him do it. At first, he'd strap it to two big trees. He burned a 60-foot channel in his woods that way, and he blew a chicken house right off the face of the earth. He's the coolest guy I've ever seen in my life. When he's got that engine going on afterburner and I'm 50 feet away, I'm scared to death that it's going to blow to pieces — they do sometimes, you know — and he's right alongside it making adjustments." — **Firestone tire rep Harold "Humpy" Wheeler, "Enemy in Speedland," Sports Illustrated, 1965.**

After Gorman the Batmobile begins to overheat again. We drive 90 mph over the entire Ridge Route, my rationalization being that the faster we drive, the less time the motor has to warp. We crest the Grapevine, begin our descent into the oil fields of Kern County and the temperature gauge finally calms down. A little.

Even though the biggest load on the motor was behind us, BZ still looks disturbed and squinches his eyebrows in disapproval.

"You know I won't be able to pull a pair of cylinder heads for you now." He wipes his brow with an oily rag.

I nod. I had used him as a source for various generic parts to replace broken or stolen pieces for the Grand Prix — an electric rear window from a '72 Monte Carlo, a headlamp fixture and a carburetor from a '73 Bonneville station wagon. I'd request what I wanted and he'd toss the pieces over the fence, to the bewilderment of the portly Mexican gal who ran the taco truck. Those day were over now that BZ lost his job.

Reminiscing about pilfered parts pitched under chain link fences reminded me of an anecdote about Art Arfons. I tell BZ about a phone conversation I once had with Art concerning the time he had scored a classified fighter plane engine from a military surplus boneyard in 1964...

Art Arfons told me that he knew back in 1964 that there was only one piece of hardware that would have enabled him to satisfy his jones for unbridled adrenaline and also reclaim the LSR from Craig Breedlove — a General Electric J79 jet engine from a Lockheed F-104 Starfighter. He acquired his for $625. "I got it when it was still classified," he said. "It had been scrapped because of foreign object damage. I had hit all the scrap yards and said, 'If you ever get a '79, I want it.' So a guy called from Miami and he said, 'I got one.'"

Arfons then called GE and asked for a owner's manual, in essence sending a smoke signal to a GE whistleblower. With something rotten in the Rubber City, a colonel from the military paid Arfons a visit. "He said, 'That's a classified engine, you're not allowed to have it,'" Arfons remembers. "And I said, 'Well, here's my piece of paper (receipt). I bought it after you threw it away.' I said, 'You can't have it.' Two years later, they declassified it."

As I replayed the phone conversation back in my mind, I visualized how Arfons chained his military surplus monstrosity to a tree in his back yard and — to the horror of his neighbors — began purging the afterburners, searching for harmonic imbalances. "There was a special wrench to take them apart," he had said. "I knew a man who worked at Wright Patterson (AFB) and he got me the tool I needed to fix it. He would sign it out and drop it by the fence for me. He'd check it out in the morning and I'd get it back before he had to turn it in that evening. I had to do that to take it apart and I had to do that to put it together. The blades were all damaged, so I just removed every third one. Never did balance the thing. I just put it back together that way and it ran fine. It had all the power I needed."

"He was armed with the biggest gun in town once he got that J79," Craig Breedlove told me in 1997 at Black Rock, laughing. Breedlove was just as smitten with the concept of thrust unlimited as his compatriot from Ohio. Cheap, abundant jet power enabled both Arfons and Breedlove to dominate the Land Speed Record scene throughout most of the 1960s. Others didn't fare so well...

BAD FOR BUSINESS

"... the professional hot-rodders — such as the Petersen magazine syndicate (Hot Rod Magazine and many others) and the National Hot Rod Association — have gone to great lengths to obliterate the memory of the gamey hot-rod days, and they try to give everybody in the field transfusions of Halazone so that the public will look at hot-rodders as nice boys with short-sleeved sport shirts just back from the laundry and a chemistry set, such an interesting hobby..."
— Tom Wolfe, The Kandy-Kolored Tangerine-Flake Streamline Baby, 1963.

"So tell me about this *Infinity,*" BZ asks again, no doubt as a ploy to distract himself from worrying about the Batmobile overheating again.

I didn't know what to tell him or where to start, except at the beginning, which was 1962 or so. I begin a rambling monologue on how the *Infinity* Land Speed Record project arose out of the success of the *Untouchable* (a jet dragster cum high velocity daredevil act that stunned the drag strip crowd) and featured many of the same players: Glen Leasher, a Type A type driver weaned on jalopies in Wichita, Kansas; "Dago," a welder who worked out of the Oakland Airport and whose christened name was Romeo Palamides; Harry Burgdt, the track operator at Vacaville Raceway (a podunk strip out among the pastures and stockyards northwest of Sacramento... Vacaville translates to "Cow Town"); and a young, fast, scientific type named Vic Elisher, a Hungarian kid who, when not wrenching on deconstructed jet engines, was dabbling in academia and beatnikdom at Berkeley...

The partnership thrived on appearance money accumulated with the *Untouchable* as it toured the race tracks of California and the Pacific Northwest. San Gabriel. Fontana Drag City. Bakersfield. Half Moon Bay. Vacaville. Fremont. Kingdon. Cotati. Medford. Portland. Puyallup, Washington.

To put the exploits of the *Untouchable* jet car in context, I tell BZ that this all happened in an era when the "official" movers and shakers of drag racing were trying to shed the unkempt, greasy image of drag racers as hot rod hoodlums hell-bent on chemical anarchy... If drag racing could clean up its act, its leading sanctioning body, NHRA, could cozy up to the deep pockets of the Automotive Power Structure in Detroit, who had no use for home-built cars with aircraft engines stealing the thunder and the headlines from the accomplishments of real automobiles on the drag strip proving grounds...

It would be quid pro quo: The Big Three, General Motors, Ford and Mopar, could market, advertise and exploit its performance and accomplishments on the official proving grounds sanctioned by the NHRA... in exchange, the Detroit's purse strings loosened and cash began to trickle its way into the NHRA's coffers...

Jet cars were not only unsafe, they were bad for business. In 1961 they were banned by the National Hot Rod Association.

No matter. Up and down the Left Coast the yokels paid their money to see the *Untouchable* jet car badda-bing, badda-boom down the drag strip, reaching seemingly unfathomable speeds approaching 220 mph. In comparison, in those days the AA/Fuel Dragsters cackled mightily and would clock speeds of 190 or so, but it was like they were standing still compared to the *sturm und drang* of the rolling pyrotechnics display what was the hermaphroditic jet car as it went BOOM! BOOM! BOOM! loud as the Wrath of God and then whooshed down the drag strip quicker and faster than anything else on wheels. Each pass was a supreme test of a man who dared to test fate on a quarter mile slab of asphalt. The paying customers ate it up like saltwater taffy.

How could they not? It was righteous entertainment. It was loud. It was dangerous. It was dirty and noisy. And it was officially *verboten* by the NHRA...

The strips that hosted these exhibitions — Kingdon Air & Drag Strip near Sacramento, as an example — were, often as not, rinky dink and unsafe... at Kingdon the Chrondek timing lights were portable and during the course of the speed meet had to be wheeled off the runway to accommodate the occasional aircraft seeking to land there... There weren't any grandstands, so spectators lined the strip and eased up as close as they dared to the fire-breathing machinery, and whenever a car got loose the spectators would scatter like rabbits...

It was under conditions such as these that Palamides and cohorts made their dough. Beyond pocketing a little coin for living expenses, the money from the *Untouchable* was funneled into the construction of *Infinity*, a much more sophisticated jet car with a target speed of 500 mph, speeds sufficient to take away John Cobb's Land Speed Record, set in 1947. Speeds twice as fast as those reached in the *Untouchable*..

∞

So yeah, at most its innocuous, the *Untouchable* and its Midwestern counterparts, Walt Arfons' *Green Monster* and Art Arfons' *Cyclops*, were drag strip curiosities showcasing brutal and brazen shards of fiery horsepower that melted the mental faculties of those assembled and frustrated the Powers-That-Be and their attempts to bolster drag racing's reputation as a test bed for automotive technology as well as a marketing tool ('Win on Sunday, Sell On Monday!') for this year's model...

I am trying to explain all of this to BZ, but he kept interrupting with questions about the junk yards in Arizona where Romeo Palamides and Vic Elisher got the J47s for *Untouchable* and *Infinity*...

"Yeah, I'll get to that. Really though, you gotta' take the taxonomy of this whole *Infinity* gag back to Bakersfield in 1962 and the Smokers Meet. I maintain that Glen Leasher never would have died in a jet car on the Salt Flats if he hadn't been jobbed at the final round of Top Fuel that year — after that he quit the *Gotelli Speed Shop* Top Fuel car and began driving the *Untouchable*. After that, *Infinity*..."

THE FUEL BAN (1959-1963)

"FBI agents descended on a Texas auto racing track last month looking for evidence that Timothy McVeigh bought a large quantity of powerful racing fuel before the Oklahoma City bombing, ABC reported Thursday night.

"Employees of VP Racing Fuels told the FBI that a man resembling McVeigh in 1994 paid $2,700 cash in Texas for nitromethane, ABC said.

"The chemical is an accelerant the government now believes may have been used to detonate the bomb that killed 168 people." — AP WIRE REPORT, 1996.

Even before jet-powered dragsters entered the mix, some independent track operators and the NHRA made no secret of their feelings about drag strip speeds getting out of control. The AA/Fuelers were unsafe.

The offender? The volatile fuel they burned: Nitromethane. Generically known as "Fuel." Pop. Cackle. Liquid Horsepower. Joy Juice. The Yellow Stuff. The Sweet and Sour Sauce. CH_3NO_2. As acrid as it is punishing, when it reaches its flash point nitromethane is an angry serpent of a hydrocarbon and its practitioners are snake handlers who have taken it on faith that they won't get bit — but they often are. Nitromethane is a monopropellant, which is a fancy way of saying that it carries its own oxygen, and therefore once it is lit or merely compressed it is as volatile as a downed high tension line dancing to and fro across the highway.

Ironically, unless under pressure, nitro is surprisingly docile as far as exotic fuels go, capable of taking out unsuspecting railroad boxcars only if under extreme duress. Mishaps off of the drag strip are rare, even when one factors in an incident of domestic terrorism a few years ago. But because of its instability (and the questionable stability of some of its handlers), nitro has developed quite an epic history and mythology, beginning with Italian rocket scientists and their experiments with it as early as 1929, followed by Russian rocket design teams testing a combination of kerosene and a nitromethane derivative a year later.

I tell BZ about the bizarre exploits of Jack Parsons, and how he would invoke pagan spirits before a rocket launch in the once-deserted, arid hills of Pasadena in what is now the Jet Propulsion Laboratory. As early as 1937 Parsons already had listed tetranitromethane as a possible rocket propellant and by 1945 the company he helped charter, Aerojet, was seriously considering nitromethane as a fuel source for their rocket engines, but demurred in deference to hydrogen peroxide.

Beyond issues of safety, it could be argued that this kind of chemical warfare in an internal combustion was a little outside of the image the NHRA wanted to present to its corporate suitors... Violent explosions, speeds that scared the insurers. Nitromethane was banned.

So at NHRA meets dragsters burned gasoline instead of the devil's hydrocarbon. Was this a red herring? Was this an excuse to cozy up to Sunoco as the official supplier of gasoline for the dragsters?

Not unlike the jet cars later, after their banishment from the NHRA the Top Fuel dragsters flourished at "outlaw" and unsanctioned tracks, where they proved to be wildly popular, case in point being the Smokers Meet, which began in 1959 and was the most popular event of them all...

The Fuel Ban. In fact, amidst cries and caterwauling of "collusion," independent trade papers sided with the outlaws and mocked the drag strip establishment as "Druids."

The Fuel Ban was an exercise in futility and beyond: Not unlike the theorem that states in order to make a bigger bang out of a firecracker all one has to do is wrap it tighter, the prohibition of exotic fuel in drag racing created an entire new scene that thrived and flourished on the contraband fuel. And it boomed loudest and burned brightest just north of Bakersfield...

If guns are outlawed only outlaws will own guns could be paraphrased as if nitromethane is banned, only the banned will race with nitromethane... and they did... just another manifestation of the "outlaw" culture insinuating itself into Eisenhower America and its forgotten nooks and crannies... while the Hell's Angels M.C. took over podunk California farm towns like a Mongol horde; similarly, under the sanction of the Smokers Car Club, the renegade fueler guys gravitated to an abandoned surplus airstrip north of Bakersfield, known as Famoso. Nitro drag racers came there from all four points of the Continental US. The "Smokers Meets" were so wildly successful that the money was loaded in 55 gallon drums and the ticket booths ran out of tickets and began exchanging toilet paper for admission...

The vox populi had spoken with wallets. They wanted their nitro. (By 1964 NHRA reversed its position on the Fuel Ban.)

BAKERSFIELD AND THE CORRECT PATH TO MINIMIZE TIME (1999)

I can feel a pinch deep in my solar plexus as we crest the Grapevine, heading north on I-5, just a few markers shy of the Highway 99 junction. The closer we get to Bakersfield, the tighter the tug upon my very psyche, id, and spirit. In the basin below lay the wide expanse of the San Joaquin Valley, encompassing Bakersfield, a gearhead's Garden of Euphony, and its corollaries of honky tonks and greasy spoons, many of which were demarcated by gaudy tubes of neon: Zingo's. Milt's Coffee Shop. The Wool Growers.

The wind is hot and stinks of oil, dung and oxtail soup. It smells of history. It summons the taste of too many cold ones in Oildale. Lefty Frizzell on the local AM radio station owned by Buck Owens. Merle Haggard growing up in a converted railroad boxcar. Famoso. Nitro. AA/Fuel Dragsters. Friggin' Nirvana.

Blazing past the "Rain for Rent" billboard that graces the east side of the 99 in Oildale and the radio is on. A female country singer that I didn't recognize burbles that:

"*A girl must live by the light in her soul The world is spinning out of control...*"

"That's what I love about proper honky tonk, BZ. Three or four chords and no bullshit. There is some greater existential truth in the simplest lyric. Nothing convoluted, straight to the point, like a drag race. Or a ray of light."

"Do you really think a country singer knows anything about the path to the truth?" He reaches over and turns down the radio. "The difference between mankind and a molecule," he explains, "is that a ray of light knows the correct path to minimize the elapsed time between Point A and Point B."

He goes on to explain how on a quantum level, the quickest path between points are two straight lines connected and bent at a pivot point... the folly is in ignoring the pivot point... he then goes on about the convergence of parallel lines, etc...

"I still think this song is right, BZ. She's saying if you follow the light in your soul, you too will know how to minimize time."

"Ahh, but is minimizing time actually maximizing time? By minimizing time do you gain a glimpse into the infinite and the eternal?"

I turn the radio off altogether. Sometimes the truth can only be expressed in action not words. Still I have to ask.

"So what is Infinity?"

"I don't know what is infinite, but I do know what is finite. What is finite is our time on this planet." He pauses. "Life is not only finite, it is also rather mundane and fucked up. We find a way to get passionate about things — like these men who dedicate their lives to conquering the Land Speed Record — as a means of not only getting through Life, but of getting a glimpse into Infinity."

I turn the radio back on. In all its simplicity, country music would provide a respite in the conversation, and an opportunity for me to digest the philosophical implications of Infinity.

BZ would not wait for me to catch up. He was having none of this. He was on a roll. His response was to riff on the notion of infinities with infinity, something that is constantly being debated in higher mathematics and string theory...

"There are infinite points in spacetime — from the Big Bang until the Big Crunch and the constant tug of war between gravity, dark matter and Einstein's cosmological constant which has created 'events.' Moments in spacetime have definite signatures, definite markers." He takes a beat. "But what about the moment between each moment? That, my friend, is infinity. The moments between the moments, which can be chopped into never-ending and finer hash marks..."

I struggle to keep up with BZ's riff about the infinities within infinities and how therein lies Infinity. I tune it out for a half a minute as I realize that each attempt at the Land Speed Record was somehow analogous to the watershed moments in spacetime that BZ mentioned. But I knew this whole trip was about seeking the moments between the moments: Infinity.

When I came back into the conversation, he has wired his notions of Infinity into a discourse on particle physics.

"On a quantum level," he says, "there is a point where a wave becomes a particle and that point can be quantified. Beyond that, there are potentially infinite sub-particles or strings that vibrate and resonate within each particle. It is mind boggling how infinitely small you can slice this stuff upon which everything — jet cars, beer cans, and the radio waves that carry the sound of country singers — is built on."

I look out the window and stare at an oil derrick slowly and methodically cornholing terra firm. It looked like a perpetual motion machine fueled by the entropy of the Universe.

I WISHED HIM GOOD LUCK

1971. Jocko pokes his head back into the scene when his Allison-powered liner (now powered by a big-block Chevy and dubbed the *Moonliner*, named not for its resemblance to a lunar module, but eponymously for its owner, performance parts magnate, Dean Moon) is used in a Budweiser commercial shot out at the Salt Flats. (Footnote: the stunt driver in the commercial is Gary Gabelich). There is another intellectual carrot dangling for Jocko: "Big Daddy" Don Garlits, having had half of his right foot blown off by a experimental transmission that exploded in his *Wynn's Charger* Top Fuel car, has shifted the paradigm of dragster design, having drawn up a crude blueprint for a rear-engine Top Fuel dragster, a somewhat novel design. (Previous attempts would, as often as not, understeer and dart (or "push") towards the drag strip's guardrail (assuming it had one).) To avoid "pushing," Garlits' pit guy Connie Swingle installs a radical 10-to-1 steering system (for every 10 degrees of steering input, the front tires would turn 1 degree) and Garlits dominates the Top Fuel scene. Jocko is piqued. Had Top Fuel cars finally caught up with his designs? Was the drag strip scene ready for streamlining for the first time since 1959? Maximum downforce with minimum drag? How fast could such as creation go in the 1/4 mile? Jocko — and the drag racing press — reckons it would go 275 mph — no jet engine, no rocket engine, but 275 with a blown hemi burning nitro. (The 1/4 mile record in 1971 was 243 mph, held by Garlits hisself.)

Beginning that year, Jocko makes the mold for a fully-enclosed streamliner body in California. And Garlits agrees to pay for a body based on the mold and have Swingle build a chassis for the car. It will be known as the *DON GARLITS WYNNS-LINER.* In the same size type-face, the lettering on the front wheel-wells will read "Body By Jocko."

But it takes forever.

1973. Fourteen years after Jocko sets the world on fire with his *Jocko's Porting Service* streamlined AA/Fuel Dragster, Garlits finally unveils the *WYNNS-LINER.* It is overweight (the bane of streamlining being the weight penalty, as the added body work will cost the car performance, and often negate the benefits of the contoured air flow.) It is behind schedule and it is *w-a-y* over budget.

None of which is Garlits doing. Garlits tours the country with his

Swamp Rat Top Fueler while Jocko and Swingle continue to build the car in Florida.

Amidst much anticipation, Garlits tests the car a couple of times before making the marquee debut at the well-publicized American Hot Rod Association race at Orange County, California, in June of '73.

Before it is even loaded off the trailer, Garlits makes no secret that he is spooked by the car. During testing, he claims the rear tires were spinning at 9000 revolutions per minute, proof that the back of the dragster was not making contact with the pavement — a most frightening and scrotum-tightening phenomenon. Garlits says later that "the car wanted to fly." Jocko is emphatic that the car is doing everything but lifting off the ground; the entire design was based on maximum downforce, thereby planting the massive slicks firmly on the track surface, just as the machines designed and driven had done when setting speed records in the 1930s and 40s.

But the lines are drawn: Garlits wants no part of driving the *WYNNS-LINER*, the radical and revolutionary car which he had so patiently patronized. Which is a problem: track promoters across the country have expressed a keen interest in what, in essence, looks like a spaceship driven not by an alien, but by the most famous drag racer on this planet: "Big Daddy" Don Garlits.

At the Grand Am, Garlits hires journeyman driver (and recent burn victim) Butch Maas to shoe the liner. Maas is certainly fearless enough (during his rehabilitation and surgical reconstruction, his hands were partially formed to grip a race car's steering yoke), but for reasons that remain unexplained, Maas drove it once during qualifying and clicked the engine at half track and coasted to the finish line a tortoise roller skating uphill.

The car qualifies 32nd. Dead last. It loses in the first round after another aborted run. Two weeks later, Garlits parks it permanently. This time drag racing dropped the curtain on Jocko — and not the other way around.

"... (I) towed to Fremont for the AHRA World Finals. It was rained out and postponed until the following weekend, on top of the IHRA World Finals at Lakeland, Florida. I decided I would run my regular car at Fremont and have "Mad Dog" Don Cook run the 'Liner at Lakeland. I won Fremont... but poor Don Cook, even with all his experience, was never able to get the 'Liner' to go straight. I had taken a cou-

ple of passes in it earlier in the weekend and vowed never to drive it again, so with Cook's failure, the entire project was scrapped and the body and frame given to Russel Mendez for a rocket engine installation. I wished him good luck. — **"Big Daddy," the Autobiography of Don Garlits.**

It is important to note that "Mad Dog" Don Cook is out of his mind sufficiently enough to drive any piece of vicious machinery on wheels. Once, after a night of excessive libation, he drove a fuel-burning dragster like a true professional despite a whanging hangover and having vomited into his facemask and firesuit.

It is also important to note that 15 years after the *WYNNS-LINER* has been shelved as a tax write-off, Don Garlits is catapulted in the air on two different occasions by conventional dragsters.

Which is parenthetical. With the failure of the *DON GARLITS WYNNS-LINER*, streamlining Top Fuel dragsters becomes a lost art. Jocko claims sabotage: "Don Garlits' ego could not stand to see another man design a car that was successful," he says.

THE *X-1, THE BLUE FLAME,* REACTION DYNAMICS AND THE WORLD'S FASTEST FLOWER CHILD ... A RAW TRANSCRIPT ... OR ... HOW I STOPPED WORRYING AND LEARNED TO LOVE THE BONE...

The *X-1.* The perfect nomenclature for a rocket-powered Land Speed racer. It's moniker was appropriated from Chuck Yeager's airplane, a piece of machinery that rode in the belly of a B-29 bomber until pod doors opened over the barren slate of the Mojave Desert, where every inch of air and space is a proving ground.

(Yeager proved that Mach 1 was not something to be feared, it was something to be penetrated. Breaking the sound barrier is an everyday occurrence for fighter planes nowadays and has even trickled down into the domain of consumer air travel in the form of the Concorde...)

In both instances, the "X" represented "experimental," and was meant to be a precursor to the real deal: in the instance of the airplane, the *X-1* was a means towards understanding and defeating the turbulence of supersonic buffeting. In the form of the rocket-powered dragster, it was an attempt at understanding exactly how much *ooommmpphhh* could be wrenched out of a rocket motor in a car.

The *X-1* dragster (aka the *Rislone Rocket*) was merely a means to an end, the end being 1000 mph — well beyond Mach 1 — in a larger, more powerful vehicle: *The Blue Flame.*

Like Yeager, Gabelich was a hired gun, a fearless hot shot who climbed into an unfamiliar situation. (After the negotiations with another test pilot who demanded a nice chunk of change in exchange for powering through the unknown, Yeager got the rocket ride when he eschewed the need for a bump in his Army Air Corp's pilot's salary.) Gabelich was hired after Suba was killed in a Top Fuel dragster.

Gary Gabelich: Who was he? His reputation was that as the world's fastest flower child. Was that accurate? This is the guy who whose parting words in a conversation were "Have a happy forever." This is also the guy who, while driving the *Sandoval Bros.* Top Fuel dragster out at Fontana Drag City would greet the track photographers with "the Bone," obscenely and mischievously sticking one finger in the air for the duration of the run...

What can you tell me about Gabelich, I mean you said he was personable and charismatic and fearless, but he was also, I mean, you guys are, you know, nice Midwestern people that uh...

PETE FARNSWORTH: The only time that we really spent a lot of time with him was at the Salt Flats. I mean he came to the Midwest here when we were fitting the car for controls, when we got everything in the right place, the window opening, you now, so that it was centered on where he was going to sit, and the depth of the seat and location of pedal controls, things like that so he could reach everything while he strapped in. Other than that, he wasn't out to the Midwest here very much and generally, he'd be out for a couple of days or so and we'd go and have dinner, but it was a whole bunch of people, a big happening.

LEAH: We heard that he was kind of wild in the California area when he was with his own element but that was not, he kind of segmented things, you know, he kept this group over here and this group over here and we weren't in the group that was, you know partying with him or anything like that and so, you hear things.

PETE: When he came to the Salt Flats, he had his own contingent, you know, people that were right around him and we met a lot of them out there.

Or was there more, you know the hippie biker kind of contingent that he had with him?

PETE: I guess all of the above.

I mean without being a value judgment, it's just that he was a different personality type.

LEAH: I would say from uh, as you said Midwest value type thing, that they were all the (*clears throat*) California crowd. They were from the other end of the country, you know, there's the Midwest and there's the California guys. No they weren't really the hippie biker type, we had that around here, too, they were just, on a different stage, but it was...

PETE: ... they were really good friends of Gary's though, boy they'd do anything for him.

LEAH: He was very mindful of his image, because he wasn't out there, he was the driver of the *Blue Flame*. That man was on from the time he got out of the car. When we went back to the motel, little kids would come up and talk to him and he'd pet their dog, he'd bend over to talk to the little old Grammas you know, get down to their level and talk to them.

PETE: Yeah, he was very good with people...

LEAH: ... he could just sell everything, but...

PETE: When he got with his own group, then he did whatever they did, but we didn't necessarily associate that much.

(*stop tape*)

After you guys set the LSR, Gabelich was hurt in a funny car crash not too long after that.

PETE: Yeah with the money he made driving the car, Natural Gas Industry paid him 50,000 bucks, plus they paid him for appearances too. He built the 4 wheel-drive funny car, they took it out and were testing it and he clipped the guard rail and crashed it and cut a foot off and a hand off and uh, pretty amazing that they put him back together —

Yeah there was a surgeon around that...

PETE: Yep, they threw him the car — and still in his fire-suit and all the pieces — and went over there and there happened to be a neurosurgeon on duty who put him back together. As I understand he won the California State Handball, Racquetball championship after that —maybe it was for handicapped people or something, I don't know — but just the same, you know it was pretty amazing. We had pretty much lost track of him by then.

I sent out e-mail queries to those who worked with Gabelich. Many went unanswered, a mute testament to how much his chums still respect him and continue to honor his privacy. The best and most informative reply read as follows:

I think I understand why those who knew him (to probably even the slightest degree) are "tight-lipped" about GG... it's because we loved him.

Like all of us, he had his "failings" if you will, or his "weaknesses"... but unlike most, he was so very open about "them" (as well as everything else), with an almost child-like naivete that you could NOT help but love him and accept him with open arms... he was just Gabelich!

You'd find his picture in TWO places in the dictionary.. the first is where it says "charm"... he was the most "charming" person I'd ever met! And I'm talking SINCERE charm... that is why he was so special... because if anyone ever had the opportunity to be "stuck-up" it would have been Gary, as he was "movie-star, drop-dead handsome," famous, daring, and with a fantastic personality, he had it all.. yet he was TOTALLY unassuming, generous, and loving to EVERYONE and NOT just when he was in the spotlight... but ALL the time... what you got was the real Gary, ALL the time. With one bright white smile he'd charm your socks, shoes, pants and shirt off!

The second place in the dictionary would be where it says "fearless"... I don't know what it was.. if he actually thought he was indestructible, if he just didn't care... or just loved doing what he did... I don't know, but, he truly had NO FEAR!

I was at Orange County International Raceway with him when he crashed.. I know what really happened... but... I'm afraid that all I can do is tease the shit out of you, in that I was one of the fortunate ones who knew him and witnessed GG "events"... usually along with others, but sometimes just me and him... or me and him and a "friend" at the shop at 2 AM... He was a super-magnet to beautiful women... but he didn't seem to overly care about the chicks... I think his "daring" lifestyle (as he did more than drive race cars... like doing stunt work in Hollywood, and being a human "guinea pig" for the Air Force... etc). was his REAL passion... And with that, I will have to tell you that I too will have to join the tight-lipped club, in that I can only tell those things that I can tell (and that wouldn't be much)... the rest I will not tell, to protect him, because I loved him.

THE DEVIL AND THE L.A. TIMES (1996)

On the last day of August in 1996, Top Fuel dragster driver Blaine Johnson was killed while setting Low Elapsed Time at the National Hot Rod Association's U.S. Nationals in Indianapolis, Indiana. The very next morning, innocently enough, I began eating my Cheerios and reading an account in the *L.A. Times Sports* pages on Johnson's demise. I was trying to come to grips with his death and glean some meaning in his passing, and I scoured the newspaper for details that I may have missed from a televised account on Channel 5 the night before.

(At one time I was an avid consumer of newsprint, but I had pretty much given up on the *L.A. Times* and its increasingly dismal attempt at credibility at reporting much of anything, which has continued to nose-dive into timid, insipid infotainment. But I felt handcuffed at this point: I needed news about Blaine's final ride in a fuel dragster he campaigned with brother, Alan, and there was only one credible source... So I walked down to the "_9¢ Store" (one of the numbers actually fell off the store's marquee) at the corner mini-mall, plucked down $1.62 for a Sunday Times and got on with my breakfast.)

The newspaper had less to say than what I already knew: the motor exploded in the timing traps, taking out a rear wing that helped stabilize the dragster traveling at a speed well above 300 mph. The right rear slick was also punctured, further hampering Johnson's ability to keep his maximum velocity missile under control. Until it impacted the guardrail Johnson was driving it like a champion, givin' 'er rudder and literally and figuratively drivin' the wheels off. By punching out in such triumphant fashion, his tragic death was a poetic statement, with an poignancy worthy of Shakespeare.

That the engine came apart like a cheap watch was a wry, unexpected occurrence. Indeed, in an age when deep pockets rule and voracious parts consumption is standard operating procedure in drag racing, it was quite refreshing to witness the way the relatively bucks-down Alan and Blaine Johnson campaigned a Top Fuel car: theirs was a very tight and clean crusade — which is to say, maximum performance underscored by a lack of part failures. Had Blaine not been killed, the taking of the NHRA Points Title was a given for this team — on a budget that was chump change in comparison to most of the hitters in Top Fuel, teams for whom grenading an engine at the end of each pass down the quarter mile drag strip was basically part of the tune-up...

Unfortunately, there will be no asterisk next to the name of 1996's eventual Top Fuel Champion in the record books – y'know, "such-and-such won their first Top Fuel title after the provisional Points Leader was killed in action at Indianapolis." Nor should there be — but in my heart Blaine Johnson was the last Top Fuel Champion. His accomplishments resonate because his team – mostly a down home family operation – slayed the competition with intellect, perseverance, and ingenuity.

But now he was dead. Blaine died as a hero, and he set Low E.T. of the meet on the pass that killed him. His efforts were noble, and his performance that day showcased his virtue — ironically, as he died. And news of Johnson's death was front page fodder for the *L.A. Times Sports Section*, which was appropriate. The *Times'* coverage of Blaine's final moments at the US Nationals was certainly takable enough. It was treated with dignity and respect and even if it was a little skimpy on details, what particulars were proffered were more or less correct – a rarity amongst the straight press when it came to covering matters of horsepower.

In this same issue of the newspaper, packaged among the coupons for designer yogurt, twinkies on a stick and other such rot, was a glossy magazine that smelled.

I mean it stunk. Literally. The *L.A. Times Magazine* was loaded with perfume ads that actually admitted a syrupy odor slightly reminiscent of angel food, anesthesia and kerosene.

The cover story that was even more offensive than the perfume coating and was equally difficult for the reader to endure. The title said it all: **"The World's Fastest Car? If You Can't Buy it Why Should You Care?"** I feared a smug, supercilious account of the impending Land Speed Record wars between Craig Breedlove, Richard Noble, and the *American Eagle-1* by some journalist with a byline that read "Bill Sharpsteen."

"... Zipping over a desert track, no matter how fast, has lost much of its heroic aura. When (Craig) Breedlove first strapped a jet engine to three wheels in 1961 and two years later broke the speed record at 407 mph on Utah's Bonneville Salt Flats, it was a wonderful novelty in both daring and backyard engineering.

"Now, it almost seems quaint. Flame-belching cars built to boast one man's - ah - engineering prowess over anoth-

er's aren't that impressive anymore; they're just loud. A car equipped with a surplus jet engine seems crude compared to the infinitely swift, silent power of a Pentium computer chip. These days, the competition for a land speed record looks more like Neanderthal breast-beating than a celebration of ingenuity. 'Setting the land speed record is not going to save the world,' Breedlove concedes. 'It's just a contest to go out and have the world's fastest car.'

"But then, pursuing land speed records has always been a fringe activity at best... The drivers made the record books, but they rarely gained lasting fame. 'How many people even know what the [current] record is?' asks Road & Track *senior editor Joe Rusz. 'I don't, and I'm in the business.'*

"That's not to say we couldn't be interested, but it would take a fundamental shift in the Zeitgeist. We've had our share of space shuttles and stealth fighters, not to mention an unrelenting bombardment of statistical trivia — from box office grosses to record high temperatures — in the daily media. Too, speed itself has become such a part of life that it would be nice if someone instead came up with a way to slow things down. The fastest car? What's the rush?" — **Bill Sharpsteen, CAR CULTURE: THE FASTEST CAR IN THE WORLD, IF YOU CAN'T BUY IT, WHY SHOULD YOU CARE?,** ***Los Angeles Times Magazine*****, September 1, 1996**

I absorbed Fag Sharpsteen's story on the imminent assaults on the Land Speed Record (the first LSR attempts in thirteen years), and I wiped my fingers. There was a real stench to this guy's work. I felt sick. Yet again, purveyors of unbridled thrust and horsepower such as Craig Breedlove were being treated as quaint freaks by some glib journalist. The writer was unable to grok the raw desire that propels visionaries such as Breedlove. The desire to reach Mach 1 on land is bold and outrageous; the related technology is the embodiment of grace and elegance.

The writer also failed to grasp that in such speed-demon endeavors things can go horribly wrong: At Mach 1, shock waves almost certainly send the vehicle careening out of control at around 740 mph. The very possibility of failure makes these efforts interesting and provocative. People die. Frank Lockhart. John Cobb. Athol Graham. Glen Leasher. Donald Campbell.

Now Blaine Johnson was dead on the drag strip, Craig Breedlove could be next on a dry lake bed and Bill Sharpsteen was a buffoon... His prose stunk like his magazine. I found his account to be emblematic of why I had already 86'd the *L.A. Times* out of my life. I had enough, so I fired off an e-mail to the *L.A. Times Magazine.*

Subject: The Fastest Car in the World
Date: Sun, 01 Sep 1996 12:35:36 +0000
From: Nitronic Research (colecoonce@nitronic.com)
To: latmag@latimes.com

Although generally appalled at the boosh-wah, latte-addled, hip, smug and ironic tone that infests the pages of your magazine, I did happen to notice a story on what is perhaps the most noble endeavor of the decade: Driving at the speed of sound on land. As an advocate of the pursuit of horsepower, I was torqued by the writers dismissive take, as well as the sub-headlines accompanying the story ("Yawn" and "If you can't buy it, why should you care?").

Oy vey — Your article on the Land Speed Record wars is emblematic of the blase, cynical hack work that passes for feature-article journalism today. Bill Sharpsteen's assertion that "a car equipped with a surplus jet engine seems crude compared to the infinitely swift power of a Pentium computer chip" showcases how clueless the writer really is. The pursuit of Mach 1 by visionaries such as Craig Breedlove, Richard Noble, et.al is bold and outrageous — the shock waves will almost certainly send the vehicle careening out of control at between 740 and 765 mph — and should be applauded as such. Sending a mocha-sipping West L.A. "reporter" to cover a story of this magnitude is tantamount to asking a porno actress to explain how research on subatomic particles might reveal the essence of life. I.e., they just don't get it.

The pursuit of Mach 1 on land is the embodiment of grace and elegance — not "Neanderthal breast-beating" like Sharpsteen mentions. And what the *L.A. Times Magazine* and its copy chimp missed in its glib post-modern attempt to dismiss the LSR efforts as Robert Bly with missile for a penis, is this: At the height of exalted elegance things can go horribly wrong. That's what makes these LSR efforts interesting and provocative. There is a nobility in accomplishment, as well as in failure. What is Mr. Sharpsteen trying to accomplish?

Also what was missing from the LSR piece was this: Unlike the endeavors of NASA, JPL, Northrop (or even the National

Endowment of the Arts), this attempt at technological triumph is financed privately — not a tax dollar in sight. Nada.

When Breedlove and Noble make their epochal record attempts at Black Rock, NV later this month, please Mr.Sharpsteen, stay here in Los Angeles with your laptop and report on something more your speed: Say, a Westside performance artist pouring chocolate syrup on her unmentionables (as a metaphor for the human condition, of course) and, ooh, what a travesty it is that her NEA grant was denied. (Just make your sure the valet didn't nick your Lexus and don't spill your mineral water, Bill...) — **Cole Coonce**

I wasn't the only person to fire off a poison letter in anger. Coincidentally, and unbeknownst to me, BZ had also read the *L.A. Times Magazine* that day and was equally torqued. The juxtaposition of the Blaine Johnson obit and Sharpsteen's piss-take was enough to fire me up; BZ was inspired by something that I had printed out off of the internet and mailed to him, a fanciful fable about a kid in the desert who stumbled across some forgotten JATO missiles and a beater of a Chevy Impala...

∞

[Collected on the Internet, 1996] *The Arizona Highway Patrol were mystified when they came upon a pile of smoldering wreckage embedded in the side of a cliff rising above the road at the apex of a curve. The metal debris resembled the site of an airplane crash, but it turned out to be the vaporized remains of an automobile. The make of the vehicle was unidentifiable at the scene.*

The folks in the lab finally figured out what it was, and pieced together the events that led up to its demise.

It seems that a former Air Force sergeant had somehow got hold of a JATO (Jet Assisted Take-Off) unit. JATO units are solid fuel rockets used to give heavy military transport airplanes an extra push for take-off from short airfields.

Dried desert lake beds are the location of choice for breaking the world ground vehicle speed record. The sergeant took the JATO unit into the Arizona desert and found a long, straight stretch of road. He attached the JATO unit to his car, jumped in, accelerated to a high speed, and fired off the rocket. The facts, as best as could be determined, are as follows:

The operator was driving a 1967 Chevy Impala. He ignited the JATO unit approximately 3.9 miles from the crash site. This was established by the location of a prominently scorched and melted strip of asphalt. The vehicle quickly reached a speed of between 250 and 300 mph and continued at that speed, under full power, for an additional 20-25 seconds. The soon-to-be pilot experienced G-forces usually reserved for dog-fighting F-14 jocks under full afterburners.

The Chevy remained on the straight highway for approximately 2.6 miles (15-20 seconds) before the driver applied the brakes, completely melting them, blowing the tires, and leaving thick rubber marks on the road surface. The vehicle then became airborne for an additional 1.3 miles, impacted the cliff face at a height of 125 feet, and left a blackened crater 3 feet deep in the rock.

Most of the driver's remains were not recovered; however, small fragments of bone, teeth, and hair were extracted from the crater, and fingernail and bone shards were removed from a piece of debris believed to be a portion of the steering wheel.

∞

BZ had been particularly smitten with the romanticism of this apocryphal incident, internet myth or no. Something about that story really rang true; its theme about bored kids using the obsolete detritus of the military industrial complex as a means for outrageous speed was a motif that could have been inserted into most of the Land Speed Record attempts since the days of Henry Ford and Barney Oldfield; Malcolm Campbell, George Eyston and John Cobb all used military technology, albeit in the form of piston-driven aircraft engines... Breedlove, Arfons,

Gabelich and others had set the Land Speed Record with some parts and pieces from jets and rockets that the military had abandoned.

Yes, the tale of the impaled Impala was a post-industrial archetype of the Jungian persuasion, BZ reckoned... vintage Detroit steel coupled in some manner of technological miscegenation with abandoned instruments of destruction left rotting in the cracked and weathered landscape of the American desert.

The implications of the internet fable were manifold, and somehow in his letter to the *Times* BZ managed to wire in this tale as a sort of hyper-metaphor, replete with tangential references to particle physics as a mental construct; the megalomania of Nikola Tesla; William Blake; and the National Science Foundation.

So, while on his lunch break at a Denny's, BZ scrawled a letter to Sharpsteen on a page out of a Big Chief tablet he kept handy and often used for spontaneous scribbling and the drawing of five-dimensional topographic knots and such. After his shift ended, he faxed it from a Kinko's in Burbank to the *L.A. Times.* He told me a smear of Denny's marmalade had stuck to the paper and the letter had to be run through their fax machine a couple of times before the transmission was consummated because the paper kept jamming. A small disturbance developed when the employee wanted him to pay for multiple faxes due to the repeated paper jams, but BZ insisted he only had to pay for completed faxes and not mere attempts.

A week later the *L.A. Times Magazine* ran his letter, on the same day they ran mine. I found this more than ironic as BZ and I often had picnics in the junkyard together, and here we were, the both of us occupying the Letters Page in the *L.A. Times Mag...*

Regarding Bill Sharpsteen's dismissal of Craig Breedlove's attempt to break the sound barrier in a car, it is true that the technological genius of this country long ago abandoned such romanticism and sensibly applied itself to the commercial manufacture of smart bombs and Chrysler mini-vans.

Utility is Sharpsteen's criterion: technology must be purified of "Neanderthal breast beating." Similar arguments killed the super conducting Super Collider. It started to look more like megalomania than physics. It blurred aesthetics and technology — what does it mean to argue whether the universe is fundamentally symmetrical or asymmetrical?

What VALUE is a seventy-mile tunnel built to smash infinitesimal objects that may or may not be objects at all, but figments of mental cognition?

Nikola Tesla's Wardenclyffe Tower was mothballed when similar questions arose. The investors realized that the gargantuan bee-hive structure had everything to do with Goethe's "Faust" and little to do with "wireless transmission of power." Tesla left his radio patent for Marconi to steal, sold the Alternating Current patent for cash and got bored with dual resonating circuits in 1898: circuits which are the basis of Sharpsteen's Pentium computer.

Faustian overreachers are less concerned with practical applications than excess of the sort that William Blake claimed led to the "palace of wisdom." Their era ended with the rise of the military-industrial complex and the National Science Foundation. And so we are left with Breedlove and the kid who reportedly strapped a military rocket to his vintage Impala and smashed into an Arizona cliff at 300 mph.

Of such gestures Blake wrote "There is a moment in each day that Satan cannot find." Breedlove's moment will be lost upon those who find sense or profit in it. The value of his run is measured not by the corrupted yardstick of technological progress; It is measured to the degree to which the *L.A. Times* doesn't get it. — **Bradford Zukovic**

BEAT THE DEVIL

"If the doors of perception were cleansed every thing would appear to man as it is, infinite." —**William Blake.**

Satan (the Debbil', Lucifer, Beezelbub, Ol' Scratch) lurks at Mach 1. Mach 1 is a dream. The pious will tell you that when you dream, you are vulnerable to possession. To dream is a Faustian bargain unto itself.

The Devil is a phantasm of 1000 faces, but one guise is very familiar to those who are pushing speed's envelope. Satan is a manifestation of the human impulse to defy mortality — an impulse that as often as not hastens and confirms our own mortality, I might add... This demon appears in the vaporous guise of pressure waves that develop around a projectile approaching the Speed of Sound. During and after World War II fighter pilots and test pilots talked about such a demon, a wind-whipped specter that would sprout wings, howl like a banshee, climb around and wrap itself around the aileron of their aircraft as it explored the outer reaches of stability.

Assuming that apparition was real — and ultimately tamed when the aircraft blasted through the sound barrier — does the Devil disappear when he has been found and conquered? Does he seek refuge somewhere else? In the very pages of the *LA Times Magazine* perhaps? In the guise of a scrivener named Bill Sharpsteen? If so, this was a preemptive move by Beezelbub, as he sensed Breedlove and Richard Noble were onto something in their pursuit of Mach 1... The Devil is a slippery bastard, after all...

"There is a moment in each day that Satan cannot find." The moment the Devil cannot find is that same moment when the doors of perception are cleansed, and the horizons are infinite. The Devil is beaten and vanquished. It is a moment of Infinity — a moment that lasts forever and disappears in an instant. In that moment those who are mad enough to dare can wrap the entire universe into a speck of a matter a million times smaller than the head of the proverbial pin upon which a thousand angels sing... it is the mother of all metaphysical payoffs... in a Nietzschean sense, the Moment of Infinity belongs to the Human Spirit at its most Exalted...

It is a rarefied and brave being who dares to Beat the Devil and peer into both the Human Heart and the Laws of mass and velocity that truly guide the cosmos...

The devil dwells in the unknown. To beat the Devil is to claim the unknown. The Devil is beaten in the moment of Discovery. The moment when discovery becomes empirical, when unknown co-ordinates are charted. When mankind stakes a flag in the turf of mystic phenomenon. Because the pursuit of Mach 1 is nothing if not a turf war of empiricism with the Devil.

The moment Satan cannot see is the moment he shows himself. And the Devil is the very thing the Human Spirit cannot see — until the moment he spreads his wings. Only then is he conquered.

THIS SYSTEM IS OBSOLETE IN LIGHT OF NEW KNOWLEDGE (1996)

Working out of a school bus in Twentynine Palms, CA, Jocko Johnson is feverishly sorting out the prototype of a something he calls the PoweRRing 3-cycle, an engine which has very few moving parts, a remarkably petite cubic inch displacement and, according to Jocko, is capable of both serious power and tremendous fuel economy. It is completely revolutionary and the size of a crock pot.

It is nanotechnology as applied to an internal combustion engine. It could change the automobile as we know it.

Twice I attempt to interview Jocko for a feature article I was doing on him for HOT ROD Magazine; the first time the '71 Grand Prix overheats while stuck in a traffic jam just west of Pomona. I am forced to use the pay phone from a hamburger stand on Foothill Boulevard as I sheepishly explain to Jocko why I couldn't make it to his shop in Twentynine Palms, California. Here he was, building an experimental radial motor with very few moving parts (no crankshaft, no connecting rods, no pushrods) and I was pulled over on the side of the surface street with a temperature gauge cooked to 12 o clock and steam pouring out of the radiator's catch can.

(In a V-8 engine, Jocko tells me later, one cylinder does work, while the other 7 work against it. No wonder it overheats...)

The next week, before traffic gets bad, I try again.

The dirt roads to Jocko's crib in the desert are wide open vistas, the kind of roads that seem to confirm the existence of the mysteries and magnetism of the desert. Even the paved roads have very few motorists, and even fewer state troopers. The kind of road the clears the mind and senses of any sclerotic gunk. Invigoration.

I pass a couple of county highways that ultimately shadow the perimeter of the 29 Palms Marine Base. On the northern border of the Marine Base, a couple of three coyote howls from Jocko's digs, a cat named George Van Tassel built — "through the guidance of other worlders" — the "Integratron," a high energy electrostatic machine designed to recharge the DNA of a person (i.e. stop the aging process). The local Chamber of Commerce describes it as a "time machine for research on rejuvenation, anti-gravity and time travel." The structure is four stories high and 55 feet in diameter and is thought by some to be "a very powerful vortex for physical and spiritual healing." From the 1950s to the 70s, the Integratron was the site of an annual "Interplanetary

Spacecraft Convention" and became famous as the site of Van Tassel's "Spaceport Earth."

As I kick up some dust on a dirt road on the perimeter of the military base, I think to myself that out on the perimeter of hell's half-acre, there is certainly ample room to stretch out and improvise. I was then buzzed by a below-the-radar F-4 Fighter. *FFFFFWHHOOOSSSHHH!!!* I haven't even arrived the mad alchemists and my senses are already overwhelmed by free-form Teutonic theater in the desert.

Jocko shows me the mock up of his new streamliner, the *Spirit of 29 Palms*, a name he had just come up with. "This town needs some local pride," he says.

The mock-up is a set of contoured bulbs with a needle-thin fuselage bridging the two sections. I point at one end. "The driver goes here?" I ask. "NO, the engine goes there," he says. We walk to the other end. "The driver goes here, then?" "Exactly," Jocko answers with pride. "C'mon, let me show you the PoweRRing."

We migrate towards a school bus.

"Current engine design," he says as we walk towards the bus, "derives from a steam engine built in 1705; it was the first engine to use a crankshaft to covert reciprocal motion into rotary motion and pass it along through various gearboxes and transfer devices." I nod my head. "This system is obsolete in light of new knowledge." I cock an eyebrow. "Since high torque is inherent in my three-cycle engine design, the engine would be placed right next to the wheel, with no gear reduction except for a reverser. This engine is very compact, shaped like a wheel and no wider than a standard auto wheel. It leaves a lot of space inside a car for other things."

Jocko's PoweRRing 3 Cycle has eighteen small cylinders arranged around a twelve-lobe cam wheel. Combustion occurs in one set of six cylinders after another, with the pistons exerting force on the cam-wheel, causing it to move. For every 360 degrees of rotation, there are 216 ignition firings, with six cylinders firing simultaneously every ten degrees of rotation.

He says he like the idea of a radial engines because it would have the lightest weight per cubic inch and they are easiest engines to cool. ("Amen to that," I think to myself.) Capitalizing on the concept of circular ignition, Jocko's engine is a radial, but with a cam operating the pistons and minus any connecting rods or crankshaft.

As we talk a military helicopter on maneuvers flies over us with two or three guys in uniform hanging on a ladder. *SCHUTTT-SCHUTTT-SCHUTTT-SCHUTTT-SCHUTTT-SCHUTTT...* Jocko doesn't even look up.

THE KING OF SWEDEN

I tell BZ about an e-mail I had received from the chief designer of *Infinity*, the Hungarian guy, Vic Elisher. Later in life, Elisher became an engineer on a physics project that won a Nobel Prize.

"You know, the prime engineer on the *Infinity* car became a systems engineer for the particle accelerators and atom smashers in Berkeley," I say as BZ raises an eyebrow. "He may not set the land speed record, but he was instrumental in allowing some physicist or another to claim the Nobel Prize."

"It's a long way from the salts of Bonneville to the King of Sweden," BZ says, and then adds, "except, of course, in fine American Literature like *Day of the Drag Racer*. And in machines named *Infinity*, apparently..."

A BEER OF OURS WORKS WONDERS

Subject: Infinity Jet Engines
Date: Fri, 18 Feb 01:54:40 EST
From: ∞@aol.com
To: colecoonce@nitronic.com

Coonce,

It was a J47-33 out of an F86D Fighter/Interceptor. And I did get after-burner turbine driven pumps. The Pumps were driven by airflow from the last stage of the compressor before the compressed air fed into the Burner Cans on the engine. The hot burning gas output then went through the turbine blades which drove the compressor and of course provided the thrust. The turbine rings were typically removed before engines were sold for parts. I don't know why? Maybe they did not want people from foreign countries to build up planes from spare parts so they disabled engines. We got a turbine ring anyway after we made friends with guys at Montham. A beer of ours works wonders.

But the best thing to do was to take an engine out of a newly refurbished National Guard Plane that was destined to be a monument. That is how I got the second engine with 40 hrs on it from the city of Medford Oregon. I talked them into giving me the engine for $750. I told them the plane would be a lot lighter without it if they were going to put it on a pedestal for a monument. They agreed. So Romeo drove up there with a Big Flat bed and I drove up with a friend in a car and I took the plane apart and removed the engine. Romeo was amazed - I rented a Cherry Picker to pull it out. It only took about four hours. It was cool! I had never seen a fighter plane like that up close before. And I got a lot of electronic and relay parts out of it as well as a silver cell battery. That battery was worth more than $750 but the city manager at Medford did not know and they got the plane for free. That was in 1961 I think?

Vic

PORTERVILLE HIGHWAY AND THE BLACK REBEL MOTORCYCLE CLUB (1999)

Just past Oildale, we take the Porterville Highway cutoff. The neon of Bakersfield is behind us. Not unlike Jordan, the landscape is barren, devoid of traffic and the biggest landmark is the lack of any landmarks. Sporadically, various monolithic totems appear in the distance. On one side of the black, sticky pavement stand some porta-potties for unseen migrant field hands; on the other side, more oil derricks serve as minimalist mechanized sculptures. Inversely proportional to the desolation are the manifold historical implications of this road itself: Marlon Brando took this road to Porterville on a Triumph motorcycle when he was researching how bikers lived for his role in *The Wild One.* ("What are you rebelling against?" "Whaddaya' got?")

"This is a shortcut," I say.

I tell BZ that Porterville Highway is a point of singularity, with a sphere of influence of extending as far as the walk-in theaters of Wichita, Kansas, where it touched the id of Glen Leasher, the guy who would ultimately shoe both the Goat's AA/Fuel Dragster as well as the *Infinity* jet car. Marlon Brando was Glen Leasher's hero and inspiration, I say.

In the third act of *The Wild One,* there is a scene where members of the BRMC motor through Bleeker's Cafe Bar on a motorcycle. Leasher would mimic this scene, wheeling his Triumph through the aisles of the local walk-in theater in Wichita.

HYPERSONIC (1959)

Boredom will send anybody in search of kicks. Testosterone-addled motorheads living in the prosaic plains of Wichita, Kansas can only cruise the drive-in malt shop on opposite sides of town for so many revolutions before the dreariness of repetition sends them into orbit, and they scatter and burst like a meteor shower across some kind of cosmic chalkboard.

These are the mad ones, the men with hyperactive souls. Hyper-intense. Hyper-real. Hypersonic. Men who can't understand the monotony of why the Earth spins in a circle when there has to be a direct route to wherever it is we are headed.

In Wichita Kansas, Glen Leasher fought the banality of human existence anyway he could, whether it terrorizing the movie theater with his motorcycle or racing jalopies round and round the bullrings of the County Fairs on a Saturday night. He raced the jalopies furiously, like he was trying to hasten the earth's rotation. True, it was small time and mercenary, but the payoff was manifold. In addition to the chump change, it also provided Leasher with experience behind the wheel of a hot job, a cache of expertise that would bolster his confidence enough to leave the flat lands in his rear view mirror and Horace Greeley it to the drag strips of California.

Before bailing all together, Leasher hitched his wagon to the mechanical prowess of "Kansas Al" Williams, driving his *Hypersonic* AA/Fueler. In 1959 they lit the up the automotive trade papers with reports of a quarter-mile Top Speed of 185 miles per hour — the fastest ever on a drag strip. And although this feat was performed on a race track improvised on an Air Force base in Kansas, the spit-and-bubble gum nature of the venue was not enough to taint the credibility of this momentous accomplishment. Leasher's star was rising and Kansas would soon be in his rear view mirror.

His résumé now read "Fastest Man On A Drag Strip," and Leasher finally motored to the Left Coast, more specifically to San Mateo in the South City of San Francisco where he found gainful employment as a bonafide, rootin' tootin' Top Fuel driver. His bossman was an ill-tempered Italian who answered to the handle of "Terrible Ted" Gotelli. Aka "the Goat."

Gotelli and his boys, the Organ Grinders, were formidable drag racers. The Goat, in specific, had accumulated a pronounced reputation for generating prodigious amounts of horsepower using nitromethane for a fuel and supercharged Chrysler hemi as a powerplant. In Leasher Gotelli found his natural foil, a young cocksure ramrod with a heavy right foot.

"Leasher was as go cat wild with his right foot as Gotelli was with his nitro percentage," I say.

BZ nods.

"When he climbed into that jet car, it was like Space Age America was a tiger that Leasher grabbed by the tail," I tell BZ.

AMERICAN HONKY TONK (1999)

We can see mecca. There is smoke on the horizon as we head east, the plume of smoke emanating from the burnout box way up yonder. This is a portent and a promise of some seriously high-octane hot rod action, and a chance to get the dirt on Leasher and *Infinity* from the Goat.

BZ and I are not alone in our pilgrimage: A bottleneck of hot rods, economy cars and motor homes crimp Famoso/Wasco Road, from the west off of the Highway 99 offramp and from the east off of Porterville Highway.

I find a Lefty Frizzell song on the AM radio. It was the one about "She's Gone, gone, gone...," anchored by a ton of reverb and a lo-fidelity fuzz bass. I didn't need the numbers on a road sign to tell me we were getting closer to Bakersfield.

"Ahhh, this is real American honky tonk," I say.

"Yeah...None of this modern county music that sounds like it was recorded at CERN in Switzerland."

I think I understand what he means, and I agree with him. As usual.

THE GOAT

The Goat ran a Top Fuel car for the a couple of decades, with a tune-up as hot and volatile as a poached egg on the highway. The *Gotelli Speed Shop* machine, eponymous tagged for Gotelli's popular high performance emporium in the South City section of San Francisco, was powered by an engine out of a '58 Chrysler New Yorker.

The Goat felt that a pushrod actuated, piston-driven mill like the Chrysler (with hemispherical-shaped combustion chambers) was the only prudent way to make horsepower while burning nitro, which was a delicate operation.

Gotelli was among the baddest tomatoes when it came to extricating copious amounts of power out of a Chrysler engine burning nitromethane as a fuel.

The partnership was perfect symmetry. Gotelli had an ax to grind (the San Francisco drag racers felt they were given the bum's rush by the Los Angeles-based "Petersen magazine syndicate") and Leasher was his blade.

DRAG STRIP RIOT (1962)

This is the moment that Leasher has been waiting for. Gotelli and Leasher enter the car in the Smokers Meet, as the klieg lights circle among the grapevines and the corn fields, heralding a showdown between the titans of outlaw drag racing.

Never before have so many Top Fuel dragsters congregated at one chunk of asphalt. It is an orgy of beer cans and nitromethane of Bacchanalian proportions. It is pure decadence manifested in the guise of the raw pursuit of horsepower.

Word of this gathering has spread to all corners of the US of A and this clarion call is magnetic enough to lure spectators and participants from across the continent. As competition progressed through the weekend, a pile of empty bent, crumpled beer cans begin aggregating into impromptu pyramids between two quarter-mile lengths of chain link fence that has been used to separate the bikers and the bleacher bums from the competitors. It is an utterly ineffectual safety barricade.

The Smokers Meet is utter chaos as dragster guys prepare their mounts. This contest of speed and debauchery has spontaneously morphed into the most prestigious gathering of outlaw men and machinery in the United States. The 2000 horsepower, blown-on-nitro railjobs' fuel consumption is matched only by the thirst of the menacing mass of humanity who have gathered to get liquored and dosed by the burning nitromethane used to propel these cars to ungodly speeds.

By Sunday, the last day of competition, the show could only be described as a bad scene — a hot rod rumble, a drag strip riot of Kern County bikers and rough trade, as well as motorcycle clubs from 'Frisco to 'Berdoo (the Hell's Angels, Gallopin' Gooses, Heshians, Satan's Slaves, the Pissed Off Bastards of Bloomington and others). The mob's collective rapacious thirst for suds is only half the story. If you wanted to urinate, you had to kick your way through the empties and the other biker-types and nitromaniacs to find a porta-potty that wasn't thoroughly thrashed. There is a fight that starts at 11 in the morning and doesn't reach a decision until 3 that afternoon.

And there you have it, a three day festival of speed lubricated by nitromethane and 80 weight motor oil as well as a couple of tanker's worth of Budweiser, Miller, Schlitz, Brew 102, various malt liquors, all of which was coursing through the veins of tattooed leather boys who were in the mood for speed and whose only possible surrogate for that sensation was raw violence...

And as the sun began to set on Sunday evening, the elimination ladder for the fuel dragsters wound down to a showdown between the last two contestants, the *Gotelli Speed Shop* entry out of South City, San Francisco and the notorious *Fuller-Zueschel-Prudhomme* machine from Los Angeles.

Finally, as the sun went down Sunday night there were two Top Fuel gladiators remaining in competition. It was decided by the Smokers that during this final round of eliminations that no false starts would be tolerated. Indeed, this would be grounds for immediate disqualification. The mood was foul and the tension was as thick as motor oil.

Both drivers jump the start. Only Leasher is disqualified.

That summer Don "the Snake" Prudhomme would be touring the country and taking on all comers as the driver who won Top Fuel at the March Meet. Glen Leasher would be dead.

NOBODY WILL BELIEVE IT'S AN EMERGENCY (1999)

On the way back to Los Angeles, and before we began our ascent back up the Grapevine, I decide to take a short detour into the Los Padres National Forest via Route 133.

It is eerie. The night is cool and black as carbon.

Bounding around a particularly sharp corner, we bounce and when the Pontiac lands back on the pavement a loose connection in the wiring shorts out, cutting all voltage to the headlights.

It is frighteningly dark at this juncture. I try to troubleshoot the short in the dark, but with no luck. I have a small flashlight but the battery is as dead and corroded as last month's takeout. The only lights still functioning are the hazard lights, which would blink with just enough foot candles to let another motorist know we were at least on the highway.

I make an executive decision to drive back through the forest — with no headlights — get 'er back on I-5 and head up to Gorman where we could either troubleshoot under the fluorescent lamps of the same Jr. Food Mart where we had scared the Middle Easterners with the geysers of steam, or we could call AAA.

We get to the Gorman exit and I shoot right past the offramp.

"I thought we were going to fix the headlights there."

"I don't know man, I kind of like traveling like this. It's like we are an emergency vehicle heading to a blood bank with a batch of particularly rare hemoglobin. I mean look at this..."

People were moving out of the way like we were a fire truck.

"Yes, it is like the parting of the Red Seas. Whatever. Try to keep it under 90. After all, we are driving in the dark."

"If I go that slow, nobody will believe it's an emergency."

IT WAS A BUNCH OF SHIT

I stick the cassette of the interview with the Goat in the Batmobile's tape deck and play it back to distract BZ.

"How did you know Glen Leasher?"

"He used to work for me. He drove my trucks. He was getting ready to go back home (to Wichita). Some guy said, 'Why don't you give this guy a chance to drive your car.' I said, 'Sure, go ahead.' He drove the car and the first meet we were in, we won it."

"So tell me about the Top Eliminator run in '62..."

"It was a misunderstanding, we should have won the race. They said that we fouled. We pulled up at the starting line and the front wheels went over the line so we pulled 'em back and Prudhomme was still coming down. He hadn't even been there yet and they disqualified us."

"So you were on a single run?"

"When he (Prudhomme) come he rolled the lights and they said, 'Shut if off.' About a half hour later they said, 'you're disqualified because you went over the line first.' It was a bunch of shit."

"You've had a lot of crackerjack drivers in your career. How would you rate Leasher?"

"He was one of the best drivers I had. He knew if the car needed some weight here or weight there. Really sharp guy."

"How did you feel about him driving jet cars after he quit driving for you?"

"I tried to talk him out of driving that big coupe. He wanted to go 500 mph. He didn't make it. I didn't want him to go, but he went anyway."

"So you were pretty hurt when you heard he was killed in the Infinity*?"*

"I don't feel too bad, because I knew that was going to happen. Anything that Romeo Palamides built was a bunch of crap. He was going down the strip at 300 and some odd mph and pulled off that black line — you're supposed to follow that black line. He pulled off and he tried to correct it and then it blew. It flipped over and killed him.

"He said, 'I'm going to drive that car up there at Bonneville.' I said, 'Oh? It's up to you. If you go up there, you are not coming back alive. Not with Romeo's stuff.' They built that car and they should have tested it. But they didn't test it. Anything over 300 mph and you lose. That is just the way it happens.

"He was saving his money so he could buy a roundy-round car. He was a helluva' driver. That sonofabitch Palamides didn't have enough decency to bring him back in a box..."

"How do you spell his name?"

"Leaser. L-e-a-s-e-r. Some made a mistake. It don't make no difference anyhow. He was a good driver. Nobody could beat him."

"Unless they have some home town refereeing..."

"Prudhomme is a big asshole, that is all he is. He goes around bragging that he beat us. He didn't beat us. I got no use for the guy. They didn't let us run.

"After they disqualified us down there, we were all down at the starting line. So I told the starter, I said, 'What went wrong? We didn't do nothing. He went over the line too.' 'Yeah, but he went over the line first.' 'We went over the line? The front wheel just touched it and we backed up. The people went crazy over that, they threw rocks at him, at Prudhomme, and everything. Everybody wanted to see us run him. We beat everybody, cars better than his. There was no money in it. It was 4000 bucks altogether. I got so damn mad that I took my pocketbook and t'rew it on the floor. There was four guys, the guy who built the car, the guy who built the motor and everything. And I said, 'I put up all my money. We run. If I win, then I take back my money. If I lose then you can have all of my money in my pocket.' I had about 3 or 4 hundred dollars in my pocket. They couldn't come up with any money.

"It was a bunch of shit. 'You four guys, if we turned you upside down we couldn't come up with a nickel. You guys are nothin' but broke.' That's why they called me 'Terrible Ted.'"

"Were the spectators as pissed off as you were?"

"People went crazy. When he went out to make his run they were t'rowin' beer cans at him. They were t'rowin' rocks and everything at him. We had to make a run too — just for the fun of it and everybody stood up and were going, 'Hooray' and all that shit. "

"It was a bad deal... Prudhomme... that sonuvabitch."

Click.

∞

We never saw a highway patrolman all the way home from Bakersfield.

LOOKING FOR INFINITY (2000)

"'Glenn Leasher was a hot rod buddy of mine,' Arthur (Arfons) explained. 'the kind of guy you run into maybe once a year but you get to like. Seeing that junk out there bothered me, it sure as hell did.'" — **"Enemy in Speedland,"** ***Sports Illustrated*****, 1965.**

At 5:30 am the phone in your motel rooms rings like a rubber band to the temples. You wake up in Wendover, a town that Craig Breedlove compared to the Western motion picture facades on the old 20th Century Fox lot in Culver City nearly forty years ago, and the one detail that makes that metaphor still applicable is the brackish coffee you are swilling out of a styrofoam cup as half of the motel's free continental breakfast. Whatever it was that the prop man brewed for Randolph Scott and John Wayne to imbibe out of tin cups around the camp fire scenes, it couldn't be any worse than this stuff, you say to yourself.

You motor out of this border town to the Salt Flats and then stop when it appears you can see forever. You are no longer on the set of a western. You are not even sure if you are on the same planet anymore. If you had ever landed on the moon, you would know it is a space with an infinite horizon, rife with possibility.

It is futuristic and it is a page out of the past. And it is surreal, although it is difficult to determine which is more other-wordly, the topography or the machinery.

As the rising sun exaggerates the curvature of the horizon, you are struck by the eerie silence of the dawn, a sonic void interrupted by the sporadic tumult of preparation for the day's record runs, the raising of canopies, the spinning of generators and the sizzling of bacon.

Your nose is tickled by the smells of pork and jet fuel, a vaporous stimulant that is much more inspiring than the motel's coffee.

You see a ghost.

∞

It is January and frigid. The Salt Flat are under water. I am looking for the jet car known as *Infinity* which had crashed out here in 1962.

The remnants of the car had been left on the Salt Flats for three years as a rather macabre reminder of how high the stakes were pushed in the Land Speed Record Wars.

The Highway Dept. had collected the remains of *Infinity* and had fenced it off in a surplus yard in the vicinity of Wendover, behind the casinos.

I am in the State Line Casino, a building divided between the two states of Utah and Nevada and their respective mores, with its coffee shop in Utah and the one armed bandits in Nevada.

On the off chance that this obelisk is still intact and not deconstructed and reconstructed into somebody's swing set, I start perusing the maze of boneyards that lurk behind the casinos, like metallic spider webs...

There is junk everywhere. It is a galaxy of metallurgical refuse, a dormant constellation that resembles nothing if not dark matter, whose gravity is sucking the carnage off the interstate and out of the skies into its lair. While looking amongst the flotsam and jetsam, debris and carnage, I stumble across some abandoned army barracks, a couple of airplane hangars and an airstrip.

The barracks appear empty and have been abandoned for decades. It is desolate, decrepit and rather eerie.

But like space itself, the barracks are not empty. There are some hot rodder-types squatting in the abandoned barracks, not unlike how the Manson Family had commandeered the miners' cabins up in the Panamint Range in California. The squatters are of the *Two Lane Blacktop* variety (drag racers with unkempt hair and angular, wiry physiques), with their muscle cars lurking outside. One of the hot rods is a souped-up, jacked-up '71 Plymouth Charger — a proper muscle car — and the other is a mid-70s Ford Maverick (!), also hopped up and with a metallic silver paint job, lettered with the moniker "AREA 51." A ratty curtain accordions open and shut and I get the vibe that these folks are very protective of their lodging and their race cars.

Next, the barrack's shutters open. These youngish, thin, blotchy-skinned hot rodding waifs demand to know what I doing with my camera around the AREA 51 Maverick. They have a gun. They look angry and territorial. I explain that I was just taking pictures of their bitchin' hot rods. They seem flattered. They put the gun down.

Backing up after taking these snapshots, I run across a naked, solitary plaque on a fencepost. It is a feeble attempt at demarcation of the buildings which housed the *Enola Gay* and *Bockscar* bombers and their crews during training missions in WW II. Yes, Wendover is where the Army Air Corp staged its operations during Operation Downfall, the mission which led to the splitting of uranium and plutonium atoms in residential areas of Japan.

I have stumbled into Ground Zero. I have stumbled into the singularity.

It's name: Wendover aka "Skull Valley Airport," according to the paint barely etched into the wooden sides of the hangar, near the threshold.

The hangar hasn't seen any paint in 40 or 50 years, its coats eviscerated by an extremely unforgiving climate which is either a convection oven or a refrigerator. The air is thick with sodium.

As I step back to frame up the hangar in a disposable camera, I inadvertently back onto the starting line of a drag strip. It is a continuation of the old tarmac. It curves and is ultimately perpendicular to the airstrip and the threshold of the hangar.

This air field has somehow degenerated into the most lo-fi drag strip I had ever set foot on. Wendover Raceway. Home track of the AREA 51 Mustang.

∞

I continue to look for the remnants of *Infinity* in the junk yards. It is completely deserted except for all of the abandoned hardware lying around.

"Fuck you, Carl! Fuck you!" I hear this off in the distance, and I migrate towards the source of the commotion. There is a Delta 88 up on blocks, but the interior is salvageable as a desert rat is scavenging through it, probably looking for a radio knob for his grocery getter.

"Fuck you, Carl! Fuck you!"

I don't know if he is aware of my presence — I doubt it as he is pretty into what he was doing.

"My name is not Carl."

He keeps doing his deal. I just clam up at that point and wait for him to finish his business. He is the one connection to the ruins of the boneyard, where bombers were launched to drop enough munitions to force the end of WW II. He seems to know the inventory of the boneyard. He is my tether to *Infinity*.

When he was done rooting around and emerges out of the Delta 88, I notice he is a short guy in a green pants from the working man section of Sears. Gas station attendants' shirt, hiking boots, green baseball cap, full beard.

"How's it goin'?"

"Fine."

"I'm looking for something called *Infinity*."

"Aren't we all?"

CLOUDS OF STAR FIRE (1962)

"I remember
When I was a star
In the night
A moving, burning ember
Amid the bright Clouds of star fire
Going deathward To the womb" — **"Star," Jack Parsons**

September 10, 1962. It is a hot, gloomy Monday morning with a mercury sky. Everything is the color of a bleached and buried coin. Or a bullet left in the sun. During the past few days the *Infinity* team had been chipping away at various stress and leak tests, ensuring that the sleek machine that resembled nothing if not an avant-garde Russian MIG fighter plane was in superlative condition to claim the Land Speed Record. Many teams had espoused the notion that surpassing the 396 mph set in 1949 by Englishman John Cobb was a matter of patriotic pride, as for once the Americans would showcase their Yankee Ingenuity as well as its hearty guts and determination in a manner arguably not showcased since Henry Ford.

It had been such a bizarre trajectory to this moment, from "Dago" Palamides' shop on the outskirts of the Oakland Airport to the bone-yards of Tucson (Vic Elischer remembers the liberation of a J47-33 out of an F86D Fighter/Interceptor while Che Guevara scavenged for spare parts for a "Globemaster" cargo plane for use in the overthrow in the Batista government in Cuba — this is a year before the Bay of Pigs!) to Boeing Field in Seattle to the Bonneville Salt Flats...

∞

The *Untouchable* had barnstormed up and down the West Coast with a coterie of drivers, first with Archie Liederbrand, next with Glen Leasher, who was fresh out of the cockpit of "Terrible Ted's" *Gotelli Speed Shop Special*, Chrysler-powered fueler.

With Liederbrand driving, the *Untouchable* debuted in April, 1962 at Fontana and goes 209 mph, a track record. But this vehicle was really just a rolling test stand for the team. The real glory, prestige and payoff was at Bonneville, all they needed was another race car designed specifically for that task, as well as fresh bullet.

While fabricating the race car at Boeing Field in Seattle, Palamides and Leasher continued to match race the jet car and generate cash. Concurrently, airplane mechanics Loyd Osterberg and Jeri Sorm shaped and riveted the aluminum bodywork around the clock in attempt to have the car ready for Speed Week at Bonneville at the end of August.

One of the locals who grew up around Boeing Fields tells me that Sorm is "a master tin man and aeronautics wizard. He grew up in Czechoslovakia before WW II and lived there during the war and when the Nazi's held the country. When the Communists were in power, he escaped in the mid 50s — he flew out in a stolen plane.

"Jeri told me once, that anybody who had any complaints about this country should try living in a dictatorship, then under the Nazis - and then the Communists... he told me that ever since he came to this country he went out side every morning when he woke up and kissed the ground. He said we don't appreciate what we've got."

Sorm had no interest in race cars per se, but took on the project as an employee of Osterberg. Many nights one or the other would fall asleep in the fuselage of the unfinished vehicle only to be awakened by the other guy's hammering or riveting.

∞

Finally, *Infinity* is it out on the Salt Flats. Breedlove is also there with his high-dollar operation, but cannot make anything work properly. Breedlove goes home.

Meanwhile *Infinity*, the intersection of hot rodding and aerospace, continues to ramp up its speeds during test runs. There is a disagreement about how much more r&d is needed, and unbeknownst to the other partners, Palamides and Leasher apparently conspire to make a record run on this morning.

As the car enters the measured mile, the left front wheel bearing seizes and locks, pulling the car off course. Then there is an explosion from an inlet/compressor stall in the jet engine, most likely the result of excessive yaw, at which point the car high sides. Then it rips into shrapnel, a torn metallic curtain... it is as if a piece of the sky folds into itself and then implodes like a dark star.

Glen Leasher was looking for Infinity. He found it — in an instant.

The biggest piece of his remains was his boot.

IT WAS IN THE BAG (2000)

The following is from a phone interview with Vic Elisher. It was a cold call, and he was watching a women's soccer match, which I could hear in the back ground for the duration of our conversation.

Why Infinity?

VIC ELISHER: Tom Fukuya and I tossed around some names and came up with it. At the time there was only Breedlove's car and his was much heavier and powered by a GE J33 with no afterburner out of a Lockheed F-80. Max Thrust around 5000 Lbs. We had a much lighter car, 4800 lbs. And we had an engine from a North American F86D with an afterburner and we could get over 10,000 lbs of thrust out of it for short periods. So our thinking at the time was that we had the most powerful car in the world. And it was true for about two years. Breedlove had a lot of money but we had a lot more ingenuity and a better car. We did run 385 without the afterburners on an early tune up run. And we only used a 5/8 the mile runup.

We routinely ran over 270MPH in the quarter mile with the earlier car (the *Untouchable)* in around 6 seconds in demonstrations at 1/4 mile drag strips around the country. That was all in 1960-61.

Did Infinity *utilize ground effects?*

VE: It was slightly curved, slightly raked. It had a slight down angle, a few degrees. The engine actually pushed it down too. Plus there was a vacuum created out of the back end. It was very stable, we never had any trouble with it, in terms of all the other runs. He just ran it off the course. He might have a little crosswind, By the way, it was the same direction that Breedlove ran his car into the lake.

Glen had a background as a dragster driver and a jalopy racer. Is that the right background for an LSR attempt?

VE: This idea that you can drive out of it like a roadster or racing car, it's just not that way.

If you think that it is a situation where there is cross-wind that is throwing... He had plenty of time to pull the chutes. It would have absolutely straightened it right out, but it would have thrown him against the harness and knocked the wind out of him. At those speeds, it will definitely do that.

He cut power once he got off the course. That probably made it worse, because he didn't have the down thrust to keep the force. I would guess that whenever you make... You don't do anything quickly except throw the chutes and that has a stabilizing effect, right? They are way out behind the car and that straightens out the car.

What else can you tell me about the attempt?

VE: It was such a lost opportunity. The loss of life was the greatest shock. Afterwards, the lost opportunity. We were so close. We had run within a few miles per hour of the Land Speed Record. And that was without the afterburner! We had no problem at all. At that time Breedlove didn't have an afterburner engine, neither did Arfons. They were both running J33s. We were the only ones with an afterburner.

The first time we were up there, we ran 385. We were so elated. It was in the bag. We hadn't even run the afterburners, there was no way we weren't going to run 409 mph. No way. It was really in the bag. I should have insisted on driving.

When we were doing it, it was the American kind of individuals. Now it's about corporations. The fact that we didn't make it wasn't indicative of us not having the right stuff; it was indicative of us missing one piece — the psychological piece.

"JET CAR" IS MY NAME

His first pass in a real race car was in the *Master & Richter* Olds-powered gasser at Fremont Raceway, back in the days of flag starts. ("Still have my Fremont 132 mph card from that pass," Smith mused. "Beat a Willys pickup.") And although the man who would come to be known as "Jet Car Bob" Smith promptly graduated into stabbing and steering blown railjobs on nitro, even that treacherous form of pavement pounding was baby food compared to his preferred from of propulsion: A military jet engine with an afterburner. Pure thrust, baby, with no power wasted on something as quaintly passe as burning rubber...

Ahhh, take a humble drag racer from San Jose, strap him into a raw, jet-powered fuselage on wheels, light some kerosene and pressurized air and Voila! Your Humble Working Class Drag Racer is now an instant Meta-Deity of Thunder and Fire! It was "Lock up your children, corral the animals or pay the man at the ticket booth! You can't have it both ways." And more often than not, the race fans and the curiosity seekers parted with their hard-earned entertainment dollar to see "Jet Car Bob," the Superhero/Anti-Hero burn down plywood fences and blast off into oblivion 1/4 mile from where he launched.

Chronologically speaking, the torch for bleeding-edge-jet-technology-as-applied-to-the-drag-strip was lit when Akron Ohio's Walt Arfons unveiled his massive, $2000 (cheap!) J46 Westinghouse-powered *Green Monster* at Union Grove, Wisconsin in the summer of 1960, but it was carried by Smith and his partner, fabricator Romeo Palamides, as much as anybody. Their cars, dubbed the *Untouchable*, were sleek, minimalist projectiles primarily propelled by military surplus General Electric J47 engines and anchored by 4 Firestone road race tires, replete with tread. Smith hung fore of the front axle in a bullet shaped capsule, naked and vulnerable to drag strip ack-ack-ack.

(And what chariots the *Untouchables* were! 12,000 horsepower, 27' long, fire-breathing uber-dildos inspired by the excess and omnidirectional audacity and verve of the Jet Age. Or "the Big Zippo," as Jet Car hisself put it.)

Originally the *Untouchable* was shoed by Archie Liederbrand who soon gave up the seat to Glen Leasher. When Leasher was cruelly snuffed, Smith assumed the hot seat in the *Untouchable* and began making history as an outlaw drag racer in a machine that, due to its aerospace propulsion system, the High Sheriffs of drag racing, as well as most of the hitter competitors, considered an unsavory, incorrigible idea.

Because of this stigma, both Smith and his race car became audacious, successful commodities. "If you just booked in one jet car," Smith quantified, "you were guaranteed a crowd." No doubt, but the *Untouchable* in specific was truly on a roll: four days after Drag News created an Unlimited Dragster class in its official "Standard 1320 Records" listings, Smith rode *Untouchable* to a 6.87/240 mph clocking at Erie, PA, a record that stood until 1967, when the records were no longer recognized by the trade papers.

Since Palamides preferred the relative calm of his Oakland Airport shop to the turbulence of traveling, "Jet Car Bob" became a veritable troubadour for the jet set, and once on the road he was more or less a one man band with the whirligig glissando of his turbine engine functioning as a melodic elements of his Teutonic folk anthem and the pop! pop! POW! of the J47's afterburner acting as the rhythm section. Like so much *sturm und drang* during this era, the exploits of Bob Smith were completely over-the-top, a career as pushed and absurdist as the contours of the rolling mutant monstrosities that carried him to fame, glory, acclaim — and a couple of emergency wards...

The hospital visits just add to the legend but the truth is this: "Jet Car" was a friggin' rock star-cum-carny sideshow, barnstorming to and fro across the benighted, backwooded nether regions of America, the Outback of the Breadbasket and beyond, in a quest to show to local yokels what an honest bunch of California hot rodders can do when given access to the same glorious shards of thermodynamic technology that was normally set aside for the military-industrial complex and its corporate welfare mothers.

Ay, after Palamides and Elischer had scoured the scrap yards of the Southwestern Desert in search of military table scraps and the crumbs dropped from the gilded spoons of the techno-industrial banquets before welding them into Frankensteinian mega-machines, Smith would roll onto the starting line of a drag strip and begin spinning the turbines and applying voltage and jet fuel to the engine's compressor and combustion chamber while the natives would cloister around the clumps of fire ejaculating out of the massive fuselage, like pygmies around a cauldron. It was ungodly; it was pagan. It was a ritual and a seance that nobody had experienced before but each paying customers felt deep in the marrow of their bones that there was something primal and good in the fire that smelled sweet and sour.

But the warmth and the comfort of the cabalistic pyromania had a flip side. On more than one occasion, the propulsion machine catapulted the fearless "Jet Car Bob," half driver, half shaman, to doom and calamity.

In fact, "Jet Car's" career crashed to a denouement as precipitously as it began. It ended with him declared dead in Milan, Michigan in 1964. But the proclamation of his demise was greatly exaggerated and ergo salutations are in order: After relegation to near-obscurity, driver "Jet Car Bob" Smith and his bossman and car builder, Romeo Palamides, have been inducted into Don Garlits' International Drag Racing Hall of Fame in 1999, a perch in a pantheon that will ensure they will never be forgotten. In Palamides's instance, who ultimately constructed six *Untouchable* jet dragsters, as well as five jet funny cars, the award was posthumous. No matter; in the case of both men the honor could not have been more righteous. But in specific, the acclaim for the man known to his friends as "Jet Car" is particularly poignant... Nobody — and I mean NOBODY — has suffered more for their art (and lived) than Smith...

∞

So "Jet Car," how did you get tagged with the name "Jet Car"?

JET CAR: We were at Dragway 42 for the Drag News Invitational, back at the hotel. I'm in the room, trying to make some dates for down the road and I'm talking to this guy on the phone from Ohio, "Hot Rod Harry" Williams, that was the way he answered the phone. All I had (written down) was "Harry Williams," duh, duh, duh, "phone number," duh, duh, duh, "Exeter Drag Strip or something." I dialed the number and he picked up and he comes on saying, "THIS IS HOT ROD HARRY WILLIAMS" and something just clicks and I go, "Yeah, well THIS IS JET CAR BOB SMITH." I was having dinner with Al Caldwell, Romeo and Doris (Herbert, Drag News editor) and I told them this story, I'm still laughing about the way this guy's answered the phone, "THIS IS HOT ROD HARRY WILLIAMS." But I've been "Jet Car Bob" ever since.

So it's pretty sweet that you and Palamides are inducted in the Drag Racing Hall of Fame. You had to be excited about that...

JET CAR: It's the greatest thing that ever happened to me, I gotta' tell you. In 1995 they inducted me into the Jet Car Hall of Fame — which is an honor also — but to us old time racers, this is the one. When I got the letter it put me right down in my chair.

You didn't know it was coming?

JET CAR: I had no idea. I was at work when my wife got the letter and she called me saying, "You got a registered letter. I don't normally do this, but I had to open it. It's from the Don Garlits Museum." I just went, "uhhhuuhhcckk." It took me a few minutes to compose myself then she read it to me.

You were driving for Romeo Palamides starting in 1962?

JET CAR: 1962, yeah. I started driving for Romeo after Glen Leasher got killed. Glen got killed on the Salt Flats in Romeo's Bonneville car, The *Infinity*.

I'll tell you a little story: I had driven for Romeo before, in a Top Fuel car. When I heard on the radio that there was a crash up there (in Bonneville) I called the airport on the chance that he would be there — and he was. I offered my condolences on the crash and the loss of Glen and wondered if there was anything I could do for him. "Yeah," he says,"I got to go to San Gabriel this weekend (for a match race); the track is supposed to find me a driver. If you could ride along and help me stay awake, maybe share the driving." I said, "Sure, no problem." I went to the airport and we loaded the jet car up and headed for San Gabriel. We started up the grapevine and the conversation came up and to who was going to drive the (race) car. Before we topped the grapevine and went over the other side, I was going to be the new driver. It took me about five seconds to say, "yes."

Just like that.

JET CAR: At that time I was driving a Top Fuel car, and of course a week before I figured I could beat "that" car. Everybody did. Everybody figured they could beat that jet car. They figured they could leave on it, but nobody added up that, "Okay, this car is running in the 6s; we're running in the 8s." Nobody wanted to thank about that. At that time the car always started from behind the starting line and slid. Then they'd fire the afterburner and the car would haul ass. Everybody figured that the car was rolling the lights and time weren't really right — me along with everybody else. But when Romeo said, "You did okay driving my fuel dragster, do want to drive the *Untouchable*?" I'm like, "Y-E-A-H."

I busted my balls running Sid (Waterman's) Top Fuel car and we're running 8.0 or 7.90 at 190. This car was going to run 6s at 220 or 230 mph. Who in their right mind wouldn't jump into a jet? If nothing else to say okay, "I ran 230 mph."

So the jet cars were sliding through the starting line?

JET CAR: Yeah. I cut some little wooden blocks out and stuck them behind the rear tires. I told Romeo, "You know the car hunches when it leaves." It would pick up and be impossible to stage. These little one-inch blocks were enough to hold it so we could stage the car.

Tell me about the first night at San Gabriel.

JET CAR: Gary Gabelich made a pass right away, then Romeo put me in the car. I wanted to go fast right away. The first run was motor only (no afterburner) and I said, "No, I want to go faster." There were a lot of switches to turn on (laughs), but I still wanted to go faster. So on the next run he let me turn on the afterburner, but he didn't tell me the whole story. I made the run and it covered the track in so much kerosene that it killed mosquitoes for thirty square miles.

Weren't you considered a turncoat by the wheel-driven community?

JET CAR: Yeah, yeah. But I was still looking at them and saying, "Hey! I'm going 230 and you're going 190, pal."

The Untouchable *was quite a hot property. Did you have problems getting paid at some of these strips?*

JET CAR: When we set the record up at Kingdon it went out UPI and AP, all over the world. I knew we went fast because on that particular run the ass of that car picked up off the ground (immediately) whereas it usually just slid then went "Boom" and then picked up speed and by the time it reached the 1/8th mile you knew it was hauling ass. However, on that particular run I felt the back of the car just pick up and nail me to the seat. After that run the phones started ringing.

So I got a listing of drag strips and I talked to (dragster drivers) (Art) Malone and (Chris) Karamesines and I asked them who the good guys were and who the bad guys were. The bad guys didn't pay you; the good guys were like slot machines: You went in and put on a show for 'em and they paid you. But there were questionables in there: they paid you but you had to be hard nosed at the pay shack. Like ("Broadway Bob") Metzler at Union Grove.

You could get money out of Metzler one of two ways: You stick a .45 up against his head and go, "Click. Pay me," and have the look in your eyes that you were going to blow his brains out, even then it was nip and tuck — he's a pretty good poker player, let's put it that way; or you give him two more dates, usually holidays. This is an hour, hour and a half in the pay shack. You walk out going, "Well, we got our money," then you go, "Oh shit, we just sold our two best dates of the year..."

There were times you really had to get mean. The second Drag News Invitational was at — I can't even remember the name of that piece of shit drag strip — it was out by Mt. Clemens in Michigan. Doris (Herbert, of Drag News) had a cut a deal with the owner. It was a signed contract. The only problem was that his guy had a drag strip that was about as wide as my living room. The week before he laid down the asphalt, and he went El Cheapo on the asphalt. We go there and the left lane of the drag strip — you couldn't run on it. No way. It was soft, squishy. But what are you gonna' do? You're gonna' race. Then it rained and everybody disappeared. Doris disappeared, the track owner disappeared. Everybody disappeared. Vaporized. There were a bunch of cars, most of 'em were depending on gas money to get home. Everybody was getting nervous, "How am I going to get home?" But I knew when I got to the motel that night I was going to have my money. When one of the lackeys gave the ol', "Ahh, get out of here," I said, "Okay, we'll do it my way." I backed the friggin' jet car right up against the tower and I said, "Get these people back here or I'm burning the tower down." We plugged that baby in and "wwwhhoooo," it started whirring. They showed up and bagged the money. It paid off like a slot machine.

What was Romeo like?

JET CAR: A super guy. A piss poor business man but a hell of a racer. The more he made, the more he spent.

He wasn't unique then, as least as far as drag racers go. It is ironic that you could have problems making ends meet with what has been considered "cheap horsepower."

JET CAR: You could build a jet car cheaper than you could build a Top Fuel car. The motors were very cheap at that time, all you had to do was go to Tucson and get them out of an aerospace boneyard over there. Then you had to have the ingenuity to bolt them into the car and make them work. There weren't too many people who were motivated to do that because this was around the time that the NHRA said, "Errmp, you're out of here." I chased (NHRA Competition Director) Bernie Partridge all down the West Coast trying to convince him that the car was safe — they kept saying the engines were going to blow up. Which could happen, but under a lot of other circumstances beyond the way we were running the car. But when the NHRA gets their mind made up about something, nothing is going to change it.

But they were even down on the Allison-powered cars. The resented anything that came from aviation.

JET CAR: True. But if we had an off weekend and there was an NHRA race nearby, I'd tow into the pits and immediately there was a thousand people around the jet car. But it took a lot of years before they came around and let us make even exhibition runs...

They are afraid of progress sometimes.

JET CAR: The next couple of three years when all the crashes started didn't help either.

"BAN THE JETS!" You guys were pretty much outlaws.

JET CAR: Pretty much. There were other associations around, plus there were a lot of outlaw strips that didn't have any banners hanging up. They had their own insurance — I think they had insurance. They paid their bills, let's put it that way.

You guys were really threatening the status quo. All of a sudden the diggers (Top Fuel dragsters) weren't necessarily the headliners anymore.

JET CAR: Right. We could draw a crowd if just a jet car showed up for an exhibition. But when we ran (top fuel racer) Tommy Ivo in a match race — that lit it off. I must say I had to go in the tank on that one.

Really?

JET CAR: Well, what would have happened if I had blown him in the weeds three runs in a row? It would have been over.

How many rounds did he win?

JET CAR: He won two, we won one.

That's harsh.

JET CAR: We came back a few weeks later and I blew him in the weeds two-out-of-three and I LET him win one. From then on, I would let the dragster win one and then I'd win two.

Rope-a-dope.

JET CAR: Hey! I knew when it started that we had a commodity and if it worked right we had a saleable item. We were putting on a show — we were showmen, that was the bottom line. What NHRA forced us to do was be showmen. Back east, there weren't that many jet cars so we'd race the favorite dragster in town, their local hero. I let him win a race so he'd look good.

And this was all on some rather dicey tracks.

JET CAR: Oh, oh, some of the tracks were shaky — in fact, a lot of them were shaky. There were very few that weren't... Union Grove (WI) was a pretty big track at that time, but you'd go through the lights and after 100 feet you'd go straight down hill. Then you'd run out to a county road that would go right across the end of the drag strip. The road was about six feet higher than the level spot right before you got there. You'd go down a hill, you go across a flat spot then you'd go up to get on the road.

You had one of your worst crashes at Union Grove.

JET CAR: I crashed the first car in town.

In town?

JET CAR: At the circle track. I put it up in the grandstands and totaled it. The second car was the one that Romeo built for (Jack) Birdwell. We sort of leased it to finish our tour — and I crashed it. That was at Union Grove. There is a bump in the track in the right lane at about 1000', and we hit the bump and that kicked the chutes out — I didn't even know that they came out. I go through the lights and hit the chutes; no chutes. I went off the end and when I got to the road I was launched 10 feet, 12 feet in the air, I guess. I cleared the road — almost. There was a big old bathtub modeled Nash Rambler there with some guys in it who had just left the races. They were going to watch Karamesines and me make the last run from over the hill. I came over the hill with no chutes and I was back-and-forth, back-and-forth trying to make three miles out of a half mile. I got to the road and there was no place to go. I hit a telephone pole and cut it in three pieces before it hit the ground, I went up in the air and came down on the Nash Rambler. There were three kids; two of 'em ran, one of 'em jumped in the car.

Oh no.

JET CAR: It came down and went "kuh-wish" and flipped it around. I went into the ditch on the other side. I broke one finger, broke my nose again, cut my lip and scraped the grafts off because I was still wrapped up because of the burns the time before. I got out of that one without much, uhh, well I killed another car so that wasn't good.

Yeah. And you say there was a kid in the Rambler? How did he fare?

JET CAR: He broke a collarbone. The real bad part was the ambulance ride to the hospital. Union Grove's ambulance was a '36 Chevy panel truck. Even worse, they put the kid in the same hospital room with me. There were all these parents there and everything... oh, man. I'm laying there — I didn't even want to go to the hospital, but "No, you gotta' go to the hospital overnight" — and who do they wheel in but this kid. I go, "Oh shit, how can I escape from this?" If they hadn't taken my clothes away I would have ran.

Were you getting stink-eye from the parents?

JET CAR: Oh, man! Oh! (Silence.) It was a bad evening...

So we've covered Untouchable's 1 & 2. *Tell me about number 3.*

JET CAR: That's the one I got hurt in the most.

Weren't you in the hospital for almost six months?

JET CAR: That was a long one. Actually, what they called *Untouchable IV* was *Untouchable III* for me. III went to Birdwell; it was the one he renamed and put a little tail on the back and called it the Scorpion.

But (after the crash of *Untouchable IV*) they tagged my toe. I was in a coma. When you're in a coma you hear things, but you can't react to them. For some reason I'm laying there — and I know there is a lot of stuff going on around me but there is this heavy fog. The shit's going on but you're taking a nap. My sister was there, she'd flown in from Germany. She's standing there with me and the doctors say, "Pffftt; ah, he's gone." They're tagging the toe and putting the blanket over my face and she let out a giant scream. For some reason I just went "Whoa" and groaned and moved around a little bit. They went, "Hold it! Let's check his beat again" and they started working on me. I started coming around and a few days later I came around some more. But at one time I was headed for the morgue...

The chute had torn off on that pass?

JET CAR: One of them came off and tore the mount off. Both (chutes) came right off the back of the car. That was not a long strip; there was a big ditch at the end of it. It nosed into the ditch which snapped the cockpit off. It came out of the ditch and just went endo six or eight times across this wheat field. The only thing holding the cage on (to the fuselage) was a throttle cable. It was like a rock on the end of a string — "whhipp, whhipp." I was basically wearing the cage.

I was conscious when they got there. They sawed the cable off and put me and the cockpit in the back of this ambulance. At the hospital they cut me out — I was telling them where to cut in order to get me out of this thing. My legs were up around my head.

Jesus.

JET CAR: When they took me out of the ambulance, the nurses thought I was black. There was so much dust and dirt on me that they thought they were taking a black guy into the hospital.

"Bob Smith, the famous Negro jet car driver." Unreal.

JET CAR: They put me in bed and set my legs; then I went into a coma. I had head injuries. For months after that there was no blue in my eyes, they were totally red. My eyeballs must've came clear out of my head. My eye sight sort of went bad after that...

You didn't drive any more jets after that?

JET CAR: That was my last jet ride.

That was quite an exclamation point. What did you turn on that run?

JET CAR: 230-235 mph. It was an average run. I don't remember the run. I remember packing the chutes before the run — that's all I remember.

Was Romeo touring with the car?

JET CAR: Romeo wasn't there. I went out with the car quite a bit by myself; he was back here welding and running the shop. In fact, I didn't even have anybody helping me. I picked some guy out of the crowd and said, "Hey, you want to help me pack a chute? Do you want to pump the kerosene?" Somebody was always willing to do that, it was quite a charge for them.

So you drove diggers after that?

JET CAR: Yeah. I was in the hospital about six months then it was six months further down the road before I could really walk and talk and put enough weight back on to look human. It was a good year before I was really up and moving around and could get a job.

Did you like the dragsters better than the jets at this point?

JET CAR: At that point, yeah. (laughs) The jet was a show. There were things you had to do in driving a jet car, but it wasn't anything like driving a digger. You didn't have the wheels spinning, the car moving around underneath you and driving it by the seat of your pants.

You were more of a passenger?

JET CAR: You were. You lined the car up right and when you fired the afterburner you were going to go straight.

But then again you were describing wrestling it in the shut-down area. That had to quite an experience with all the weight on the ass end.

JET CAR: Oh yeah. It was like a Greyhound bus.

Did you do any racing at Bonneville?

JET CAR: No. I didn't go with them when Glen got killed. Romeo and I talked about another car to go to Bonneville with. In the three or four year span that I drove for him in the jet car, we never made it long enough into the year to get there.

70 PERCENT IS A LOUSY ROCKET FUEL (1973)

"The skies were black with clouds and the season was late, so any storm represented the official end to the runs for the year. Gary made a successful first run, the car was turned and fueled for the return through the 'Flying Mile,' it was a moment of 'should he or not?' The timers gave Gary the radio call that the decision to go or not was his. He sat in silence (he was always sort of spiritual). Suddenly the clouds parted and a ray of sun pierced the windshield, Gary's words were: 'That's a sign from God' and he lit the match for the record setting run."-- Blue Flame **crewmember Paul Stringer.**

Inspired by the US moonshot and Gary Gabelich's achievement in the *Blue Flame* (a cool two-way average speed of 622.407 mph on October,1970), Craig Breedlove uses the drag strips to shake down his *English Leather* rocket dragster, powered by a hydrazine-fueled lunar module motor. His ultimate target speed with the rocket is the Speed of Sound, but Uncle Sam intervened and confiscated Breedlove's eye-dropper and chemistry set. Or as Craig puts it, "We actually built the *English Leather* rocket car as a prototype test vehicle to develop a hypergolic rocket system for a Land Speed car... We ran that engine on unsymmetrical dimethyl hydrazine and nitrogen tetraoxide for an oxidizer. We were able to order it at will, TRW was able to vouch for us that we were not a bunch of dingbats out there. In 1974, all of that was outlawed."

Nonplused, Breedlove begins to r&d a hydrogen-peroxide rocket car. Different design, same results. "We changed the design of the car to four peroxide thrusters because they had not yet restricted hydrogen peroxide in any way," he explains to me in the *SOA* compound on Black Rock in 1997. "After we made the switch, all of a sudden you couldn't manufacture or sell peroxide in any concentrations higher than 70 percent. And 70 percent is a lousy rocket fuel. At that point the entire rocket-powered land speed vehicle was trashed." Disheartened and almost destitute, Breedlove jettisons his dream of going Mach 1 and began living on his sailboat, a sad statement on the Spirit of these here United States. With the government putting the kibosh on lunar module fuels in the private sector, Gabelich's rocket-powered record run was the final chapter for Bonneville as the playpen for truly unlimited thrust. Bummer.

I/0

A MODERN FUEL

What was the budget going in, I mean what did you guys think you could deliver for?

PETE FARNSWORTH: We signed a contract I believe for $165,000.

Um hm, so that's almost a half a million by the time it was done?

PETE: It was a little more than half a million when it was completed run and a movie made about it. It was all part of the budget.

So I'm assuming the chassis's 4130 chromemoly?

PETE: From the back of the driver to the front of the front wheels, structure in front that held the pressure tanks for the fuel systems was chromemoly 4130 and all the structure from the driver back was 4130. I heli-arced that whole thing together.

And the propulsion system, did they end up using the liquefied natural gas?

PETE: Um hmm. That was a bi-propellant engine, hydrogen peroxide, liquefied natural gas. We did break the primary injection system for the liquefied natural gas on one of the early runs and bypassed and ran the secondary system which we were going to put 3/4 of the fuel through the secondary injection system and 25% through the primary system. We broke the primary system and ended up only through the high speed, the high powered section of it.

Okay, so there was two injection systems but either one used a combination of the two propellants.

PETE: Yeah, yeah...

Because here's the confusion, some people don't think that there was LNG running through the car.

PETE: The Gas Industry insisted on that, there was definitely LNG running through the engine. It helped in creating heat in the combustion chamber on the run and we were way down on power. We went out there, the engine was designed for 22,000 pounds of thrust at full power; the first year we didn't need nearly that much, we only were going to run the primary fuel injection system, with the 25% fuel flow. We ran it at that and we sunk a big steel post in the Union Grove (drag strip) down in their shutoff area way down at the far end. We tied the car to it and put strain gauges between the car and the post and the post was down in several yards of concrete below ground with a nine inch diameter steel post and, uh, tied it to the car with 5/8 steel cables and we were consistently getting 16,500 pounds thrust cutting the engines. That's we went to the Salt Flats with.

Okay I'm trying to understand what you said — The 16,500 pounds was strictly out of the primary injection system? Not even using the secondary?

PETE: We were not going to use the secondary system the first year. We had enough power, we were going to upgrade it the second year supposedly to go supersonic, but in order to do that we would have to have gone to Schenectady, New York and check out the rocket — the Lowell Rocket system on their rocket test — and check it for combustion instability and that would have been probably well, we're not really even sure, but we think it would have been 50 or 60 thousand dollars additional just to test it in those days. 1970 dollars.

And so you guys wanted to go Mach 1 but the Gas Company just wanted to...

PETE: Well, they got the record and that was enough for them. They toured the car around the world it was the first car to exceed a thousand kilometers per hour in Europe. It was a tremendous hit, over there, Jesus, one thousand kilometers per hour on the ground, but it was just a number. Speed of sound... THAT was the number.

A physical barrier, yeah?

PETE: We were restricted the first year as well by Goodyear: no more than 700 miles an hour with the tires, till they could evaluate the design and take the tires, cut them apart, make sure that everything was all right. So we went 660 with it, with a broken motor, we ended up having 10,500 pounds thrust on the record runs. A very interesting project, but just heartache after heartache. But you know, (these were) experiences that you wouldn't trade for anything, no matter what.

On one level it sounds like you got jobbed out of you know, going Mach 1.

PETE: No, no, we never said that. You know, we would have liked to have the attempt at it.

Okay, I mean basically that next year you wanted to break...

PETE: They never agreed that they were going to do that, (but to make) an evaluation after we ran the first year.

If the car hadn't been repossessed and had you guys still had some cash or maybe derive some cash from the car, from appearances and in car shows and what have you, that potentially you would have gone out the next year.

PETE: Perhaps.

BLUE FLAME POSTSCRIPT

After setting the Land Speed Record, Gary Gabelich drives a 4 wheel drive Funny Car, a car doomed to make one run. During a closed photo-op for some drag racing magazines at Orange County International Raceway, it is agreed that Gabelich will merely "smoke the tires" for photographers. Caught in the moment, Gabelich stays on the throttle and the car climbs onto the guardrail and rolls, unraveling like a tin lid on a can opener. Gabelich's body is not exempt from the slicing and dicing and a hand is severed as well as other limbs sliced open like so much canned fruit. Through a stroke of luck, after being stuffed into a station wagon and raced to the hospital with severed limbs in tow Gabelich is sewed back together by a crack team of neurosurgeons. He was said to never be quite the same, unfortunately. He is later beheaded in a motorcycle accident with a diesel truck on the streets of San Pedro, CA. As a testament to free-wheelin' lifestyle, he is eulogized more in biker magazines than in any hot rodding publications.

∞

"Gary was very upset when the car was sold because he wanted to attempt a sound barrier run with the car. In 1970 when they raced it, they had many mishaps. The most damning was they burned out the retro in the rocket and had to get a loaner or a gift motor to finish. As I remember the original rocket had about 40,000 pounds of thrust and the actual motor they used to set the record had about 14,000. That would lead you to believe that the car could go much faster given the space limitations of the Salt Flats, and the ground effects of going supersonic.

"I can't even describe how many hours we spent talking about where the air goes (under the car). Would the air flip the car when supersonic 'splits the air?' They talked at great length about lengthening the rod on the front tip of the car to split the air farther out in front to prevent any negative effects. Craig Breedlove was a very close friend of Gary's and he as well was always helpful in helping Gary advance his efforts. Craig and Gary where from the same town in California and I met Craig in 1966 on a water skiing trip. Most would think that they would be strange bedfellows when Gary got picked to drive the car, but Craig was one of his biggest supporters and fans.

"Gary was trying to figure out how to stop the new car going supersonic also.

"The problems are: no air for chutes and brakes won't work over 400MPH. He was working on a splitting tail like the Space Shuttle and body panels that popped out. Of course, he never considered running anywhere but the flats.

"Gary's feelings about the car being sold was this: the car was owned by the Natural Gas Association as a publicity stunt. When the car got the record, they received millions of dollars in promotion which they never could have bought. They never saw it as a race car and felt that a return to the flats and the risk of an accident would become negative publicity. Hence, the car was sold.

"Gary even pursued contacting the new car owner about another run. Apparently, the car had been dropped being off loaded from a ship when it left the country and there was some tweaking of the frame and that ended his interest.

"Gary then began trying to raise sponsors for a new car he'd named *The American Way*. While he raised some eyebrows at the time, he raised no money for the project as interest in the LSR had waned by then, this was in 1979 nine years after the last true attempt and he wasn't breaking another's record, he would only be raising his mark and sponsors wondered how much interest this would raise. To raise the interest, he and Craig Breedlove stated they'd create some new interest by building two cars and they'd 'drag race' for the record on the flats. Wow, a 700MPH drag race! Of course, Craig would have to change his thinking to a rocket as a Jet vs. Rocket race would be no race in a drag event the best I can remember is something like 0 to 500 in 10 seconds (more than a few G forces).

"One of the reasons Gary was chosen to drive the car (*Blue Flame*) was because his full time job was he worked for

Rockwell International in Downey, California as a 'Test Astronaut.' He tested all the space suits for the Apollo space missions. This is a glorious title to say he was the guy going around in the centrifuge. He was used to a lot of G forces, they were always concerned that the driver would blackout during acceleration.

"As far as Gary's life being cut short, while we all miss him lots, few of us could picture him dying an old man. Gary's life was lived on the edge from the time he was 15 years old. Gary started racing by cleaning up the grease/oil mess for some kids in his neighborhood who had a drag car. He did this for a few years on the promise that someday they'd let him drive it at the drag strip. That day came when he was 15, on the first pass he went faster than any run ever in the car. One year later, he had his own car and became a legend in California drag racing. He was the ultimate crowd pleaser being a lot 'nuts & wild' and being EZ to spot as he always wore an ostrich plume on the top of his helmet. He'd love to taunt his competitors on the starting line by shaking his fist and sometimes getting out of his car to yell something. Of course, it was all in good fun and I never met another racer who didn't love his magnetic personality.

"While setting the LSR made Gary infamous, many of his friends consider it a high point in his life that made the rest of his life chasing a dream. After the record, he didn't know if he was a career LSR car driver or needed to return to his career in Drag Racing. Before his death, he nearly lost his life four times to my count. He flipped a drag boat @ 200MPH and as he went in the water the motor hit him in the back, nearly killing him. His kidneys were badly damaged and he was on dialysis for two years. He had two accidents in the same Funny Car (*Beach City Corvette*). Once, he lost the chutes and ended up on fire on a freeway and the second accident, the car caught on fire during a run and burned to the ground (he jumped out at over 100MPH). That accident burned holes clear through his goggles and helmet but he had only minor burns to his face and head. The fourth accident was a crash in his own funny car. It had 4 wheel drive which made it very fast off the line. On a photo shoot for a magazine, the throttle locked down during a 'burn out' and he lost control. At about 160MPH it went through a guard rail twice and flipped end over end.

"Gary had one of his hands cut off to the outside skin, one leg was behind his head and one was wrapped around the steering wheel. That leg became the problem. While his hand was re-attached and the leg behind him was dislocated, the surgeons wanted to remove the other leg as it was nothing but shattered bone from the ankle. Gary would not let them remove the leg, so they inserted a long rod to replace the bone. He adapted to the handicap, but spent about a year trying to get rid of gangrene." --***Blue Flame*** **crewmember Paul Stringer.**

ALSO SPAKE ZARATHUSTRA (1973)

"Man is something that must be overcome; and for that reason you must love your virtues — for you perish by them."
— ***Thus Spoke Zarathustra.***

DUMMMM........DAHHHMMMM.........DEEHHHMMM........ DEEMMMMMM........DA-DUM....... to the accompaniment of an orchestral overture, somewhere in America four mechanics in white shirts and slacks push a shaved albino carrot of a motorcar onto the launch pad of a drag strip... the rocket car is shrouded by four motorcycle tires and looks rather docile, like a soapbox derby racer with a slight thyroid condition... horns blare out of a series of lo-fidelity loudspeakers wired in parallel, with cables sagging down the length of a drag strip... *DUMMMM..........DAHHHMMMM..........DEEHHHMMM..........DEEMMMMMM........DA-DUM...BOUMP....BAMMPP....BOUMPHH...* as tympanies rattle, smoke silently wisps from hydrogen peroxide gas chilled to near absolute zero... the caustic vapor stings those close enough to read the lettering *POLLUTION PACKER* stenciled onto the racecar's aluminum-skinned fuselage.

The *Pollution Packer.* The moniker itself served as a fantastic portent of an age when outrageous hyper-velocity will be absolutely effortless and won't degrade the Air Quality one iota. The rocket car is a postcard from the future, a day when there is no smog and warp speed for the populous is commonplace. The fuel is hydrogen peroxide, suggestive of experimental hydrogen-burning engines that produce water instead of smog.

(Although hardly as pure as the driven snow, as far as rocket fuels go, hydrogen peroxide is decidedly less toxic than, say, hydrazine, a radically unstable fuel additive that would explode upon contact with just about anything. Vintage film of Nazi Luftwaffe pilots with nasty and gruesome burns from dicey landings with experimental rocket airplanes are testament to the chemical's volatility. In the 1960s, a few of the braver nitro dragster racers would splash hydrazine into the fuel tank after the motor was lit and the dragster was running on the start line, creating a cocktail of nitromethane, benzol and 2% hydrazine. Surreptitious use of hydrazine is credited with the first 200 mph clocking by a fuel dragster (Chris "the Greek" Karamesines in 1960, a feat not matched for another four years). As per the instability of hydrazine, one top fuel driver said that, "I do know if you spilled the straight stuff in the trunk of the tow car you had instant fire. Had first hand experience with that one. I really think there were more guys running it than were willing to admit (it).")

∞

"... it didn't take the Talmud to see that folks would pay good money to see death-defying displays of horsepower and cockpit acumen at their local drag strip... jet amd rocket dragsters became a way to subvert the system and ensure that the racers were in the loop in a fiduciary sense... it was a means for hot rodders to be paid in full..." — **Gus Levy, SCHTUPPING THE SYSTEM WITH MAXIMUM THRUST, previously unpublished.**

"NHRA was founded in response to a demand among thousands of hot rodders in all parts of the country to organize a legitimate, purely American motorsport. And NHRA, under Wally Parks' guidance, did just that. We're all very proud of 50 years of achievements.

"If you're so fond of airplane engines, race 'em the air, in airplanes, where they belong. Yes, drag racing is about automotive engines, and as long as I have any say over it, the sport will stay that way." — **NHRA muckety-muck, Dick Wells.**

Meanwhile, back at the drag strip's launch pad, the music is all midrange and sounds like a hangover feels. As a string section join the horns and the percussion, and everything swells towards a crescendo that distorts the speaker cones and attempts to cloak the lack of any real noize out of the race car resting in a wistful and dormant manner on the drag strip's starting line. Noise from the twisted and besotted crowd swells in time with the trumpets' flourish and a smattering of beer cans and trash are tossed ineffectually in the general vicinity of the track.

From the rocket motor comes a a discordant harmonic, a high-pitched whistle — like the sound of a negligent housewife's tea kettle set to a high burn. The opera overture reaches its apex and continues blaring out of tin speakers, oblivious to the whistling, which is in a different key altogether. Every head hurts just that much more from the atonality.

As the start lights turn green, the rocket car smokes in the drag strip with a heavenly mist of steam. The air stinks like ammonia with a hint of rubber gloves burning in a landfill faraway in Valhalla. As it zips down the race course, the *Pollution Packer* burns H_2O_2 in a quantity and concentration that would keep an Aryan nation of Rita Hayworths platinum blond for life. The white vapor is a gentle and clandestine nerve gas, silently tweaking central nervous systems and fogging the brains of those assembled like mosquitoes in a culvert.

It is fitting that the soundtrack to the launching of a rocket car is "Also Spake Zarathustra," Richard Strauss's ode to Frederik Nietschze, a pompous piece of music appropriated by motion picture director Stanley Kubrick as the opening theme in his space epic, *2001.*

Nietschze was a firm believer in the elevation of the human spirit, and how man could take his endeavors to ever-spiraling heights. If life had any meaning, he reckoned, it was to raise the bar on all matters spiritual and intellectual — and by extension, technological.

2001 was a 1960s production and an exercise in inscrutable bombast. The movie's message was garbled by the gobbling of *w-a-a-a-y* too much LSD by its filmmakers as they read the Arthur C. Clarke book upon which the script was based... one precept of *2001* was the notion of uroboros or bookends and how everything in the spacetime continuum comes full circle... at the beginning of the film, barbaric simians gather at a monolithic totem left behind by a future civilization of humans who have vaporized their very existence... during a total eclipse of the sun, the monolith generates an unheard cosmic wail that tweaks the psyches of the primordial chimps who have discovered technology in the form of a zebra bone that can be used as a billy club... they haven't yet discovered the wheel nor fire, but these hairy precursors to humanity have found a way to beat each other's brains into a pulpous ooze... this same totem mysteriously manifests on one of Jupiter's moons, whereupon the nervous sounds of a planetary eclipse drives a handful of space explorers to their doom... civilization has gone full circle, back to the species upon which humans evolved...

There is an echo of Kubrick's ethos by the whooping and hooping of beer-battered bleacher bums, dangling precipitously by the top rails of a temporary grandstand. The drunks are an embodiment of verisimilitude and simulacrum, an example of *2001*'s apes either somewhat evolved or somewhat de-evolved. The shrill pitch of the rocket engine is a physiological device that tweaks the primitive id of the beastly crowd of trackside tipplers.

The rocket whizzes by and the drunks scream even more belligerently, dazzled by the raw display of speed and stoned by the surreal cloud of rocket vapor. Up in the grandstands just shy of the finish line, two hippies blowing weed drop their jaws. "That was *too* fast," one exhales, like he had just seen the monolith and thy monolith's name is the *Pollution Packer.*

And perhaps it was too fast. Or perhaps tossing beer cans in the presence of a rocket car is just a monkey throwing a bone to the heavens.

THE MAD! ROCKET SCIENTIST

As a totem, or a weapon, or a propulsion system — whither from Biblical times through the days of Mongol Invasions, beyond the Dark Ages into the bomb factories of Germany, from the launch pads of NASA and finally touching own onto the drag strips of 1970s' America — the bark of a rocket has always been as fierce as its bite. It is the stuff of the physiological. It is the stuff of Ernst Mach — sensory and tactile and now hard-wired into our metaphysical fabric. It is the stuff of visionaries, daredevils and crackpots. It is also the stuff of dairy farmers moonlighting as rocket scientists...

∞

"You couldn't see the person next to you," says Brent Fanning, aka "the Mad! Rocket Scientist." Fanning is reminiscing about when he and and his wife Vicky ran the *Outer Limits* rocket funny car at drag strips across America to supplement their incomes as dairy farmers.

Outer Limits was supposedly a Corvette with a rocket engine, but by the time the Fannings were done deconstructing and reconstructing the fiberglass body by installing a series of colored bulbs they had bought at the hardware store and then wired in a hokey chase circuit, it was basically unrecognizable as anything off of a Detroit assembly line, much less of anything on this planet. If the no-budget sci-fi film *Plan 9 From Outer Space* needed a car as a prop, this was their interstellar baby...

Yes, at a Texas dairy farm whose barn is transformed into a garage for a rocket, the hydrogen-peroxide powered monolith known as *Outer Limits* would dwell silently and become quite the conversation starter for an agrarian culture not exactly known for its verbosity. The Fanning's neighbors, most of whom were also farmers, would gather around the monolith and kick the tires, like goats looking at a watch. Brent would tell them the principles of running the rocket car, which he had researched over at Texas A&M, using the university's networked computers as a font of knowledge and rocket science. He told them how the NHRA muckety-mucks had reluctantly attended a test of the rocket car way out in California and the men in suits were less than enthusiastic about even watching it run, much less signing off on a license for somebody who calls hisself the "Mad! Rocket Scientist" racing something called "the *Outer Limits.*" Fanning told his buddies how they even had flown in a bonafide NASA engineer into supervise the test, who was actually kind of baffled about how Brent has put this particular system together.

∞

While discussing rockets over a couple of beers one night, I tell Fanning that Craig Breedlove once said to me, "Everybody know that anything under 70 percent hydrogen peroxide makes for a nearly useless rocket fuel." Fanning couldn't disagree more about watered-down hydrogen peroxide as a monopropellant.

"We used to dilute it with water so we could make more steam. I'd put Vicky in the stands while we made a run. After the car run, if she said she couldn't see the person next to her, we considered the run a success, regardless of the speed."

The speed. In those days, the rockets were running so much faster than the Top Fuel dragsters, track operators would lie about the elapsed time and terminal speeds so as not to upset the National Hot Rod Association and its insurers. This was an ironic about-face to the rather common practice of hyping "popcorn" times over the public address system and in the trades as a way of generating more interest in a given race track and its events.

Indeed, the same muckety-mucks who reluctantly oversaw the Fanning's rocket test out in California, sent out threatening letters about revoking the licenses of drivers who went too quick and too fast. Philosophically and intellectually, the rockets were beyond what the Druids could process.

Fanning's *Outer Limits* was the last vestige of the rocket car subculture, a once-burgeoning scene whistling across the drag strips: the names of the cars underscored a weird synthesis of nationalism, post-psychedelic individualism and futurism: the *X-1, Vanishing Point, Miss STP, Stratosfear, Moon Shot, Screaming Yellow Zonkers, the Free Spirit, Spirit Of 76, Age of Aquarius, Captain America,* the *Pollution Packer*, the *American Dream, USA-1,* the *Conklin Comet, Concept 1,* the *Courage of Australia,* etc...

The future was now for hot rodders across America, including Brent Fanning, who, due to the screwy economics of Jimmy Carter America, couldn't afford a nitro Funny Car but could afford a rocket (!).

"I got to see a rocket car run and got to studyin' 'em and stuff. I thought, 'Them things can't tear up hardly,' y'know? 'We got to make money somehow, enough money to get a nitro Funny Car' — that's what I always wanted. So we ran a lot of match races with that rocket car. The first year we ran the (hydrogen) peroxide car, it would cost me $250 a run for fuel. When we quit four years later, it would cost $1200 a run. The last year we ran, I bought more hydrogen peroxide from FMC (Food Machinery Corporation, the manufacturer and distributor) than the U.S. Government. They had doubled the price. Basically, that put us out of business. It was only good for a flower pot so I gave it away and took a tax write-off."

One of the finishing strokes for Brent's career as a Mad! Rocket Scientist was when the NHRA tech daddies vetoed some of Brent's ideas for propulsion enhancement. "Since I had a really weak rocket," he clarifies, "I was actually going to try to inject a little nitro in it to increase the specific impulse on it — NHRA wouldn't let ya'. I can't blame them; it would have made it a little more... unstable."

ZARATHUSTRA POSTSCRIPT

"... supposedly when I lifted off the throttle, that was one fuel shut off device and when I popped the chute it was supposedly another one. Well, none of the fuel shut off devices worked so both chutes pulled off the car because it wasn't very firmly anchored to the chassis and off I went, till I ran out of fuel. When I got down to the end, there were two guys waiting to pick up the chute and help me get off of the track. Well, here they start walking out in my lane, I'm in the left lane, I mean, I knew I was in trouble, but they didn't realize that the chutes came off and then I steered the car — not knowing the chutes came off — I pulled over to the right and that aimed me, fortunately down a dirt road, when I went through a 14 foot cattle gate and missed a chain link fence. Otherwise I would have impaled myself right through the fence... I went up a hill and I don't remember anything else, I remember seeing blue, then that's the last thing I remember..." — **Paula Murphy, on her crash in the "Miss STP" rocket dragster when she set both a local speed and an altitude record in a race car.**

Chuck Suba's 5.41 second run remained drag racing's all-time Low E.T. until November 11, 1971 when Vic Wilson clocked a 5.10 pass at 311 mph in the second hydrogen peroxide rocket dragster, Bill Fredrick's *Courage of Australia.* This transpired during private testing at Orange County International Raceway in Southern California.

Despite the reluctance (actually, refusal) of the NHRA to sanction the rockets as a real class (the NHRA remains the de facto arbiters of all things drag racing and they refused to acknowledge or publish any jet car "records" as the cars were relegated to the "exhibition class" status (or "exploding clowns" as the dragster crowd sniffed)), the rocket car scene flourished like a comet. Its luminescence was just as brief. The triumphs, mishaps and tragedy left in its wake were legion and belie the brevity of the rocket car's moment in the sun. To wit:

1972: Craig Breedlove crashed his *English Leather Spl.* (nee *Screaming Yellow Zonkers)* while testing an experimental aero package (sans wheel fairings); in her first (and only) pass in a rocket car, Paula "Miss STP" Murphy breaks her neck while setting both velocity and altitude records in Sonoma, California when the parachutes are ripped from the car's chassis, and the car subsequently launches up and over the rolling hills of Wine Country...

1973: John Paxson tests a new motor in the *Courage of Australia*, and after a parachute failure, drives through the sand traps, pole vaults and lands upside down on the vehicle's vertical stabilizer. Paxson was uninjured...

1974: Dave Anderson crashes in the *Pollution Packer* in Charlotte, North Carolina... Anderson's chute doesn't deploy and the dragster first slides into a parked race car at the end of the course — killing two crewman — then impacts a retaining wall and nearly bends in half, killing Anderson...

1975: Upon impact, Russel Mendez frees his spirit and is beheaded by an aluminum guardrail in Gainesville, Florida as his body ejects from the *Free Spirit*...

1976: "Fearless Fred" Goeske wrecks his *Chicago Patrol* rocket at a speed of 275 mph and merely bruises his collar bones from the shoulder harness...

1977: Stunt woman Kitty O'Neil rips a 3.72 at a crushing 412 mph in Bill Fredrick's *Rocket Kat* dragster... Jerry Hehn is killed in his *American Dream* while doing thrust tests in a gravel pit; Hehn is strapped in with the vehicle anchored down, when the car breaks loose of its restraints and impales the side of a hill...

1981: Among the most bizarre of all rocket cars is the *Vulcan Shuttle*, a Volkswagen Bug dissected with a solid fuel rocket stuffed through the middle of the passenger compartment, which, unfortunately for driver Raul Cabrera is not throttleable. His destiny was the same as that of Mendez: Garish, ghastly and gruesome. The demise of both car and driver transpired while testing at an airport...

1994: The last hurrah for the rocket went down on an abandoned Royal

Air Force air base in England. "Slammin' Sammy" Miller stopped the clocks at mind-warping 3.58 seconds at 386 mph in the *Vanishing Point* rocket funny car. Miller, who had his crotch burned off in a nitro funny car fire in the early 70s, routinely kept his foot in the throttle until he would pass out (!) from the excessive g-forces, which was usually 660 feet into the run. According to crewmembers, Miller routinely got his thrills from waking up in the car after the car stopped accelerating, coasting through the speed clocks at nearly 400 mph.

(As an addendum, "Slammin' Sammy" Miller possesses the only 1 second e.t. on a time slip; circa 1980, at an 1/8th drag strip in Holland, he actually tripped the clocks 1.60 at 307 mph. He was relegated to Europe after an NHRA blacklisting...)

Brent Fanning explained Miller's method cum madness thusly: "He had the brake handle rigged with a brass knuckles type grip (it was a push brake) so his hand would stay on the brake should he black out when the car ran out of fuel, which it had been calculated to do, at just past the 1/8 mile. Then the deceleration would move his arm and brake handle forward applying the brakes and also releasing the chutes which were attached to the brake handle in some manner. Thus slowing the car until he regained consciousness."

∞

Military grade hydrogen peroxide is getting used up. As with hydrazine, because of environmental concerns, no more will be doled out to those rocket car renegades. Even if the private sector could summon any more of it, the drag racing authorities and their insurers had no interest in sanctioning what they considered to be hyper-speed death traps.

But even Fanning alluded to a problem with the rockets; an actual lack of *sturm und drang*. Not enough noise, not enough walla-walla... "We always felt the fans wasn't gettin' their money's worth, so we rigged up a little act to go along with the rocket car," Fanning smirks through a cigar chewed to cud. "We'd tell the ambulance drivers to be ready because we had something special to race against the rocket car. We'd put my brother in the other lane with a firesuit on, strap a fire extinguisher on his back like he was Roger Ramjet — it wasn't nuthin' but baking soda packed into the extinguisher, y' know, and we'd line him up against the rocket. The light would go green and the rocket would take off and my brother would pull the lever on the fire extinguisher and all that pressurized powder would begin spraying all over and my brother would begin runnin' around in circles; he'd spin around like he was out of control, then bang into the guardrail, and flip over it. The ambulance would come down from the finish line with the bubblegum machines on and the siren blaring. That was nuttier than the rocket."

1995: the *Vanishing Point* car is seen by the author parked at an auto repair shop in a bad neighborhood in Los Angeles (on Fairfax, two blocks south of Washington). Its tires are flat.

PART THREE:

PUSHING THE ENVELOPE

PULP FICTION (1996)

"The writing's on the wall: The day of the backyard mechanic is over." — **overheard in Bruno's Coffee Shop, September 1997.**

"I just got this nutty fax from Jocko." On my phone machine is a message from the editor of HOT ROD Magazine. Jocko's fax said the magazine did not have his permission to run the feature on him, which he likened to "pulp fiction." If it ran, he would sue Petersen Publishing.

One of Jocko's many complaints was that I had referenced one of his neighbors in the story, an outside thinker and engineer named George Van Tassel, who had built a time machine known as the Integratron at a place he called Spaceport Earth. "Everyone knows Van Tassel is a kook," Jocko said.

They run the story anyway.

THE PHONE CALL (1997)

The phone call comes from Shell Oil's media power center in West Los Angeles. It is the day after Labor Day, 1997. The voice on the other end, an oil company's flak who apparently had drawn Craig Breedlove as his assignment, is clueing me in as to how, beginning tomorrow and after a year long hiatus following the 675 mph mishap, the speed trials are back on for the *Spirit of America* at the parched alkali of Black Rock, Nevada. It is official, the first proper supersonic Land Speed Record attempts are a green light. I am to get credentialed tomorrow at a hotel in Reno, NV, whereupon Craig Breedlove will rendezvous with the press and lead a caravan out to the desert like some latter-day man-machine Mohammed. At the press conference he will explain the modifications and improvements administered to a land speed machine that had become unstable and crashed at transonic speeds.

In the days following Breedlove's 1996 near-calamitous daredevil act — near the speed clocks, Breedlove got out of the groove and began bicycling his sleek J79 jet engine-powered manned missile like a circus act, the 5-wheeled vehicle riding on the front tire and one rear wheel rolling and yawing off course until it made an abrupt right hand turn and was aimed at some Snowbird-types in an RV (by the grace of the All-Knowing, by a whisker had Breedlove missed torpedoing these senior citizen motorheads who had hoped to witness history, not aware that unwittingly they had almost become new members of the Good Sam's Club in the Sky) — the more dubious members of the motorsports press had surmised that Breedlove's speed was closer to 475 mph.

"Performance incentive clauses" was the phrase bandied about by these cynics, in reference to the reality that Craig would need beaucoup greenbacks from his sponsors to repair his exotic race car. The only confirmation of the actual speed of the vehicle as it became unstable came from the *Spirit of America* itself. (Breedlove showed data from the run which corroborated his speed, apparently.)

Whether the streamliner was traveling at 475 mph of 675 mph was rather moot; the *Spirit of America* had failed to reach its objective of reclaiming the Land Speed Record from the clutches of the British in general and Richard Noble, OBE in specific. The recent improvements to the race car's contour promised to render 'er even sleeker than last year's model, a design which already resembled an arrow from the quill of the Pauites.

There were also conflicting reports about whether Craig intends to crack the sound barrier or if his intent is to get the car up to trans- and sub-sonic speeds, and then remove himself out of the hot seat, install a remote controlled drone system and then go supersonic.

In other words, there was a chance that when the *Spirit of America* went Mach 1, it may not have a driver.

To get the skinny, the publicist tells me, I have to be at the Reno press conference by noon tomorrow. The flak kindly asks me to be sure to include references to Shell Oil in the article on Breedlove I was to pen for HOT ROD Magazine. I assume he means in relation to its continued patronage of Breedlove's increasingly-streamlined fuselage, a relation that dated back to 1962, and not its recent alleged complicity in the political assassination of Ken Saro Wiwa and genocide in Nigeria, when some of the locals were less than happy with what they considered exploitation... Ultimately, notions of tyranny and subterfuge in the Third World are now dormant in my mind. The important thing is that the Grunions are Go! The Land Speed Record is about to be raised...

The hour is late... I have just enough time for loading a camera bag with lenses and a half dozen plastic canisters of Ilford, cramming some clothing and toiletries into a shoulder bag, brewing up a thermos of Cafe Bustello, jumping in the Batmobile so's to make time to the Burbank Airport, throw a credit card down on an airline counter and catch a plane to Reno.

Because of the haste and my appearance, I would fit the profile of a terrorist: unshaven, jittery, amped on caffeine, paying with a credit card and demanding to be put on an airplane that was just about to taxi... but that routine would be repeated often during the next six weeks or so and was part and parcel of chasing the Land Speed Record, I would find out that Richard Noble's adage about "Going fast is slow business," is not accurate: it is slow business with a co-efficient of chasing airplanes.

My journey would only take a few hours. In Newtonian terms, the Land Speed bunch had taken an eternity to arrive at this moment; in four-dimensional respects, an infinity.

BAD DAY AT BLACK ROCK (1997)

On the eve of the press conferences in Reno heralding the Mach 1 attempts, I arrive at the Reno Airport after spending the flight engaging in heavy and heated discourse with a geeky film buff about the aforementioned Spencer Tracy movie. I am heavily mythologizing not only the flick, but the actual location of Black Rock itself. He's not buying it.

"Yeah," I said with authority, "there is a coffee shop called 'Bruno's' that is right across the street from the train station used in *Bad Day at Black Rock*. It has the be the same diner coffee shop where Spencer Tracy — with his only good arm — karate chopped Ernest Borgnine in the throat."

"Well that can't be," the geek in the seat next to me sniffs, as he ramps his bifocals up the bridge of his nose. "I have the laserdisc in my library and on one of the Second Audio Programs the director, John Sturges, explains at length how they used these abandoned railroad tracks they found in Bishop, California for the train scenes. That fictitious coffee shop was actually a set on a back lot in Burbank."

"I'm telling you they shot this film in Gerlach, Nevada. I've been there AND I've seen the movie. Spencer Tracy gets off the friggin' train in Gerlach."

"That sir is empirically impossible," the geek bleats. "The production never set foot in Nevada. Rent the laserdisc."

"Laserdiscs are Satanic."

When the plane lands, en route to scoring a rent-a-car I go to the Information Booth in hopes of procuring a map of the Gerlach area — I've been there before, but this is the kind of terrain where you just don't want to get lost. There is a kindly, slightly senilitic Chamber of Commerce croater behind the counter who asks me where I am headed. I tell him, "Black Rock," so he says, "Lovelock, it's right here, " and he points to the town of Lovelock on the map.

"No," I say, "ummm, Black Rock, out by Gerlach."

"Ohhh; Tomahawk, it's right here, just take I-80 east past..."

"No, no, no," I interrupt and point to my destination on his map, crinkling it a little bit. "Black Rock, out by Gerlach."

"O-h-h-h, Black Rock. That's easy: Just take I-80 east to Fernley and take 447 north to Gerlach. It'll take you right to the station where Spencer Tracy got off the train."

"Actually," I pipe up, "that movie was shot in Bishop, California and on a back lot in Burbank."

"You have a nice drive, sir."

THE CAB RIDE (1997)

The press conference isn't scheduled until noon. I sleep kinda' late, saunter downstairs in the casino for a leisurely breakfast and grabbed a copy of the *Reno Gazette.*

I drop my fork.

The bottom left quadrant of the front page has a small feature about the arrival of the Brits and their *Thrust SSC* jet car that notates — in so many words — that after seven years of research and development as well as "dancing-as-fast-as-I-can" cajoling of corporations, the joust is finally on: A quintessential California hot rodder (Breedlove and *Spirit of America*) arm wrestling a permutation of the British military industrial complex (Noble and *Thrust SSC*).

And although the match is on, there are still many obstacles in the path of both teams, not the least of which is negative cash flow. To facilitate the arrival of the Brits from Farnborough into Reno Int'l Airport — keep in mind it required 250,00 gallons of jet fuel to top off an Antonov AN-124 Russian cargo plane (the only vehicle in existence with enough trunk space to transport the *Thrust*'s 80-ton portable skunk works) — Noble appealed for alms via the London Daily Telegraph and the internet. The vox populi responded with a vengeance, mailing checks and forking over credit card numbers in a frenzy worthy of St. Vitus. *Thrust SSC* gets its jet fuel all of which is documented in the *Reno Gazette* I continue to peruse while hailing a cab outside the casino. (Ultimately, 20 percent of the funding for the *Thrust* effort came from Noble shaking the virtual bushes of cyberspace and the print world. Amazing.)

So I grab a cab, a two-toned yellow and black beater that pings and knocks, and is driven by a guy who has the look of a fallen factory worker from Oakland who has decided to culminate his working days here, shuttling tourists who can't quite raise the capital to gamble in Vegas to various casinos and cathouses just beyond the city limits. He asks me if I want to go to the Mustang Ranch and I tell him no so then he asks where I am going and I tell him I'm in a hurry to get to the Peppermill Casino for a press conference that will announce an attempt to capture the Land Speed Record.

"The press conference for the Land Speed Record is at the hotel you just left," he says.

"No, that's the venue for Craig Breedlove and the *Spirit of America*'s announcement," I tell him.

"You mean there are two guys trying to get the Record?" he asks.

"Oh yeah," I say, "there is a British team that arrived last night in a massive cargo plane big enough to transport their crew and their race car."

"You mean that' s why that Russian plane is parked at the airport?"

To a paranoid survivalist like this cab driver, whose sense of history ended with the Fall of Saigon, the Brits represent the unholy union of NATO, the United Nations and the Beatles. As we pull into the parking lot, the *SSC* rests on an open trailer, raked at a 45 degree angle, pointed towards the sky. Milling about is a local Betacam crew with a blond news correspondent, flanked by a camera operator and a soundman umbilically tangled in their cables. This is the only electronic media I can see, although a couple of reporters are scribbling notes while chatting up the British team, who are resplendent in a sort of Royal Air Force green. The cab driver gives me his card for a ride back to my hotel once the *SSC* conference is done and I pay the fare. All the while though, the cabbie keeps a distracted eye fixed on the dual jet engined monstrosity resting placidly like a black widow in a tennis shoe.

To my cab driver, this wicked land speed streamliner may as well have been a black helicopter.

THE KEY THING IN THIS IS STABILITY

In 1983 Richard Noble turned 633 mph at Black Rock and reclaimed the LSR for Great Britain in his *Thrust 2* jet car, taking it away from the late Gary Gabelich, who clocked a 2-way speed average of 622 mph in a hydrogen-peroxide powered rocket in 1970. Noble's conquest struck a raw nerve in Craig Breedlove's craw — and in his sense of patriotism. As Noble had tea and crumpets with the Queen, Breedlove immediately began drawing eyelid diagrams of a third-generation *Spirit of America* he felt was sleek enough to not only enable him to procure the LSR but also slip through the last great barrier: Mach 1.

But to sell his dream to America and to his sponsors, Craig needed an adversary like Ike needed Khrushchev. So he approached the then-LSR record holder, Noble, and confided in him his aspirations towards conquering the Sound Barrier. Noble took the bait. Immediately both men jettisoned their relatively prosaic lives — Breedlove was now a realtor, Noble was now marketing recreational aircraft — and focused all of their energies towards their new goal.

A funny thing happened en route to the epochal "Duel In the Desert '97" in the Great American Southwest, however...

You see, both Breedlove and Noble had ambition but were lacking three other elements critical to his success: 1)Venture capital; 2) A crew; 3) A design for a vehicle that would somehow subvert the laws of physics and aerodynamics as applied to the turbulence inherent in supersonic travel — forces which would most likely launch and/or shred the vehicle and its driver. For in a steed traveling at that speed some of the pressure and shock waves which would envelop the vehicle would have no way to diffuse themselves as they hit the floor and then reverberated UNDER the vehicle, acting like a 750 mph catapult. As Noble himself described it, "At Mach 1, you're either on the ground or you're ten miles in the air at a force of 40 g's." Blimey.

So, yeah, Noble sets off to meet the esteemed Ken Norris, co-designer of Donald Campbell's revolutionary *Bluebird CN7* LSR machine, to explain his plight, i.e. that he had the "want to's" real bad but no design team nor plan. And in a crucial and profound stroke of luck, Norris's earlier appointment, Ron Ayers (a retired guided missile designer from the Brit military-industrial complex who is as renowned in his field as Noble and Norris are in theirs), is caught in crosstown traffic and arrives at Norris's digs the same moment as Noble.

Before the chance encounter with Noble, Ayers had no desire to design a Mach 1 motorcar (and very little interest in motorsports in general). "My immediate reaction was to distance myself from the project," is how the elderly, erudite, avuncular aerodynamicist recalls the moment that Noble pitched him the project. "To drive at supersonic speeds would clearly be extremely dangerous, and indeed, it could well be impossible. I pointed out to Richard that even keeping the car on the ground would be extraordinarily difficult." But Noble knew fresh meat when he saw it, and commenced to dog-and-pony-showing his way into Ayers' id and sense of purpose. Suffice it to say, Ayers became the *Thrust SuperSonic Car*'s first conscript — and its prime architect.

Indeed, the next day Ayers went to his garden, got out a pad and pencil and began free associating... *"How can we keep a motorcar stable as it passes from the transonic to supersonic speeds..."* Ayers continued to sketch and *Thrust* began to take shape. *"... it will need two jet engines, not for thrust but for weight, drag and downforce... they will have to live on either side of the cockpit..."* His approach to cannonballing through the turbulence of Mach 1 was an aerodynamic application tantamount to the bigger hammer method. *"... we will not finesse this per se, but punch through the sonic barrier... the center of gravity must be forward, but no so fore that it actually burrows into the desert floor and resurfaces in Eurasia..." "Everything that isn't lift is downforce..."* The only logical shape this beast could assume was the bastard, mutant spawn of the Batmobile and Lockheed's SR-71 *Blackbird* spyplane — i.e., the gnarliest, baddest contraption to attack the jet stream since the Cold War ended. It was gorgeous.

And for all its designed inefficiency, it was practical. Richard Noble concurred emphatically with Ayers' take on attacking Mach 1. "The key thing in this is stability," he told me out on the playa. "Anybody can stick a jet engine on a chassis and light the fuse. Ron and I sketched out something and we thought, 'My God, this is really rather good. This could work very well. Right: twins engines, aluminum wheels' and then Ken (Norris) says, 'There is no room for steering' — and it started to build from there."

(You can imagine the conversation amongst *SSC*'s design team: "Yeah, Ron it's bitchin' — but where do we put the torsion bars?" In an epiphany, *SSC* Chief Mechanical Designer Glynne Bowsher — one of a succession of aerospace hitters hornswoggled by Noble and intrigued by the notion of breaking the sound barrier on land — concludes that in order to shoehorn a steering system between the framerails, *SSC* must turn by the two in-line rear wheels. Talk about form follows function...)

Thrust SSC was housed in a spare hangar in Farnborough, UK, the locale of the what, in essence, is the British Skunk Works (in other words, the hangars for her Royal Majesty's stealth and supersonic aerospace programs). Suffice it to say, the bulk of the *SSC* engineers who became intoxicated with Noble's dream already knew where Farnborough's commissary was well before Noble approached them for help...

As the design came to life at Farnborough Airfield, Noble canvassed the breadth of the Jolly 'Ol, banging on boardroom doors for financial support and hosting seminars at campuses and air shows in order to recruit a pit crew. Interestingly, his stirring pitches appealed to the hoi polloi more so than the suits in the corridors of power. The hoi polloi formed the Mach 1 club — "give us a few quid, drop what you're doing and come with us to America to break the sound barrier" — and was another indispensable element to the *Thrust SSC*'s eventual success.

And finally, another crucial element was in place. That is, Noble's choice for a shoe: A softspoken-yet-buff, dashing, Royal Air Force pilot named Andy Green whose physique, psyche, and demeanor were ideal for the project. Indeed, Andy Green could have been culled straight outta' Central Casting. The team was in place.

And after some Computational Fluid Dynamics and rocket-sled testing "confirmed" (at least in the virtual sense) Ayers' theories on supersonic travel, the vehicle was completed. But before the conquering of Mach 1 in America was to commence, the team trudged off to an RAF air base in the Al Jafr desert in Jordan during November of '96 for some shakedown runs, with the blessing of ol' King Hussein. Testing the synergy of all systems on this technological marvel commenced: Computerized suspension, telemetry, satellite uplinks, communications, aluminum wheels, rear wheel steer, twin Spey 202 turbofan engines, support vehicles, etc.

(The active suspension was perhaps the most crucial piece of software and hardware. Calculations by some of *SSC*'s engineers warned that if the vehicle's angle of attack relative to the earth's surface varied by even one quarter of a degree, driver Andy Green would have been launched upwards of 1000 feet... a potential altitude that would have dwarfed Paula "Miss STP" Murphy's mimicking of a moon shot in 1972.)

All that was left was empiricism.

All systems seemed to be speaking to each other, but a full dress rehearsal for the upcoming mission in the Black Rock desert would have to wait for then came the prerequisite trial, error, and anguish that, if you study your motorsports history, seems to accompany all LSR efforts. In a Middle Eastern desert that is dryer than microwaved kitty litter, it rained. And rained. And flooded.

Indeed, as Ron Ayers related in retrospect: "According to the weather statistics, November should have the ideal combination of moderate temperature, low wind, low precipitation, and few dust storms." It was, in fact, quite the antithesis. The *Thrust SSC*er's arrival at this arid Middle Eastern desert was akin to fording a river: At the air base where *Thrust* was stationed the flooding was moving so fast that it appeared to be pushing stones ahead of it. Finally, Glynne Bowsher pointed out that the stones were actually floating camel droppings...

HOORAY FOR HOLLYWOOD

"For most of its runs, the SMI Motivator/Budweiser Rocket *car ran on a hydrogen peroxide monopropellant motor developing 5,000 to 6,000 pounds thrust. At Edwards, this motor was replaced with a peroxide/polybutydiene (synthetic rubber) hybrid motor developing roughly 9,000 pounds of thrust (maybe at the most 11,000 pounds). The best electric eye clock speed run using only the hybrid motor was 677 mph. When the hybrid motor proved insufficient, it was supplemented with a sparrow air-to-air solid fuel missile motor developing an average thrust of about 5,000 pounds for 5 seconds. The best electric eye clock speed ran using the hybrid motor/sparrow combination was 692 mph."* — **Franklin Ratliff, previously unpublished.**

The most abject comment and manipulation on the American Dream of going Mach 1 comes not from the military-industrial complex, but from Hollywood... One of Tinseltown's movers and shakers, Hal Needham, a stuntman-cum-producer/director (and whose greatest claim to fame was gracing the world with Burt Reynold's cornpone movies), purchases the *SMI Motivator* rocket dragster, retrofits 'er with a hybrid liquid/solid-fuel rocket engine, hires *Courage of Australia* mastermind Bill Fredrick to turn the wrenches, re-badges the machine *Speed of Sound* (nee *Budweiser Rocket*) and hauls the operation out to Edwards AFB...

"The thing about the car you have to realize is that it did not have enough fuel on board to make a full land speed record run," Breedlove states. "They applied to have the rules changed so they could make one run (timed) over 1/100th of mile — instead of a mile." With clocks installed by a drag racing organization over a timing trap of 52 feet — instead of the traditional measured mile — Needham points driver (and fellow stuntman) Stan Barrett at the timing cones and lights the fuse.

Needham proffers as evidence of a Mach 1 clocking the data from a handheld radar gun. Why radar instead of the drag strip clocks? The rocket car ran out of fuel before it reached the timing traps!

The whole misadventure is documented by *CBS Sports Spectacular* and is passed off as authentic, with additional corroboration by Chuck Yeager who writes in a letter that, "Having been involved in supersonic research since the days of the *XS -1* rocket plane, which I flew on the first supersonic flight on October 14, 1947, there is no doubt in my mind that the rocket car exceeded the speed of sound on its run on December 17, 1979."

The jet set sees this as poppycock — Chuck Yeager or no Chuck Yeager. "It degraded the whole Land Speed Record business. It took a wrong turn," says Richard Noble. "The most outrageous thing about that whole project was that they wasted the time giving Chuck Yeager a ride in it the next day when they could have done it again (properly)."

Breedlove debunks the Needham claim this way: "There was a water truck that was driving in the background," he said in reference to the corruption in the radar gun's data. "On this specific run, when the operator was hand-tracking the car, the range finder targeted the water truck because it was a bigger target. They had no actual third data point," Breedlove postulates in reference to co-ordinates of speed, range and angle needed to gather data via radar. "The following day, they had the car drive down the course and then took the data from the range of the other vehicle and substituted that into the calculations and then extrapolated data in that manner. It is just so unbelievably flawed; the manufacturer of the radar says it's not even calibrated to do that. You've got an uncalibrated radar — hand operated — with the third leg of the data being substituted. Can you imagine a guy trying to claim a drag racing record that way?"

Indeed, this, umm, whole stunt attempt is fraught with arrogance, ambiguity and unresolved issues. Hooray for Hollywood.

HAVE YOU SEEN THE NEW TRADE-A-PLANE?

I get an audience with Breedlove in his trailer at Black Rock. I ask a couple of simple questions. He responds with some most elaborate and thorough answers.

∞

Why a jet instead of a rocket?

CRAIG BREEDLOVE: The primary reason is because of the unavailability of fuel at the present time. Along about 1974 the government restricted the availability of certain fuels based on their toxicity and — in their judgment — hazardous materials. So we built the English Rocket car as a prototype for a hypergolic rocket system for a land speed car. That engine was designed by Jerry Elverum at TRW and Jerry did the Apollo lunar descent engine among other things. That's probably the most remarkable thing he's done because that was the first throttleable rocket engine that the astronauts could fly to the surface of the moon — it was like a jet engine with a throttle. And that's what allowed America to make a soft landing on the moon.

We ran that engine on unsymmertrical dimethylhydrazine and nitrogen tetraoxide as an oxidizer. It was a hypergolic engine which means that as soon as the two chemicals come together in the chamber they ignite instantly.

It is a very reliable system. It is also a very powerful system. Those chemicals... we bought the nitrogen tetraoxide oxidizer from Hercules, a powder corporation. We bought the unsymmetrical dimethylhydrazine from FMC, Food Machinery Corporation. The oxidizers came from Northern California and the hydrazine came from Wilmington, Delaware. We were able to formerly order it at will. The companies did request that they be apprised on how we were using it and that we were not just a bunch of dingbats out there. TRW did that for us, they were able to vouch for us. They did their own policing and then they just sold it to us because there were no restrictions against selling it to us. In 1974 basically that was outlawed. Now there were restrictions. Also TRW is a US fuel depot, we had hoped we could get the fuel shipped to TRW and have it stored there. But the problem was we can't transport it by rail, they even had a difficult time getting it into Vandenburg AFB to make launches.

Then we changed the design of the car to four peroxide thrusters because they had not yet restricted hydrogen peroxide in any way. It was shortly after we got the car changed over to peroxide that they restricted peroxide.

You could not manufacture or distribute peroxide in higher concentrations than 70 percent. 70 percent is a lousy rocket fuel. You need 98 percent. At that point in time the entire Land Speed vehicle was trashed at great personal financial cost to myself. Frankly, I just completely backed off.

The jet idea came back... of course Richard Noble had run the jet engine. The J79s are not easy to get and they are not necessarily cheap, either.

I took a sabbatical and we took the rocket car mock up to a car show in the San Francisco Bay area and some guys approached me — they were from a surplus aircraft and electric parts company called Radcom — and they had a particular deal going with a French company where they had purchased the F-104 contingency from the NATO Belgian Air Force. They had forty-three 104s and spare engines and wings. They offered to give me two F-104s to do an air speed record with and also to supply me with engines for both Land Speed and Water Speed Records. That deal fell apart because the French company cut them out of their stock and they actually ended up with nothing. They ended up not getting the engines and got cut out of the deal completely.

During the period of time I re-designed the car around the engine. The only problem was I had a car design, but not an engine. We began looking for an engine and Mike McCluskey called me up and said, "Hey, have you seen the new *Trade-A-Plane*? There is an ad where the government is selling sixty-seven J79s out of North Island Naval Station." Ed Ballinger went in, inspected those engines and we put a bid on three lots of three. We were unsuccessful. The entire sale was sold to International Engine Parts in Chatsworth. I called them right afterwards and much to my surprise International Engine Parts was owned and operated by Elmo Idavia who supplied me with my afterburner in 1965. El said, "Sure Craig, we'll sell you a couple of engines and you can have the pick of the lot."

Later El gave me another engine.

HOORAY FOR HOLLYWOOD (REDUX)

But conversely somebody did run a solid fuel engine and that was Needham?

CRAIG BREEDLOVE: No, that was a peroxide car. The thing about that car that you have to understand is it did not have enough fuel on board to make a full Land Speed Run. They applied to have the rules changed with FIA and FIM — it was a three-wheeled vehicle — to make a one-way run over 1/100th of a mile and that was denied by FIM.

It made a run at Edwards and was clocked at 666 mph on Earl Flanders clocks — a 52 foot trap.

I spoke with Earl in 1983 and I asked him what was the circumstance around the supersonic claim that was made by the Budweiser effort. And he said, "All I can tell you is that the car went 666." And I said, "You mean you clocked the car on the run," and he said, "Yes I did." He said he was under strict contract to Hal Needham and the *Speed of Sound* group not to divulge anything. I said what was the deal with this 739 and he just rolled his eyes and said, "It didn't happen."

Subsequently, I looked for years to get a clocked speed of the car and finally somebody sent me a paper that was delivered to the AIAA convention (aerospace engineers) and on that paper it states very clearly that the electronic time of the car was 666.234 mph. The claim that had it gone supersonic was made because of a radar tracking of the car when it was approaching. Now, typically you accelerate all the way to the traps. This is odd that the car would be going 740 and then go through the traps at 660. Then on further investigation, Dick Keller (of *Blue Flame* fame) contacted the radar company and the radar is not activated by the car. It is activated by an operator who tracks the car by hand. So the speed produced is not by the car, but by the operator. The operator then tracks the car on a television screen with crosshairs, by swinging a tripod antenna or transmitter to track the car. Then when you look at the data, they simply average the three highest peaks in the data. Then they claimed that the Air Force sanctioned that. Dick Keller furnished me with a letter from the head of the Air Force stating they disavow any sanction whatsoever and they simply provided Speed of Sound with raw data and any interpretation of that data was purely *Speed of Sound's* interpretation and not that of the Air Force. The Air Force disavows any sanctioning or underwriting or statement as to how fast the car went. There were two guys there — Pete Knight — who said he felt the *Speed of Sound* had reached their objective and General Yeager who said that in his opinion the car reached their objective. But if you look at the data, it doesn't bear itself out. It is totally uncalibrated.

I'm told that the contract was written in such a way that they were to receive a million dollars upon a successful achievement of setting a new Land Speed Record and breaking the sound barrier. First of all, they could not qualify for the Land Speed Record because of the measured distance and the one-way run thing.

I understand that the (use of the) letters from Yeager and Pete Knight were trying to enhance the possibilities of getting the payment. I don't know if the payments were made or not. I was told that it was, but I don't have any way of knowing.

So, simply there are photographs of the car in the lights with the engine still on and the rear wheels off the ground. My question is if, in fact, the car is running out of fuel before it gets to lights, why don't you go out the next day and move it a little closer to the lights? And get your supersonic time through the lights? They said they couldn't afford to do it, yet they could afford to fuel the car up and have Chuck Yeager take a joy ride.

The point is the car has not set a World Land Speed Record, the car had no sanction and the Air Force has disavowed any underwriting or support of that data. In my judgment, a claim has been made, but no documentation has been furnished that make me believe it went that fast. I have stated this before and every time I do Hal Needham threatens to sue me.

700 MPH IS OF NO INTEREST TO US (1997)

"Ladies, gentlemen, and members of the press, we are here to go Mach 1. Getting the record back does not interest us. Going 700 mph does not interest us. We are here to go Mach 1."

Thus sayeth Richard Noble hisself from the podium at a press conference in a downtown Reno casino a couple of days after Labor Day, 1997. His audience is a motley mix of motorsports journalists, a couple of local betacam crews, some curious tourists who stroll away from the keno girls after gazing through the tinted casino windows at what looked to be a phallic-shaped 10-ton spaceship that had landed by the valet parking, and some local street people who are intrigued by the commotion and have sniffed out the prospect of free danishes and coffee.

Noble's "No Sleep 'till Supersonic" gauntlet is throw down just hours after his exhausted troops had arrived in Nevada on blitzkrieg rock-and-roll-180 flight from the Farnborough hangar, jet lagged, sleep deprived and immaculately clad in matching green uniforms. They really don't seem chagrined at the nearly 1-to-1 ratio of street people to electronic journalists...

Indeed, the *SSC* cadre is in a rare mood, as blithe as they are determined. One team manager describes how the two LSR efforts will share time on the playa with one team securing the lake bed in the morning, the other to use the course in the afternoon, and with a coin toss to settle any disputes over the right to valuable.

"Will that be an American or a British coin?" I ask.

WE'RE VERY HAPPY

"It doesn't have two engines for performance reasons," says Ron Ayers, aerodynamicist for *Thrust SSC*, at the press conference in Reno. "Two engines will give us a geometry which is much more stable. So two engines for stability, not for performance — although the extra engine does no harm for performance whatsoever. It enables us to get the weight well forward and the front wheels wide apart, so that means the weight is between widely spaced front wheels, stabilizing roll, pitch and yaw simultaneously." *A-n-d* he concluded, "We're very happy with a 15 mph crosswind."

I REALLY DON'T THINK YOU NEED TWO

Cut to: the *SOA* press conference at a casino across town. Craig Breedlove is nonplused by the *SSC*'s arrival and is holding forth on the different approaches to reaching Mach 1. "I spoke to Richard early on in his design process and he'd said that he'd decided they needed a twin-engine design and that was where we differed.

"I said, 'Well, I really don't think you need two,' and he said, 'All land speed record cars have always underperformed.' I said, 'I really haven't found that to be true — I had a J47 that I really think I could have reached 600 mph with. Maybe you experienced a lot higher drag numbers than I have.' In any case, that was their philosophy: Really screw the car down, just suck it down with a lot of ground effects. Just power it through — (and) it's a very stable way to do it." But not the *SOA* way.

"The problem I saw at Black Rock early on in this design concept was Richard was sinking in," Breedlove continues. "I went to Ken Norris and asked what their (*Thrust 2*'s) ground loadings were and he told me they were at 13,000 lbs. (of downforce). I asked how they were distributed and he said, 'No, that's on the front wheels.' I said, 'Well, you're aware that you guys are going to have so much rolling drag that you guys are never going to get the record.' He said they've been discussing that and the only thing is that Richard is very reluctant to point the car up any because of the flying problem."

Conversely, for his Mach 1 endeavors, Breedlove in essence eyeball-aeroed a projectile in the shape of an arrow. Using a hot rodded J79 General Electric jet engine from a Navy F-4 Phantom fighter aircraft for motivation, Craig visualized a sleek, narrow dart that would partake of the J79's 22,650 pounds of thrust (45,000 horsepower) and finesse the shockwaves that emanate when a vehicle climbs through a transonic slipstream into — BOOM — a supersonic slipstream.

"When we ran *Sonic 1* at 600 mph (1965) we had no weight on the front end. I'm not saying that's a prudent way to do it, but that's just the fact of the matter. Somewhere between 13,000 lbs. and zero is the speed record."

BRUNO'S (1997)

In May of '97 the Brits had made a return trip to Jordan for more shakedown runs — they managed to get the *SSC* up to 540 mph, which was apparently all that patchy surface could handle — and they were treated like royalty. Pomp and circumstance is not much in evidence in Gerlach, NV when the *Thrust SSC* mates first arrive. The Brits are homeless. Gerlach is a town of 300 — counting the scorpions — and lodging is sketchy. There is one motel, "Bruno's," which is also the name of the bar and the coffee shop, all of which are tagged eponymously for the town czar, a lanky, bent elderly Italian with the kind of disposition only slightly surlier than that of Benito Mussolini's. Despite *Thrust SSC*'s scout team undertaking a reconnaissance trip in April to secure the permits and lodging crucial to their mission, it has all turned to shit: Bruno double-booked all the available lodging and ultimately rented his rooms to the highest bidder: the *SOA* contingent.

THE PHONE BOOTH

I am waiting to make a phone call to the editor of HOT ROD Magazine. I wait outside the booth as Richard Noble is fumbling for the proper change to dial out, and I notice all he can summon is lint and some British coins.

Here he is, Richard Noble, the fastest man on the planet, desperately trying to make lodging arrangements in the middle of the American Outback, the weight of an entire LSR operation on his shoulders. The *SSC*'ers got no rooms and their leader can't even make a fucking phone call.

The Brits are boycotting that turncoat opportunist Bruno. They adjourn to the bar next door, "Bev's Miners' Club," and discuss Plan B. After enjoining Bev the barkeep to "Give us a fag, wouldya' love?" (Loosely translated, "I'd like to purchase a package of cigarettes"), the affable Brits begin making friends with the locals, particularly Bev.

So picture this: Richard Noble and his lads (twenty-odd clamoring Brits clad in matching RAF-khaki) are hoisting Coors in a dusty, desert Dew-Do-Drop-Inn (this about as bizarre as it gets, in my book) when one of Noble's crew members shushes the entire bar. The local teevee news is reporting on that morning's press conference ("Going 700 mph does not interest us. We are here to go Mach 1") at the casino in Reno. Suddenly the videotape cuts to the chipper studio humanoid broadcaster who closes the report with this coda, "Noble and his team are taking Saturday off in observance of Princess Di's funeral."

Simultaneously Richard Noble, OBE does a *"say wot??"* double take while his overworked and underpaid entourage cheer and Bev pours more drinks and opens more cans of beer.

They didn't get the day off. Nor did they care, really. All of which underscores this question: What is it about Noble that inspires his troops, his lads to persevere in high-desert heat to erect a portable self-contained military-industrial complex that meets the criteria for the digital era's standard for data gathering, all on a dry lake bed that time forgot?

(The massive amounts of hardware assembled by the *SSC* to facilitate the penetration of this phantom waveform amounted to nothing short of a hi-tech paramilitary invasion of a forgotten lake bed that — excepting for the war games and impromptu fighter plane dogfights staged sporadically by the military back in WW II and the alterno-tech paganism of the annual Burning Man Festival — had more or less been bypassed by the techno-industrial revolution of the 20th Century and had never seen electricity, much less microwave satellite uplinks, portable airsheltas, rescue vehicles, hundreds of channels of real time telemetry and supersonic motorcars.)

The answer is not explainable by the notion of "technological enthusiasm," a phrase that has recently come to explain everything from hot rodding to the Apollo moonshot. The answer is deeper, more atavistic and completely primeval. The answer has roots which extend into the quintessence of matter: The universe is expanding. By extrapolation, consciousness is expanding, constantly encroaching into realms of the unknown. The technological enthusiast must go *THERE*, the technological enthusiast will devour and outmaneuver whatever is in his or her way: Pauites, the laws of aerodynamics, Newtonian physics, whatever.

Thus you have some of the finest minds of our lifetime sleeping on other people's couches, on their hands and knees picking up pebbles off the desert floor (to keep them from getting Hoover'd into the jet engines intake), all so they can have their moonshot.

PICKING YOUR BRAINS

What's your take on what Bill Fredrick did with the Courage of Australia *and the* Budweiser Rocket?

PETE FARNSWORTH: Well, they were all, after we built the *X-1* and I saw what the potential for the quarter mile rocket car was, I didn't want anything more to do it (*rockets on the drag strip*). I figured it was just a matter of you know, how big the guys balls were as to how fast you were gonna go and how quick you gonna go. I didn't want anything more to do with it. I could just see the next step was going lighter and lighter and more power and there was no limit to it really.

But when Fredrick and those guys did their deal at Edwards, did that torque you a little bit?

LEAH: *(laughs)*

PETE: More than a little. I admire the idea of them wanting to go fast. I had no problem with that, it's just the fact that the car was never built for a Land Speed Record, that all it was was a publicity stunt uh, to try and break the speed of sound. They had no idea of turning it around within one hour, it was never designed to do that. It wasn't an automobile in the first place, according to the records, it was a three wheeler and it was more the size of the vehicle that we had designed originally, but uh...

... but really, the fact that it wasn't a measured mile, it was like 52 feet that they finally shrunk it down to...

PETE: Yeah, motorcycle trap or whatever it was I mean we, we'd have gone 660 if we'd done it that way.

Well, also it was hand tracked radar, um, the radar run with some guy holding it in his hand...

LEAH: The *Blue Flame* could have set a record the first week if all we had to do is just put together.

PETE: We worked up in speed. We worked up in 50 mile an hour increments.

LEAH: But we had to do a whole mile and turn it around.

PETE: Ours was never, it wasn't a publicity stunt. It was designed to set the world's speed record.

Even though the fuel didn't allow the car to ever go through a whole mile I give Barrett a heck of a lot of credit for the courage to ride that thing.

WHY WE BURN THE MAN (1997)

Later that first day out I go to a photo shoot for Breedlove out on the playa. He is like Captain America, Buzz Lightyear and Neil Armstrong. Short, stylish, blow-dried and futuristic. Betacam crews from Speedvision are rolling tape and zooming in and out and around Breedlove in an over, unders, sideways down manner, the desert wind acting as a prop man's fan, giving Breedlove's hair the illusion that even when he is standing still things are still in motion... News photographers and motorsport beat writers try to stay clear of the swooping camera crew and its gold reflector boards.

I wonder why the Speedvision crew wasn't at the *Thrust SSC* news conference and am informed by some of the press that Speedvision has signed an exclusive deal with Breedlove. I remark that this is kind of like reporting on Pearl Harbor and you can't mention the Japanese and people laugh. It is hard for me take Speedvision seriously as a news-gathering entity, but this bought-and-paid for journalism is increasingly the way of the world, isn't it?

The photo shoot wraps, I motor across the dry lake bed and chat up some members of the *SSC* team. After soaking up the sights and sounds of Gerlach, I spend the night in my car, parked next to the railroad tracks and Breedlove's media compound, which is Gerlach's vacant Chamber of Commerce building. As I struggle to sleep, I think about what is transpiring right in front of me and how Noble KNEW it would be more dramatic if he and Breedlove set up a drag race (of sorts). Indeed, this "duel" was supposed to happen LAST year, when Noble ran out of cash and Breedlove ran out of aerodynamic stability.

Ergo, this year both camps are completely winging it on some level and are following a letter-perfect game plan on another; what makes this fascinating is the differences in constructing the dueling massive porta-skunk works installed on this uninhabitable dry lake bed. The Brits are a completely disciplined hive of worker bees, who have summarily *fhwwooped* together an inflatable quonset hut, parked a coterie of tractor-trailers and space age support vehicles. It is lickety-split and it is focused. Breedlove's encampment is coming together in a much more lackadaisical manner, as if he falls short of the delegation abilities and the manpower to simultaneously star in a photo shoot and oversee a portable installation.

But “target dates” are really “moving target dates.” There are just too many variables in pulling a run off; Breedlove is supposedly going for the record on Wednesday, but who knows? This may take six weeks to play itself out...

The locals are bemused and rather enthralled by the LSR war that has taken root in their county. It is certainly a kinder and gentler invasion than the Burning Man art festival that has just wrapped there.

This is the conversation over breakfast at Bruno’s, as I am speaking to the Fly Ranch Hot Springs land owners (a scruffy, pot-bellied gent named Vann and his wife, Annie, who looks like Peggy Lipton after the gas has been shut off), who are telling me that before the festival they “had 120 head a cattle; this morning we counted 25.” Vann pulls on his overall straps and reckons the animals were spooked by the festivities, and were not fodder for the festival goers’ bbq’s, as many of these folks were militant vegetarians anyhoo... In addendum, Vann and Annie don’t expect to see any coin from the festival promoters — who apparently owed them five figures — because of the County’s predilection for asset liquidation and financial opportunism.

(It seems The County hijacked the dosh and the gate receipts from the Burning Man promoters... the local gov't claims the organizers owe The County 40K for “services”; the promoters liken it to “protection money” (I’m paraphrasing), including fees for forty eight (!) fire trucks on standby.)

Annie says, “It makes me realize why we burn the Man in the first place.”

HOT SPRINGS

There is no lodging. For anybody, except the *SOA* bunch. The Thrust *SSC*ers are sleeping anywhere they can, including in the hallways of local residences.

That night I am to rendezvous with Vann and Annie at their place way out in the middle of nowhere. They are lending me the use of an abandoned trailer on Fly Ranch. I am to meet them at their Hot Spring and they would escort me to my lodging. I had made nice-nice with a couple of members of *SSC* and I suggested they follow me out to the Hot Spring and just bask in the infinite warmth of the geysers of hot water.

As we lie in the hot springs, we are talking about the road out to Gerlach. There is nothing this wide open in Britain they are saying. There is no way you are going to find 80 miles of open road, with the only opposing traffic being that of the ghosts of Indians who have died in battle on the mesa. To these two blokes, this transport from Reno to Gerlach was an even more fascinating journey than the Antonov flight across the Atlantic two nights before. They said that the "*gee*-zer" was so fantastic that had it been used as a set in a motion picture, the audience would have scoffed at its authenticity. As it gushes blue and green under the stars and a full moon, I couldn't argue.

As the night progresses, I marvel at the irony of the Brits tapping into the Spirit of America. They were soaking up and drinking in what many of us have taken for granted, ignored and attempted to bury: Americans *are* free-er than those who dwell both across either pond or north or south of any line of demarcation.

It is bliss. It is one big mind orgasm, as our brains explode like Chinese rockets of another millennia. The fireworks served to welcome the spirits, not chase them away. As we groove on a pict of infinity and isolation, there is nothing but scorpions, bighorn sheep and supersonic cars within a 50 mile radius of us. I doubt these gents have experienced anything even remotely similar since returning to Ol' Sod. Our bliss is a function of climate and geography, and underscored by the contemplation of the cosmos whilst naked in a natural free range hot spring in the Nevada desert.

Later, I try to sleep in the abandoned trailer. It is disturbingly peaceful. It is so quiet my mind begins filling in the blanks. It begins creating noise to emulate a night in civilization. The sounds that are spontaneously generated are a series of white noizes.

Danny Jo the Blind Hippie and His Woman the Earth Momma were squatting on the same property. I wouldn't meet them until later.

BEAT THE SYSTEM (1997)

"There is a kind of craziness to Britain and the British, you know, the 'mad dogs and Englishmen' and all that. We go out and we do crazy things. We invented a lot of the great sports of the world, even bob-sledding. We haven't got any snow, but it took British people to go out to Switzerland to invent crazy things like bob-sledding. Speed records are all part of that same thing. We kind of built an empire on this pioneering spirit. I'm not saying everything we've done is right. A lot of it was wrong. But we do have this pioneering spirit, as you have in the States. Part of it seems to be record-breaking endeavor. We just have that tradition." — **Nigel Macknight, British Water Speed Record contender.**

"My best wishes to all involved in Thrust SSC*'s attempt to be the first through the sound barrier on land. This project is a graphic illustration of British enterprise and engineering at its best. Good luck. The whole country is behind you."* — **Tony Blair, British Prime Minister.**

"It's all about beating the British system. If there were any British government involvement (in Thrust SSC*) we would end up with somebody on our board, okay? And this has to be a little organization that is very flexible and can dance and weave. The last thing we want is that sort of person on the board."* — **Richard Noble.**

THE SHOT GLASS

Nobody exemplifies "technological enthusiasm" more so than Ron Ayers. Although retired and in the twilight of his stay here on Planet Earth, Ayers was as active as any of the fresh-faced Mach 1 Clubbers on holiday from the university.

Nearly a month after the *Thrusters* had arrived and were continuing to creep into the transonic speed range, I eavesdropped on Ayers as he was explaining his theories on supersonic travel in a motorcar to a bewildered and besotted patron in the Miner's Club. Ayers uses a shot glass as a prop that represents the *Thrust SSC* and gingerly slides it along the surface of the bar to illustrate his theories about subsonic, trans-sonic, and supersonic pressure waves and how they would affect the handing of the *Thrust SSC.*

The guy at the bar asks Ayers why don't you Brits just put the hammer down and go Mach 1 and be done with it?

Ayers explains the *SSC* design teams rationale for chipping away at ever-increasing speeds: "The aerodynamic forces would be simply enormous, enough to lift the car and throw it around like an autumn leaf in a gale," he says. "The crux of the problem is knowing how the flow would behave underneath the car at sonic speeds and what would happen to to shockwaves in that region."

The guy on the bar stool next nods as if he comprehends Ayers' riff.

"The most important thing," Ayers concludes as Bev the bartender repossessed the shot glass and put it to less theoretical use, "is that we don't obliterate *Ann-dee.*"

BALL OF FLAME

A writer for RACER magazine sees me in Bruno's with a "Jocko's Porting Service" t-shirt on and comments on it.

I tell the guy from RACER that I had done a feature on Jocko for HOT ROD and was a big fan of his. I then add that Jocko had been nominated into the International Drag Racing Hall of Fame.

Jocko had called me and ran his acceptance speech by me. He says he was to take the podium dressed in a tearaway tuxedo. He would begin his speech with the words, "I'm really honored to be inducted into Don Garlits' 'Mall of Blame'... I mean 'Hall of Shame'... I mean 'Ball of Flame'...." while he gradually tore away the tuxedo and stripped down to a "Jocko's Porting Service" t-shirt.

"Jocko's not going to be in the Drag Racing Hall of Fame."

"Sure, he is. He called me up and read me the first paragraph of his acceptance speech. Jocko's in the Hall of Fame."

"Not anymore. He changed his mind."

ART DAMAGE

"Thrust SSC, Thrust SSC... Hey Kids, you need to come to see Thrust SSC" — **Danny Jo, the Blind Hippie, singing to the Thrust SSC team members.**

"I'm a loo-ser, and I'm half the man I appear to be...I'm a lo-o-o-o-ser..." — **Flash, the bartender at the Gerlach saloon, serenading from the street to anyone who will listen, but pointing his guitar in the specific direction of Craig Breedlove's ad hoc press center.**

There is a heavy air of psychosis that envelops the playa, like an invisible asbestos cloud. Breedlove has fodded an engine. One unofficial report was the fod was not a pebble on the desert floor, but a bolt absent-mindedly mislaid upon the fiberglass inlet of the jet engines, and sucked into the turbines when the engine was spooled up. Breedlove's prize jet engine is junk. Like many things, the days of scoring a J79 cheap has passed, as has the day of the backyard mechanic shoehorning a massive jet onto a piece of pipe, strapping himself in, lighting the candle and making the newsreels. Sheer bravura was once synonymous with the Spirit of America, but like Roy and I discovered when we drove through that massive passenger car pile-up and crash in West Los Angeles, the Spirit of America is now a ghost — and it ain't a friendly one.

"The day of the backyard mechanic is over..."

What has changed? Why is Breedlove lost? He seems confused. It had all been so straightforward before: design a car shaped like a dart or an arrow and make 'er as light as possible, crank up the thrust, push the envelope and bask in the ensuing glory. Now he has augmented his approach with Dezso Molnar as his crew chief, a young pony-tailed post-modern boho from San Francisco, an artist whom some of his old gang of hot rodders labeled as "art damaged." Dezso was a tenant at the "art explosion laboratories," south of Market in San Francisco. Before his stint with Breedlove, he had been robotic/jet engine technician for the *Survival Research Labs*, a guerrilla art group notorious for blowing up sculptures under bridges and then running from the police.

(Molnar is no stranger to Black Rock. As early as 1995 at the first Burning Man Festival, he had attempted some performance art with a pulse-jet-powered go cart, which was carted out to the desert when strapped and mounted onto his roommate's Ford LTD. According to festival organizers, out at Black Rock Molnar attempted to "cross the 8th dimension" with his go-kart. Uh huh. His techno band, "Rocket Science," also serenaded the post-industrial revelers...)

Go Karts and Techno Music. The old time land speed guys had no time for such pretense. This guy Dezso's background was in blowing up sculptures in the warehouse district and calling it art. An acetylene torch was his paintbrush and various pieces of surplus steel was his canvas. Now he has an opportunity to get involved with slightly higher stakes — Craig Breedlove's life — and the hot rodders in Craig's clique put up with his selection of crew chief, but it reeked of desperation, like a Dorian Gray-ish attempt to tap into the energy of youth. Had Craig forgotten his roots? Or were his roots showing? Doesn't Dezso have more business with the Burning Man than being the crew chief on the supersonic missile with one of America's greatest heroes strapped inside? If so, the folks who had supported Breedlove throughout his career began to feel betrayed. Even the Gerlach locals and the Land Speed loyals had turned against the *Spirit of America.* The queue of desert rats, speed freaks and survivalists who lined the circumference of the playa also are troubled by the dubious performances of the *Spirit of America.* The American flags that dot the impromptu trailer park seems to droop impotently, even when the winds kick in. When the local bartender grabs a guitar and starts serenading Breedlove's camp with "I'm A Loser," the bleakest existential ballad out of the Beatles' ouevre, Craig has to know it was time to regroup.

Breedlove had fodded an engine.

So now what? Come midnight, Breedlove loads up his tractor-trailer with his wounded racer and turns the rig around, and heads home. More trouble. It is so dark on the playa the truck driver cannot find the tire tracks that lead to the highway. Instead, he is transfixed by the lights of Gerlach, which act as a siren's song of sorts and summons the drivers into a muddy, *terra-not-so-firma* section of the lake bed, whereupon the rig promptly sinks to its axles...

The *Thrust SSC* team is called to the rescue, using Supacats to pull the truck out of the muck. The Brits more than magnanimously rescued the *SOA, esprit de corps* and all that British chivalry. It is like the *Bridge on the River Kwai,* when the British, interned as prisoners of war, built the bridge for the Japs ... and just like the William Holden movie, the Brits are *so* together, a veritable Swiss watch of organization, while the*SOA* camp come across as the Japanese, a slow exercise in chaos and self-destruction. (The only thing that runs on time is Craig's morning jogs with his personal trainer and his publicist.)

The *SOA* has degenerated into vaudeville and the butt of jokes.

Back at his shop in Rio Vista, the team performs an engine swap, installing a weaker J79, which Breedlove has kept in his inventory to scavenge for spare parts.

Yeah... it looks bleak for the *SOA.* But is this the darkness before the dawn?

THRUST SSC (THAT BRITISH INVASION)

The next morning is a wash... the weather is bad, the winds are in full song, Breedlove is on the road home, nothing is happening and the entire town is in the throes of maximum boredom.

Over coffee in Bruno's, I hammer on a laptop.

A waitress asks, "Are you looking at poor-nog-gra-fee on — what's that thing called?"

"The internet," her co-worker answers.

It is the usual gathering at Bruno's: land speed engineers, bighorn sheep hunters in fatigues, retired rocket drag racers and slumming physicists from Berkeley, all of whom are within earshot of the waitress's prurient queries and gathered at the counter or at tables, and none of whom put down their forks or the cups of coffee.

I assure the waitresses that no, I am merely getting working on an article about the Mach 1 attempts.

Later that morning I run into Vann and Annie and they introduce me to four hippies who are staying out at their ranch. Vann and Annie look a little frazzled, having had to throw a couple of trespassing journalists from *People Magazine* off of their hot springs. What's more, their other "tenants" are beginning to use up their welcome. The hippies had come out for the Burning Man and had just never went home.

I start talking to one of them, Danny Jo, the Blind Hippie. He tells me he had written a song about the *Thrust SSC.* I asked him to sing it. So he does: *a capella.*

Now let me tell you about
The latest automotive sensation
With happiness, watch out
Here comes that British Invasion

Instead of one jet engine it's got two,
and rear wheel steering
To see it through

You really need to come and see Thrust SSC

Now let me tell you boys and girls
Who love art and science
That British team from the start
So much reliance

So just like them
Be real good in class
And you can do things with so much class

Hey Kids, you need to come and see Thrust SSC

(CHORUS)

Thrust SSC, Thrust SSC
It's a different car in a rare racing sport
Which is good for the family (x2)

Let me tell more about
That latest automotive sensation
With mystery, look out
Here comes that British Invasion

Secret ways of things
Under that shell I got some ideas but I'm not going to tell

You really need to come and see Thrust SSC

Now let me tell you boys and girls
Who love ultimate thises and that
With a sense of humor
They have got more than mere figures and fact

So just like them
More than come to task
Be good to people and you'll have class

Hey Kids, you need to come to see Thrust SSC

(REPEAT CHORUS)

I drive back to the airport. With the radio off.

BEFORE DAWN

A few days later, things begin to heat up again: Breedlove is back, still trying to save face and preparing to strap one on and show *Speedvision* and The World he isn't bullshitting about this Mach One gag... that an American hot rodder can still stare down the entire planet and prove his mettle. That one man can overcome the bleakest of obstacles and stake his rightful claim as the fastest man on wheels.

So, with Breedlove back on the playa, I drive up with BZ, pulling an all-nighter out to Gerlach. (We had driven up from LA in a rentacar, a three cylinder Geo that was not really the right vehicle for the drive, but one that BZ insisted we take instead of the '71 Grand Prix and its chronic overheating.)

Our itinerary is loose, predicated only by a 7 AM arrival on the dry lake bed of Black Rock in time for more record runs...

After watching both Breedlove and Andy Green abort record runs, the day ends with us cruising around the measured mile, watching the sun go down. The sun drops like a biscuit and there we are, blanketed by darkness just like Breedlove's truck driver. I tell BZ I can't see the access road towards the paved highway. The one thing we aren't supposed to do is drive towards the glow of Gerlach, lights shining from Bruno's coffee shop and motel, Bev's Miner's Club, the Black Rock Saloon and a couple of hundred porch lights... but it is very easy to get disoriented out there in the Outback and Gerlach — the only beacon — pulls you away from your destination and into the mire...

And just that quick, I drive us into an absolute root beer freeze as the parched, impermeable playa dissolves into quicksand... I stomp the gas pedal on the anemic little Geo, giving 'er full rudder as well as full throttle, telling BZ that it would be a long walk to the Brits encampment and even harder to explain to them what we doing on a racing surface that is in a quasi-lockdown mode...

THE PHONE BOOTH, TAKE TWO

The next morning the winds blew in at full song, creating a white out condition and canceling any attempts at record runs from either Breedlove or Andy Green.

We head home. While BZ is scoring some liquids, fruit and junk food outside the general store in Empire, (five miles from Gerlach, and it's only source of food that isn't from a coffee shop), a free lance photographer with pinwheel eyes hits me up for a quarter for the phone booth. I'm having a variation on deja vu, what is it about this place that everybody from the fastest man on Earth to Dennis Hopper's doppelganger doesn't have the proper coin for a pay phone?

I give him some change. "Thanks," he says. "I got to call my bureau."

So that's what they are calling it these days, I think to myself.

He's got a frayed and frizzled coiffure, a two and a half day beard and an ack-ack-ack cadence as a co-efficient to his New Yawk accent. He asks if I am out here for the record runs and I say yeah. BZ is still in the store, so I make the mistake of mentioning Breedlove's shut off run, thus sustaining what I have mistaken to be small talk and what is really a run-on screed about the desert and those that it attracts.

"'The Spirit of America.' Is that what this is about? 'Don't tread on me because I want to shoot guns in the desert.' This as a gesture?"

I tell him we got to make time back to LA.

"'Make Time.' You can't 'make time.' Time makes you. What is this pre-occupation with time anyway? With Speed? Mach One? What is it with you people? Do you think that by sticking your head through the placenta of the spacetime continuum you are going to cheat mortality? Don't you know you are hastening it? Do you know it wasn't until caffeine and the clock were invented that the Western World woke up from its hangover and built what we now know as Civilization? Speed? Do you really think that is the way the winds are blowing? Do you realize you are upwind of Ground Zero?"

A MOTHERFUCKING PHONEBOOK

Andy Green vaporizes Richard Noble's record. He sets a two-way average of 714 mph, but this is just a drill. The goal is Mach 1, baby. (*"700 mph is of no interest to us..."*)

They keep creeping on it. The Mach 1 runs are imminent. I'm in LA, weighing my options. The weather reports out of Reno seem to indicate that foul weather can hit Washoe County and wash out any activity.

I call operation information and ask for Bev's Miner's Club in Gerlach, Nevada where I know the Brits are gathering for a beverage and discussing run profiles. Nada. The only number I can extricate out of the operator is for Bruno's coffee shop.

I call. Bruno answers. I politely and quickly tell Bruno my name, my job and how much money I have spent in his coffee shop. With all that being said, I am trying to reach somebody, anybody on the *SSC* team who I know are at Bev's next door and do you happen to have a phone number for Bev's?

"What am I?" he thunders. "A motherfucking phone book?"

S-L-A-M. The next sound I hear is a dial tone.

I catch another plane and rent another car.

SPIN

While en route to watch Craig Breedlove lay down a disappointing 400 mph run, I am in a press shuttle along with a van load of other reporter/feature writer types...

Ethnically and nationalistically speaking, the press corps is pretty diverse with print and electronic stringers from the BBC, ITC, a French newspaper, the Reno Gazette, etc., etc. It was a real multi-national rainbow coalition; everybody introduces themselves to each other. I asked one guy — he was definitely artier looking than the rest of the corp and I thought his name was "Arjae" or something — where he was from and I thought he said, "Spain," so during the course of the van ride I tried to engage him in a discourse on Hemingway and the Spanish Civil War, while feebly trying to wire that machismo trip into the Mach 1 pursuit on this godforsaken lake bed...he looked at me very bewilderedly and didn't say anything... I figured he didn't speak English all that well and left it at that.

Later, at Bruno's Coffee Shop in Gerlach I overhear him ordering a cheeseburger in perfect English; "*WHO* do you write for?" I ask. "Spin," he says. "O-h-h, SPIN!" I reply...

Turns out "RJ" lives in my neighborhood in L.A. — we probably hear the same car alarms going off. So we have a burger and a chocolate malted, talk about the neighborhood and get along famously — poor kid didn't know much about the pursuit of horsepower but his piece in SPIN Magazine wasn't half bad.

THE SOUND OF SPEED

The only thing as intimidating as the speed of sound is the sound of speed.

One feature incorporated into the design of the *SSC* was something that Andy Green referred to as his "bravery switch." When Mach's Demon, the howling banshee of the supersonic winds, begin to gather as compressed molecules of air and began pummeling the race car, Andy hits a switch that samples the sound of the dark wind and processes it, creating and pumping out a mirrored tone exactly 180 degrees out of phase from the original howl.

Due to the cancellation from the dueling sound waves, the sound level in the cockpit drops to a very takable whine from the spinning turbines on either side of the cockpit. This is like Ernst Mach's experiments in sensory terror (the whizzing of the bullets was what damaged and terrorized battalions as much as the bloodshed and the bullet wounds, or the Ancient Chinese who tried to psych out the spirit world with their rocket displays.)

Andy Green's battle is with a demon. Now the demon is an adversary who is at least muzzled.

HAIKU FOR THE TECHNOLOGICAL ENTHUSIAST

And so it went at Black Rock that September and October: It was a month replete with sandstorms, rain, and incessant fod. After Breedlove had "fodded" his engine and when the winds would murmur and bellow, it was like *Waiting for Godot.* It was a month of hurry-up-and-wait, hey maybe tomorrow is the day. It was an exercise in endurance. Occasionally sandstorms would kick in and nullify the very thorough "de-fodding" (removing debris from the 13 mile courses) that took place during the day. In addition to the capricious, recalcitrant weather which made a mockery of the Mach 1 clubs perpetual de-fodding efforts, the Brits were plagued with a malfunctioning on-board computer that would sense non-existence turbulence and kill both engines at 400 mph. The *SSC* software phreaks would chase after the jet car at 180 mph in a hot rodded XJ12 Jaguar and blow some fresh code out off a laptop into the onboard computer's serial port.

Through all of this both Bruno's and the Miner's Club in Gerlach became an Algonquin Round Table for the LSR maniacs who gathered on the playa in search of the Big Bang. The conversation was always good. It was during these nights I engaged Noble in a dialogue about overcoming obstacles. He insisted that the two forays into Jordan prepared the Thrust team for any possible catastrophic eventuality.

"The problem with Jordan," he said, "is that we built a car that was extremely unconventional and very complex. We took it out there with a very green crew, so we had the problems of sorting out the crew, sorting out the car and, even worse, sorting out the desert. It hammered the hell out of the car... (after) we cleared 170 miles of stone. And a lot of that was on our hands and knees."

Another night I got a similar recollection from Andy Green. "We had gone out there with a car with a lot of features that people said couldn't work: rear-wheel steering, twin engines, the computers," he said. "We went out there and we had a lot of problems with rear-wheel steer. And the engineering fixed it out there in the desert — we got the car to work right out there in Jordan. Everything that could have gone wrong with everything we had did — and we fixed all of it. The only thing we couldn't fix was the weather."

"The biggest obstacle wasn't the fod or the weather," said Simon

Rogers, one of the *Thrust SSC* microlight pilots whose job description was to patrol the desert looking for fod. "Some days we would have to abandon a run because I would spot camels straggling across the track or Iranians rampaging across the desert smuggling massive amounts of petrol in a lorry (tanker truck)."

But perhaps the finest quote I was able to extricate from the Brits came from Green when I asked him what possessed him to be the first driver of an automobile to burst through the Sound Barrier. He said, "Nobody knows what is there because nobody has ever been there."

It was
a haiku
for any technological
enthusiast.

HOLIDAY

I ask Andy Green to describe the differences in handling a Tornado fight plane and *Thrust SSC.* "The car has a lot more acceleration than a jet fighter," he says. "It has two jet fighter engines with half the weight of a jet fighter — tremendous acceleration." He says he enjoyed his "holiday" from the RAF while moonlighting with the *Thrust* team. "You only run when the weather is nice, everything is good for you and the vehicle is perfectly sensible."

THE HUMAN PUNCH CARD

Colours, sounds, temperatures, pressures, spaces, times, and so forth, are connected with one another in manifold ways; and with them are associated dispositions of mind, feelings, and volitions. — **Ernst Mach, THE ANALYSIS OF SENSATIONS (1886)**

As night enters its own rapid eye movement, Danny Jo lay back at the Fly Ranch and closes his eyes. Why a blind man closes his eyes to sleep is a mystery, but he does. And he gets lost in thought...

Due to his preternatural and extraordinary sensory awareness, Danny Jo the Blind Hippie now serves as an auxiliary participant in the quest for breaking the sound barrier in an automobile. Danny Jo volunteered his services to the *SSC* team as a sort of data analyst for the Mach 1 Land Speed Record attempts at Black Rock. His mission as he saw it would be to provide analysis to complement other data gathering designed to prove the existence of a true, physical barrier — an invisible, longitudinal wall created by the energy generated by any entity attempting to travel faster than thunder.

Danny Jo would be working without any of the modern accoutrements desired by contemporary systems analysts. His method of telemetry is completely primeval and organic... For the sensors used are his fingers, toes and bottom. He receives the sound waves generated by a jet-driven motorcar as it reaches speeds of almost 800 mph, analyzes the shape of the waveform and its pitch as it enters and massages the nerve endings in his body and then plots the reaction of the wave's characteristics as it attempted to punch through this much hypothesized invisible brick wall.

He is a human punch card.

This sound barrier has never been penetrated by a motorcar and the blind hippie is well aware of the significance of his assignment. The slightest miscalculation on any of the data recorders and the results could prove fatal to the driver... As the stars shift and the earth continues its rotation, Danny Jo contemplates the ramifications of dealing with a concealed phenomenon and its ability to capsize any vehicle loaded with the chutzpah to penetrate its hidden threshold... he reasons that his offer to monitor data was accepted because it takes a blind man to see and hear both into and beyond the invisible...

As his earth momma woman sleeps beside him, the blind hippie continues to meditate in the black. He remembers a free verse poem he had composed and began to recite it to himself, *sotto voce. "Sound occurs within spaces. Like natives, vibrations interact in a circle."* He repeats it to himself, this mantra interrupted only by the infrequent doppler of a military plane or satellite — it sounds like a detuned pedal steel guitar slithering out of a trucker's jukebox in Reno — and the accompanying ultraviolet tones emanating from the blinking lights. He also hears a train, just like the Spencer Tracy movie. These sensations make the blind hippie smile...

The blind hippie tunes out the psychic waves that beep and click from the satellites like Morse Code from the dead; waveforms Teutonic in origin are what he needs to focus on; he is here to witness and interpret a high white noise generated by a space age, supersonic motorcar; any signal that was not of a technological nature is to be rejected...

But on a metaphysical level, he knows he is to do more than encode and decode raw data. Although not in the job description, part of the gig is to diagnose and analyze the distant echo of the white sound most men never hear. To monitor such phenomena, a detector must be as sensitive as possible. The trade off, unfortunately, is that a detector that sensitive is also subjected to noise, in this instance being the poltergeists of genocide as well as an extraterrestrial force that seems to seems to congregate at sites where spy planes and black projects frolic and dogfight in maneuvers above the desert lake beds; indeed, there are still shell casings as well as undetonated carpet bombs on the desert floor, more flotsam and jetsam from war games and simulated battles dating back to WW II.

(The dormant ammunition gives off its own weird and twisted energy, more information that crept into the mind of the hippie mystic...)

He attempts to summon the sound of an oncoming train, but his efforts are continually hampered by the strength of the signals from the Pauite Injun' burial grounds. The sounds of the locomotive are drowned out. The blind hippie relaxes, slips into a trance, and communes with the soul of ol' Chief Winnemucca hisself, a Pauite Tribal Leader summoned to the Father Land over 100 years ago.

And so the supernatural powwow begins. The Chief says that back in the day he was enthralled and fascinated by the technology of the white man — *weapons that made a great noise like thunder and lightning, houses that moved, "big houses that go on a mighty ocean and travel faster than any horse."* In those days, he considered the white man his brother.

The Injun' speaks to Danny Jo of the beginning and how there were four children of the Good Father in the Spirit Land: A white brother and sister and a red brother and sister. Their bickering was divided upon color lines and the Good Father segregated the siblings along those lines. The great paleface emigration of manifest destiny was seen by Captain Truckee née Chief Winnemucca as an opportunity to heal the wounds... to reunite the red man with his white brothers and sisters, an opportunity which had turned to shit and utter dysfunctionality when two wily sons of jackals/fur traders kidnapped two young Pauite squaws and hid their nubile quarry in a trap door — technology that was beyond the kin and comprehension of the redskins.

(*What is a door to an Indian?*)

Before the squaw's abduction, the Pauites were on copacetic and neighborly terms with the paleface emigrants and squatters. But the Injun's demanded justice in the form of the sons of jackals' blood, which led to the merciless bloodshed in the shadows of the mountains to the East, the Great War of 1860. Kit Carson, enjoined by the Forked Tongue Power Structure to whoop up on some redskin ass, led the attacks. The fallout from those battles was self-evident to anybody en route to Gerlach. And suffice it to say, ol' Captain Truckee was not quite enamored with the new technology of his white brothers and sisters after the smoke had cleared off of Pyramid Lake...

As the Chief finishes this tale, the telepathic tête-à-tête is interrupted by another spirit, not unlike a lurker in a chat room. The blind hippie tunes into these new vibrations and deduces that its origins were much further away, hundreds of miles east on I-80; indeed, the source was as far away as the abandoned air strips at Wendover, Utah or perhaps its adjunct, the Salt Flats of Bonneville where a few moons back Land Speed warriors plied their trade with jet-engined automobiles until the potash mining had finally fucked up the salt's water table so badly that high speed record attempts were fruitless. Captain Truckee reckoned that the voice was that of a white brother, although not one of the white brothers whom had plundered the mesa.

The signal is weak at first, but when he rolls his eyes, they act as a rotary dial on a ham radio or the swiveling of a pair of rabbit ears and the reception improves; still, the transmission has to penetrate entire mountain ranges — Cortez, Sulphur Spring, Shoshone, etc. The blind hippie admires the channelers' tenacity and likens the signal itself to those seemingly massless subatomic particles that could penetrate and pass through the earth, a handful of which were captured in a detector in Japan.

Once dialed in, the voice from beyond the mountains tells of his experiences with a great noise like thunder and lightning and houses that moved; indeed, the voice from beyond the mountain range actually used the thunder and lightning itself to move the house, a notion that Winnemucca found amusing as he was fascinated by the white brother's technology but wondered at what point does this technology become a coyote with two heads? The blind hippie deciphers what the voice from beyond the mountain was actually referring to, an automobile powered by jet engines on the Salt Flats of Utah. *Exactly*, said the voice from beyond the mountains. *Oh yes, I have seen those from the Spirit Land*, says Captain Truckee.

Did you not use the weapons of thunder and lightning to further the expansion of the white nation? Not exactly, the voice from beyond the mountains answers. *We borrowed the thunder and lightning for another purpose: not to just travel faster than any horse, but to travel faster than the sound of the thunder itself. We were attempting to get closer to what you call the Spirit Land. The only warriors who died were ones who allowed themselves to be sacrificed by the thunder and lightning itself.* Captain Truckee says he understands the desires of the new white brother warriors to use the thunder and lightning to enter the Spirit Land. He then told of a high white noise above most folks' hearing range. It is, to most, an unheard music. Danny Jo interrupts, saying that this music is only for those who are tuned in to the ethereal, the existential absolutes. *Yes*, acknowledges Captain Truckee: *It is a noise for those who are unafraid to die — and it is as loud as the thunder when the warrior is closest to his own death.* The Injun' muses that e*ven though the first white brother had given me a new name that meant "very well," perhaps those were not the white brothers that the Good Father in the Spirit Land had meant at all.* Captain Truckee reasons *that perhaps you were the correct white brother as you are a fallen warrior whom in death has joined me in the Spirit Land.* The Good Father talks of *koyaanisqatsi*, the world out of balance; *until we as brothers reconnect, the universe will not be whole.* The blind hippie marvels at the bookends of this cosmic situation and nods his head.

SSC IS ROLLING

Einstein proved that space and time both bend. Empirical confirmation of this phenomena manifests at Black Rock on the day the Brits go supersonic. There is a parallax of cones which delineates the boundary of the race course, from the shut down area through the "measured mile" speed trap all the way to the launch pad. With the human eye, the cones gradually meld into the floor of the lake bed itself. Off on the horizon, a puff of dusty exhaust blossoms like Teutonic smoke signals as the crewmembers spin *Thrust SSC*'s turbines and purge the afterburners of its Spey 202s. But this dervish of pyrotechnical activity transpires approximately 45 degrees off axis of the parallax view. Space bends. You are witnessing the curvature of the Earth.

"*Thrust SSC* is rolling," the *SSC* radio hums. For the first mile of the record run, the machine is merely cruising at speeds which would not bat the eye of a highway patrolman in Montana. This is precautionary, to avoid creating a vacuum in the 202's intake which would suck pebbles and arrowheads off the lake bed and into the motor. At the Mile 1 marker Green stomps on the loudpedal. Instantaneously, copious amounts of thrust sock the RAF hero in the solar plexus and he's blazing across the lake bed, with a rooster tail of dust and exhaust in his wake as tall as Noble's phone bill. The trajectory of the vehicle appears to be bending on an exponential curve, even though it is straight as a Southern Baptist. Everything is strangely silent, despite the fact that the machine must be making prodigious thunder in its wake. (*Isn't it?*). Suddenly, the trajectory appears to change and is completely linear... it is absolutely boogeying... *Thrust SSC* enters the measured mile and pushes through a shock wave the size of a football field... silence... a mushroom cloud begins to manifest itself in the wake of the vehicle and then *WHHHOOOOSSSSHHH...* fuck that is loud! The sound of two fighter plane engines with turbines spinning at warp speed rattles the playa and the schoolhouse in Gerlach.

Time bends.

RIGHT THEN

Richard Noble has taken our car keys.

"Record breaking is very dangerous business," he says.

In the first of the required back-to-back runs, *SSC* has, in fact, gone Mach 1. The parachutes are torn from the ass end of the race car. Parachute failure is what sent Craig Breedlove into a brine pond and what launched Paula "Miss STP" Murphy into the back forty of California's wine country. In this instance, however, the damage is minimal. There is so much drag built into the design of *SSC* , that it can slow down from a speed of 760 mph with room to spare. The Hand of the Supreme Consciousness began to push onto the race car and slow 'er down, a gentle tug that decreases the machine's velocity to where Andy Green can actually begin to apply the brakes and not melt them ala Breedlove in 1964... Breedlove, of course (and unlike Green), did not have the benefit of lights blinking in the cockpit and buzzers and beepers whooping as warnings to the driver that it was now safe to apply his foot to the brake pedal... so, with all of this in place, Green judiciously hit the brakes, well aware that he has had a chute failure, and after seven miles or so of coasting, brings the beastly black behemoth to a stop.

Which has really fouled up the routine. Here they are, in the first leg of a back-to-back record run with an hour turnaround time, and *SSC* has overshot its mark — where the support vehicles are waiting — by a mile or so.... The support team has to fire up the tow trucks and chase Green down, mount the massive race car onto the trailer hitch, turn back around and begin to service the car, replenish the kerosene, download data, pack the parachutes....uhhh, pack the parachutes... yeah, pack the parachutes...this is the nexus of the crisis, after so much grunt work and sleep deprivation in a couple of utterly uninhabitable climates, here they are, they have gone Mach 1 and all they have to do is turn this sucker around and the parachute lines are tangled into knots of macrame and a lattice of spaghetti. What to do?

Richard Noble manages the crisis. "Bloody hell, cut the goddamn parachute off." So they do.

The assembled smell blood in the water. A supersonic speed record is imminent, and these guys are going after it with the parachutes cut off. Flash, the bartender from the Black Rock Saloon, is waving the Union

Jack and sporting a t-shirt that reads. "the Empire Strikes Back." The tension of waiting is as thick as the dirt on Noble's rentacar. And then the stress tightens even more, as nobody is prepared for what comes next...

Breedlove's publicist pulls Richard Noble aside and tells him that Breedlove is out on the access road, and wants to offer congratulations for actually breaking the sound barrier, but doesn't want to spoil or interrupt Noble's moment of glory. All the journos and photographers gathered around the dusty rentacar crane their necks and tilt the axis of their hearing ability to eavesdrop on the incessant whispering and weaseling from Breedlove's boy.

This is a moment of crisis and for all of Breedlove's recent folly (bungled communications which led to structural damage of his racer — and nearly a motorhome and its inhabitants; his return to the desert with the notion of making a drone run at supersonic speeds; a engine fodded because somebody left a bolt on the engine's inlet duct; getting the rig stuck in the mud as they pulled out of Black Rock; the exclusive penny ante deal with Speedvision that reduced video uplinks of his efforts to a near blackout; and when the team got its shit together enough to actually make a run, the miscues that led to series of rather unspectacular runs on the playa), here he was, hovering off of the lake bed in a white van with the motor and a.c. running, relaying his congratulations to the guys who were on the verge of pulling the whole thing off. If these scenes were not running in fast forward through Richard Noble's cranium, they were certainly running through the noggins of the gathered journalists who had endured the last six weeks in the town that Bruno built.

"For fuck's sake, tell him to get out here."

"Well, Craig feels it would be unsportsmanlike to impose on your moment of glory."

Some journalists chuckle. Others arch their eyebrows in mute bemusement.

Noble reprises his suggestion for Craig to join him. The *SOA* flack nods.

W-a-y off in the distance, a bubble of heat waves and smoke *s-l-o-w-l-y* grows in dimension. It looks like a mirage, but is actually Breedlove and his minions, making their way onto the lake bed at a speed of 35 mph.

It takes forever.

He gets out of the van and he looks like Mick Jagger. The journalists rush him and turn on microcassettes and shutters click and flashbulbs pop. It is unfuckingbelieveable. Here is the moment that Noble and his *SSC* compatriots have forsaken their lives for and All eyes are on Breedlove. As Craig makes his way across the press area of the measured mile, his handlers part a sea of news gatherers with the swift assuredness of James Brown's bodyguards and Noble is left alone by his dusty rentacar.

Gradually, Breedlove makes it to the rentacar and shakes Noble's hand. They are now enveloped by journalists who are fluid in an experiment in the Bernoulli Effect.

"Richard and I both agreed (*ka-buszzhh ka-bussszh ka-buszzh*) that Andy Green is the first person to break the Sound Barrier. (*ka-buszzhh ka-bussszh ka-buszzh*)." The light reflects in Craig's aviator shades. He is oblivious to Flash waving the Union Jack.

Six and a half miles away, *SSC* is rolling again.

They light the beast, Greens eases 'er down the lake bed for a mile or so and then hops on the throttle.

"USAC timing, can you confirm that we did it within the hour?"

"Unfortunately, *SSC* you missed it by 43 seconds."

Richard Noble doesn't miss a beat. "Right then, that's record breaking."

NOW I'M GOING TO DROWN (REVISITED)

My ride back to the motel in Fernley is a grizzled, hippie drag racing writer. It is an 80 mile drive back to the motel. We talk about the magnitude of the spectacle we have witnessed. We are both taken aback by the sheer audacity of Breedlove sheepishly stealing Noble's thunder. After all the misfires: the Speedvision deal, the hipster crew chief, the fodded engine, the rig getting stuck in the mud... I remember that I have a cassette of the Breedlove crash, and I put it in the car's tape player.

BREEDLOVE: (*loud, over laughter*) I gritted my teeth and that pole just sheared off like nothing. You know, "DOUMM" and no pole! (*breathes in*) UUNNHH... I looked up and I thought, "Oh Boy! Another chance!"

VOICES: (*giddy laughter*)

BREEDLOVE: I looked up...

VOICES: (*giddy laughter*)

BREEDLOVE: ... I hit the water and the water started slowing me down and I seen (sic) this big old bank coming up and I thought, "OHHH NAWWWW." (*laughs*)

VOICES: (*giddy laughter*)

BREEDLOVE: I hit the bank and it just went right over the top there. I was flying through there about thirty feet in the air and I thought, "NOW I'M GOING TO DROWN!"

VOICES: (*uproarious laughter*)

"After the way he screwed up his chances of being the first guy to go supersonic, drowning would have been a better fate," the grizzled, hippie drag racing writer says.

THE NEXT DAY

The 50th Anniversary of Chuck Yeager's supersonic flight goes by. There is no activity on the lake bed, except for maintenance on the machines.

Standing outside of Bruno's, I see Danny Jo and we start talking about the spiritual nature of machines and how technology may be filling a metaphysical void. "Kant says that experience is the key to the Universe," he tells me. A train goes by. "The faster you go, the closer you are to God," he says.

RUN SIXTY-FIVE

They see something and then they hear it. Puffs of smoke off in the distance and then an audible blast out of the jet engines' tailpipes. Empirical — and sensory — confirmation that light is faster than sound. Ernst Mach would be proud.

Members of the *SSC* support team are standing by in Supacats. They are aborigines gathered around a fire.

"The car is beginning to yaw," Andy Green says, a master of understatement. He is coming towards the Supacats, slightly weaving between parallel white lines. It appears to the observers, however, this machine is coming from an arc. It is empirical confirmation that the earth is round.

He manhandles ten tons of machinery back into the proper groove and passes through the measure mile at 763 mph. Boom. Boom. Windows rattle at Bruno's and glasses on the bar wiggle. A shot glass is knocked off the bar and breaks.

"Man, that was hard work," Andy Green reports through his mask.

At Mile 13.5, the support team turns the beast around and pack the parachutes, replenishes the fuel and interface the starter motor, spinning the turbine blades and injecting voltage and kerosene. The moment is nigh. Back to back, baby. *Supermotherfuckingsonic.*

THE DESERT EXHALES (RUN SIXTY-SIX)

"*SSC* ready to roll ... *SSC* is rolling ..." Andy Green keys his mic and leaves it open... (*inhale*) ... *SSC* slowly creeps up to a 100 mph ... a very careful, calculated application of thrust ... the white line fades ... (*inhale*) "two good nozzles, looking for max ..." (*exhale*) the afterburners glow with an orange flame... "350...jeez-us" "450..keep your foot down..." (*inhale*) ... compressed molecules of air pile up against the massive black missile of a marital aid like football players running in place against the closed door of a locker room... the winds begin to howl as Mach's Demon spreads his wings ... (*inhale*) even with the "bravery switch" the winds are deafening when molecules of air come together and create a unique form of primordial intelligence ... Green continues driving the shit out of it, giving it rudder while grunting in his brainbucket's headset, a measured breathing, phone sex for the supersonic set......in the measured mile the shaman closes his eyes, which is redundant as he is already blind, but whatever...

Andy Green is giving 'er full rudder at 700 mph... the machine has yawed off course and the steering yoke is pointed completely vertically...

NEGATIVE GRAVITY

Ernst Mach was right, Einstein was right....

SSC is fifty feet off of its white line that serves as the guide down the desert, a perilous conundrum reminiscent of the fate that claimed Glen Leasher... it is very easy to get disoriented in the desert, and Green is following the wrong white line... Green is fighting this vehicle, something that was designed as a model of stability in supersonic chaos and the car is blown off course by fifty feet... "I'll say that was fast... 450, chute out, yes, everything is wonderful."

Danny Jo goes into a singular trance, in tune with the manifold harmonics of the jet engines and the sound of molecules compressing into a pane of glass to be punctured like this was Vienna in 1868... he hears the singing of the angels, dancing on the proverbial pins... the desert exhales... it is like some bodacious, preternatural breath of relief, a post-coital moan of exultation worthy of tantric monks and snow leopards.

The blind hippie reaches for his sock, wiggles his toes again, and smiles.

∞

Ron Ayer's approach to Mach 1 — use a ton of weight and downforce and just suck that baby onto the playa — proved to be the correct one. Poetically, on October 15th, 1997, one day after the 50th anniversary of Chuck Yeager's supersonic flight, Andy Green recorded speeds of 759 and 766 mph, which translated to Mach numbers of 1.01 and 1.05, establishing a supersonic LSR of 763 mph. "The car becomes unstable at around Mach 0.85 as the airflow starts to go supersonic underneath the vehicle and requires very rapid, precise steering inputs to keep it on the white guide line," Green clarified afterward, ironically using the present tense to describe his benchmark performance. "The car becomes slightly more stable above Mach 0.9 and can then be steered fairly accurately through the measured mile. The shockwaves formed visible moisture on the front of the car, which could be seen from the cockpit and which moved back along the body as the car accelerated." Green continued to describe how *Thrust SSC* exquisitely but firmly punctured a hole in the sound barrier. "The car then remains reasonably stable as it accelerates through Mach 1, with the rate of acceleration dropping off as the vehicle generates the huge shockwaves which cause the sonic boom." BOOM. Mach 1 was no longer theoretical. The bigger hammer method prevailed.

Noble, Green, Ayers, et. al, achieved their technological imperative — designed a race car that wouldn't disintegrate as it punched a hole in the sound barrier — convincingly. Art Arfons put the magnitude of this achievement in perspective: "Everybody has been bragging — me included — that we'll go out there and go supersonic when we really couldn't," he said. "This guy did it. This has got to be the living end."

Arfons nailed it: It is the end of an era and it all transpired at the end of the century, during the waning moments of the millennium. Regardless of the heroics and foibles of Sir Malcolm, John Cobb, Craig Breedlove, and Art Arfons, future historians will regard Richard Noble's and Andy Green's feat as the last epic gesture of the fossil fuel age, because. . . hot rodding is over — the gearheads have reached the Holy Grail.

After Mach 1, what else is there?

I/0

IT'S ONLY EMPIRICAL WHEN YOU GOT THE TIME SLIP

The Blue Flame's *design is um, for a layman it's similar to Breedlove's. It's like a dart, you know, the car is designed like a dart and his cars are designed like a dart or an arrow as opposed to say, the* Thrust SSC *which is, designed like a barn door.*

PETE FARNSWORTH: Yeah, massive.

You know and basically "We're going to push this barn door through this other wall." Their design slowed considerably when it started getting into trans and subsonic and super-sonic regions, but is this a correct design to puncture the sound barrier?

PETE: Yep.

... because the whole idea was to stabilize the car... That's why they had the two Spey 202s. It wasn't for thrust, it was to anchor it. If you take your design and get it into those same regions, it could have gotten a little strange.

PETE: It certainly could have.

LEAH: It could have, we never were gonna stand up and go, "We could have done it," because nobody who has really really been into racing knows that you can say, "You could have."

So it's only empirical when you got the time slip.

PETE: Absolutely. We learned that from drag racing a whole bunch of years. You don't make six changes at once you go a step by step by step by step by step. It takes time, and you don't how the outcome is gonna be, you just make judg-ments. Now, with the computers that record a hundred things at once, you know, it's great they could make several changes and uh, know how they're, you know what each one is doing, but uh, the thing is you tend not to do it anyway.

SINGULARITY

"Nothing is true. Everything is permitted."
— **Hassan i Sabbah**

This is a paradox worthy of Ernst Mach hisself. If "nothing is true" then "nothing is true" is not true also. And according to Einstein, the only thing that is not permitted is motion at a velocity greater than the speed of light. If motion is detected at a speed greater than warp speed, Einstein's entire cosmology crumbles.

Which may or may not happen. But traveling faster than sound in an automobile was also deemed preposterous — including by Ron Ayers, who reversed his position only upon sketchpad meditation in his garden.

Thrust SSC entered the realm of the empirical. They went Mach 1 and became Ernst Mach's post-mortem favorite sons.

This book bills itself as a history of the Land Speed Record. It isn't, per se. It is about the pursuit of a moment of singularity. It is a chronicle of the search for a Teutonic dharma; i.e., a romantic yet irreducible accomplishment that would encapsulate what is cool, weird, noble and absurd about technological pursuits in general and the pursuit of massive amounts of horsepower, in specific.

The moment of singularity that this book documents is the puncturing of the sound barrier by a motorcar, a feat I have come to understand as the ultimate romantic gesture (although "romanticism" is not equated with futility, in this instance) in the field of hot rodding.

With the Land Speed Record a mortal cost — in either lives lost or ruined — could almost be keyed in as a co-efficient to the equation which states that breaking the sound barrier in a car is equal to the eradication of cherished notions about physical limitations and human perseverance.

"It can't be done," is a refrain that echoes throughout the pursuit of any advance in maximum velocity. When it is done, the naysayers are not only humbled, they are rattled. Moments of triumph and defiance — such as traveling at the speed of sound in a car — are crushing to those who do not like their fundamental principles of living fucked with. They can't process the inevitability of change as well as having the drawers dropped on heretofore cherished notions. Moments such as the breaking the sound barrier, whether by air or by land, change how we see ourselves and by extension, it changes who we are.

If one were to endeavor to write a history of special and general relativity as it applied to cosmology, or on quantum mechanics and particle acceleration, string theory via number crunching on supercomputers, nanotechnology, one might find representation of any of these elements in research of the traveling at the speed of sound in a race car... All of these elements coalesced on a dry lake bed in the Fall of 1997 when the sound barrier was, in fact, broken by an automobile.

If you talk to practitioners in any of those fields (cosmology, experimental physics, advanced mathematics, race car engineering), most specifically those who can both pride themselves on pushing the envelope as well as intellectualize and articulate their pursuits, their rationale for taking their disciplines to such extreme boundaries — a topological space that befuddles the comprehension of the masses — is to "get closer to the mind of God," or words to that effect.

I can't help but think that when one is actually rubbing against the compressed molecules of air against a race car as it reaches a supersonic speed, that one gets really chummy with whatever one's God may be. I never asked the driver of *Thrust SSC* what he felt when he reached that sublime moment of Transubstation, but when I saw a motorcar go Mach 1, I not only felt closer to a Supreme Manifestation of the Collective Consciousness, I felt sad — and according to Zen Buddhism, life is, in fact, sorrow...

Perhaps I was gripped by some other metaphysical and philosophical implications of the whole Mach 1/LSR trip. This wasn't about ensuring stability of future supersonic commuter trains between LA and San Francisco.

This was about the pace of technology and how how it took the speed of transport to triple from the Stone Age over a million years ago when ancient Man was first hunting in China (and if he was running from a pissed off mastadon, at a speed of say, less than 15 mph an hour, which translates to the coveted 4-minute mile achieved by Roger Bannister); sometime around the Bronze Age, Man figured out how to tame horses and use those as a form of transport and as a necessary device for jousting matches, all of which was maximum velocity until steam engines and electric motors were put to use in the 19th century.

The first LSR was going about the same speed as a jockey on a horse:

39 mph in an electric car. Less than one hundred years later the speeds were ten times that (John Cobb, Craig Breedlove); within another three years is another 1 and half times as great (Breedlove, Arfons, Gabelich, Noble); and slightly less than a century after "Never Satisfied" did its thing, Andy Green went Mach 1. 763 mph. 25 times greater than the 30 mph speed of Gaston Chasseloup-Laubat in 1898.

We are traveling 25 times faster today than we were 100 years ago. We are Glen Leasher rushing headlong into *Infinity*. And I cannot sort out if we are rushing towards an Age of Enlightenment as we explore the cosmos at speeds nearing that of Light of if we are hastening our own obsolescence.

(When news of Breedlove finally packing it in '97 hit me, I was having a beer with Cuz'n Roy. "The failure is ours," he said. Perhaps.)

We are speed. We are mass. We are energy. But at what point are we $E=MC^2$ and at what point are we intelligent beings?

This LSR gig is about life, contrary to the mortal rate that has ridden shotgun with this whole trip. On a more prosaic and less cosmic level, when that twin-engined jet-powered streamliner known as the *Thrust SSC* went Mach 1 I knew that a statement had been made. As a gesture, the moment was antithetical to the banality and the drudgery that contaminates our daily lives... It seemed to undermine the notion that We as a society live in an age of limits... Life as we know it is a bottleneck and we spend more time bargaining with the Devil to loosen his grip than we do talking to whatever any of us perceive God to be. Raw, unmitigated speed has always been the release from the trappings of this asphyxiation of the mundane and has always been a metaphor for freedom.

My sorrow at that moment of singularity was manifold: a) like the man said, the era of the back yard mechanic was over. Never again, could scrappy individuals in the mold of Breedlove and the Arfons's build a spaceship-looking motorcar and set a Land Speed Record with it; b) I knew the moment was fleeting; c) I also knew that there would not be another gesture to be made in hot rodding, the general arena that I have endeavored to study: that of making a motorcar go faster than what is prudent or even sane. The natural extension of this is to take it to a place where there are no limits and no rules — the ultimate libertarian Big Go!.

(I'm sure there are a litany of logical arguments for all of the restrictions that all of us face in our day-to-day existence, most saliently how rules and regulations "save" and "protect" us, but what I'm saying is that there is nothing to "save" at this point; it is too late, as romanticism is dead, cooked, toasted, fossilized. The very notion of "limits" is antithetical to hot rodding's mantra of "run whathca' brung and hope you brung enough."

Mach 1. The ramifications are vast: If Einstein hinged his entire body of work on the premise that all subatomic events transpire at the speed of light (the crux of Relativity is that this constant barrier is absolute and NOT relative), what happens when an automobile crushes a similar physical limit — the speed of sound, whose number fluctuates with altitude, temperature and barometric pressure, but whose crushing and malevolent force remains a constant upon any vehicle that passes through its threshold?

On a philosophical level, I came away from the LSR with this knowledge: Limits exist only to be eradicated and mocked.

Like I said, the ultimate barrier or restriction is the speed of light. Einstein postulated that no action can transpire at a velocity greater than 182,262 miles per second. If that were so, his entire cosmological handshake of spacetime, gravity would come apart like a cheap watch.

The last bastion of unlimited performance — and again, to most folks the notion of "unlimited performance" is what made hot rodding interesting in the first place — is the pursuit of the Land Speed Record. It is the last scene where there are damn near no rules, where freedom of expression is limited only to one's imagination, where barriers exist only in the mind. It is where there still dwells the strange, powerful energy which envelopes the id and psyche of its subjects with the same grip as the physiological phenomenon known to fighter pilots and astronauts as "Go! Fever." It is where everything is permitted... and like I say, when everything is permitted, it really disturbs those who feel that some things are not permitted... it is a classic struggle, is it not?

PUSHING THE ENVELOPE (1997)

Washington, DC, October, 1997. We are now on our second margaritas. I am cranking into high gear as I tell the Curator of Technology Emeritus from the Smithsonian Institute about the hijinks and absurdity that transpired on the Mach 1 gag out at Black Rock.

I was telling him how the guy from RACER magazine had spotted my "Jocko's Porting Service" t-shirt and commented on it. The Curator was a member of the Selecting Committee for the Drag Racing Hall of Fame — among his choices for inductees was "Jet Car Bob" Smith and Robert "Jocko" Johnson — and he had something to say about Jocko's refusal of the honor.

"If anybody ever asks you where you got this, you tell them you don't know." He pushes a manila envelope across the table, between the basket of chips and my salted glass. "If anybody ever asks me if I gave this to you, I will tell them 'No.'"

I open the envelope. Inside is a xerox of a fax, addressed to the Don Garlits' Museum of Drag Racing, home of the Hall of Fame and whose board of selectors included Wally Parks and Don Garlits. It reads as follows:

October 16, 1997

Museum of Drag Racing Ocala, Florida

In reply to your letter of October 9, 1997 I hereby inform you that due to my disgust with Don Garlits' handeling (sic) *of my streamliner known as Wynnsliner I do not want any connection with him or anything he has a hand in. It is no honor to be connected with Garlits, the liar and thief. Another major reason that I decline induction is that statue of Wally Parks standing on a plinth with the names of all the inductees carved below his feet. I was never under Wally's direction at any time and want no connection with him in the present or future. It is politically incorrect to have any man standing above all the others. An inanimate object such as the starting lights would be more appropriate. This statue should be dismantled. In the meantime the pigeons will do on it.*

Drag racing is a pollution institution and should be abolished and forgotten. DRAG RACING SUCKS!!

My feelings were hurt by Don Garlits playing a game with my 'liner and telling everyone that it lifts at 150 MPH then giving it to some one other than me (its rightful owner). Then he supposedly bought it back later for the museum. All the other people who I gave a 'liner body for trial gave them back when they were finished, but not Garlits, he made a mockery of it and tells how it cost him money when in fact it made him a lot of money when he brought it to OCIR in 1973, this including sponsor money.

I heard from a crewman that Jim Tice paid the biggest show fee ever paid in the history of drag racing for that car to appear at OCIR and I got $0.00 for my year's worth of effort creating the body that attracted all those folks to witness the 1/2 runs Butch Maas made according to Garlits (sic) *mandate. So, is it any wonder I'm so pissed? Garlits called me to inform me I was voted into the Hall of Fame. I don't believe he called out of friendship, but feared that I would do something to upset his ego trip. If that is the case he was right on. I will upset him and his quest for domination of all drag racers. I am sending my story to the TV networks because people like to get the truth. If they see my video and decide it is "news" they will do what is right.*

My personal integrity means more to me than anything you people can do with all your agrandizement (sic) *routines. So delete my name and lose my address and phone number.*

Sincerely,

Jocko Johnson

Then, there was a follow-up addressed to Garlits:

Garlits,

It's been 25 years since you screwed up big time and threw away your chance to show how to run the 1/4 mile with a true downforce streamliner body. Your own idea was a bust when you showed how to go airborne and do backflips with a drag-

ster. Boy did I get a big laugh when I saw you go airborne with two of your own designs. I bet you can't produce photos or videos of the Wynnsliner lifting off the deck because it didn't happen and can't happen.

Now that all those mindless followers have all had a taste of Garlits-aero I think it's about time I build another 'liner that looks just like "our" Wynnsliner but with some major differences, no Don Garlits, no lies, no ego driven motives, just proven aero that gives the desired results. You did delay the coming of streamliners, but you did not stop it. You held me back and now you want to categorize me into the Hall of Blame or is it the Wall of Shame, no the Ball of Flame that all of you has beens are in, but I'm just starting my run at the straight line race track. I'm not a has been or dead so don't even think of putting my name at Wally Parks' feet!!! Like it or not you are HISTORY Don and there you shall stay.

Jocko

INSIDE DRAG RACING (1997)

A few weeks after my dinner with the Curator, I am channel hopping and catch the last few minutes of the weekly television talk show, INSIDE DRAG RACING. Drag racing is not the topic. Interstellar forms of propulsion is. Don Garlits, an ardent and obsessive UFO buff, is trying to get to the truth about the back engineering of UFOs as sanctioned by the Air Force. He was interviewing self-proclaimed UFO mechanic Bob Lazar.

As the segment closed, Garlits asks Lazar if, while in the catacombs of Area 51 back-engineering spaceships, he'd ever seen one of the extra-terrestrials. Lazar takes a beat, then blurts an emphatic "NO."

∞

Kate holds up the phone, points at the mouthpiece and whispers *sotto voce*, "It's 'Big Daddy.'"

Garlits is on the line and he is pissed. He is livid because I had run parts of Jocko's letter of refusal in a national publication. "And this is not for publication, but all of those recreational drugs and living in isolation in the high desert has FUCKED UP his mind."

I don't have the heart to tell "Big Daddy" that while he was looking for the truth about spaceships, he actually has one mothballed in his museum. The DON GARLITS' WYNNS-LINER.

THE VANISHING POINT (1996)

Cuz'n Roy and I are coming back from Black Rock after Breedlove's 600 mph mishap...

"Man they just don't write 'em like that anymore," I say to Roy, as the main guitar riff to "Set the Controls for the Heart of the Sun" comes crashing back in.

"Ah-men," Roy howls and pounds on the Pontiac's cracked upholstery with his mammoth mitts, simultaneous to Syd Barrett banging out the barrage of interstellar power chords that propel the Pink Floyd tune to its crescendo and coda. "It's like this guy is talking about the car crash we drove through today."

"... *And everything will keep moving until the Universe collapses into itself*-uh," the voice on the radio rattles the fabric of the speaker cones like a dime store popcorn maker. *"It is a matter of chaos*-uh *and prob-*uh*-bil*-uh*-tee as the tendency towards disorder is the most universal manifestation of time's arrow. Our galaxy is traveling at 600 miles per second towards a collision with in-fin*-uhh*-ty and oh-bliv-ee-un*-uhh...."

"This guy is cool as shit," Roy burps and rips the tab off of a beer can.

"...and there is a man in the desert who endeavored to defy physics and common sense by uhh-*temp-ting*-uhh *to break the sound barrier in a stream*-uhh*-lined, jet-powered five-wheeled ahh-tow-mow-beel. He has failed...* " The station cuts to commercials about radar detectors and military-quality ready-meals.

"Well I'll be dipped in the primordial soup," I laugh. "This guy is talking about Breedlove."

"He sounds just like a weird, soda cracker version of Cleavon Little in that movie about benzedrine and muscle cars," Roy says. "You know, the one where Cleavon played the soul brother deejay, *'Vanishing Point.*"

The deejay cues up "Journey to the Center of Your Mind," by the Amboy Dukes.

"That's exactly what this dude is talking about," I say, leaning on the accelerator. "The vanishing point. Like he said, 'the intersection of infinity and oblivion.' Defying the physical laws of that intersection is what makes this whole trip fascinating." I give it a beat to organize my thoughts. "It's like we — as a society, as individuals, as gearheads, as land speed record setters, as wannabes or whatever — go racing to the vanishing point like lemmings or something, like splinters of iron drawn to a magnet, no, like an electron to the nucleus of an atom and when we get there we disappear, like the collision of matter and anti-matter." I pull on my styrofoam cup and silently wonder exactly where from the center of my mind that last outburst came from.

Meanwhile, Roy laughs and then nods like he understands exactly what that last outburst meant. I knew that he did. Probably even more than I did, and I'm the guy who said it.

The radio show returns from some commercial breaks and the noises in the car become a jumbled cacophony of confusion and overlapping dialogue with me trying to find the intersections of the biological and cosmological imperatives, the voice on the radio riffing extemporaneously on Craig Breedlove not heeding the laws of some Grand Unifying Theory while the intro to the Chambers Brothers' "Time Has Come Today" tick-tocks in the background. Apropos of nothing and everything, Roy begins speaking in tongues, which I gathered was a loose recitation of chapter and verse from either Genesis or Revelations (I wasn't sure which...) and keeping time on the dashboard while singing in unison with the Chambers Brothers ("Time has come to-day... TIME!" and then he'd knock the rear view mirror off its axis).

Finally, the deejay ducks down the music and begins a pretty heavy metaphysical/relativistic rap about the futility of attempting to go Mach 1 in a car: *"Yes, my friends*-uhh, *time has come today. Light is always going 186,000 miles a second faster than the person observing it, but to try and subvert time is fatal... traveling through time at warp speed and beyond will require the passage of a black hole, the massive gravitational forces of which would rip the time traveler to shreds*-uhh..." The voice on the radio is on fire, briefly modulating in an intermittent tremolo interspersed with emf noise as we pass under some high tension lines. *"Light is traveling*-uhh *at the speed limit of the Universe. No vessel bound for the stars can travel*-uhh a*ny faster than that. And no man can travel*-uhh *at the speed of sound in an ahh-tow-mow-beel. When a time traveler*-uhh *moves towards an opening in the wall of spacetime, the mass of the hole increases to in-fin*-uhh-*tee. So, in the end, the traveler*-uhh *is torn to taco chips. As of today, Craig Breedlove nearly met his black hole... He nearly met in-fin*-uhh-*tee..."*

"There are no speed limits to the Universe, you Luddite Quaker Flat Earth philistine," I shout at the voice on the radio. I drive like ball lightning. We have a preponderance of pavement to cover before the trip is done. As Roy begins rolling a left-handed cigarette the voice on the radio segues to a rambling rumination about *"anti-particles traveling backward in time*-uhh*"* and then it hit me...the cosmic significance of the *Spirit of America* and potentially breaking the sound barrier in the Great Southwestern Desert of the USA are one and the same: "I know what this guy is trying to say," I bellow to Roy, between sips of some tepid godforsaken excuse for coffee. "By going Mach 1, Breedlove's not only trying to subvert the passage of time and prove the cynics wrong. He is a post-atomic Prometheus, trying to steal fire from the Gods, y'know?"

"Whoa..."

"Breedlove is riding time's arrow towards glory."

"What?" Roy asks and stops rolling in incredulity. I had lost him and I am disturbed.

I exhale. Roy whistles and then sparks up. My stomach and brain implode and then expand like a sponge, physiological effects from a night of truck stop coffee. The radio has broken for a commercial about 1-800 numbers and hand crank short wave radios that would still function despite the advent of Armageddon. The break ends and the voice on the radio continues its exegesis in excited tones.

"...uhh-*ccording to Ernst Mach and the Mach Principle acceleration*-uhh *can be defined only relative to the distant stars, the farthest corners of Val-hall*-uhh. *Ernst Mach thought the universe was mostly a vacuum. He didn't take into account the dark matter that makes up ninety percent of the heavens."*

The voice out of Reno says that if Breedlove screwed the pooch at 700-plus mile an hour that he too would join the great void of dark matter. *"Yes, my friends,"* he says. *"The vanishing point*-uhh. *In-fin*-uhh-*tee."*

Roy drops his lit left-handed cigarette and begins laughing. The deejay cues up "Time Won't Let Me" and conversation stops.

"*I can't wait forever...*"